Zola's Crowds

Zola's Crowds

Naomi Schor

The Johns Hopkins University Press
Baltimore and London

This book has been brought to publication with the generous assistance of the Andrew W. Mellon Foundation.

Manufactured in the United States of America

The Johns Hopkins University Press, Baltimore, Maryland 21218
The Johns Hopkins Press Ltd., London

Library of Congress Catalog Card Number 78-1564
ISBN 0-8018-2095-2

Library of Congress Cataloging in Publication data will be found on the last printed page of this book.

For Serge

Contents

Acknowledgments

Acknowledgment: 1. an acknowledging or being acknowledged; *admission; avowal.* 2. *recognition of the authority or claims of.* 3. a recognizing and answering, as to a greeting. 4. *an expression of thanks or appreciation.*

These acknowledgments are arranged in ascending order of intimacy, for as the dictionary reminds us, an acknowledgment is more than a ritual expression of gratitude: it is first a form of confession, a moment of truth.

I wish to thank the Columbia University Council for Research in the Humanities for a grant which allowed me to devote the summer of 1974 entirely to the writing of this book. I was privileged to have as close readers of my manuscript several men whose teachings and/or writings have, over the years, shaped my work; their influence is gladly acknowledged: Victor Brombert, René Girard, Henri Mitterand, and Michael Riffaterre. It is with great sorrow that I acknowledge my debt to another, not the least of my mentors, the late John Lapp; I shall miss his precise commentaries and his strong support. The expert readings of David Baguley and Philippe Hamon, as well as the sure commentary of Léon Roudiez, helped smooth out many rough spots. A special word of thanks to the women in my Zola seminar (Fall 1973); this book and its author owe much to their response. Nancy Miller, friend and colleague, did more than edit the translations—a tedious task; she shared the adventure. While absolving her of any responsibility for the persisting margin of awkwardness in the translations, I wish to say that I relied on her strong and always lucid voice. Serge Doubrovsky, my companion, gave not only the love and faith that sustained me throughout the long haul; by his own example, he taught me excellence. As for Dr. Gerald Epstein, had he not patiently helped me ravel my myth of origins, this book would never have been written.

Acknowledgments

Before and After

This book is and is not about Zola's crowds, or rather is *about* but not *on* them. This ambiguity is evident in the books I have chosen, which include, alongside the conventional "crowd-fictions" in the Zola canon (*Germinal, La Débâcle*), works in which the crowd plays a purely peripheral or potential role (*La Conquête de Plassans, Le Docteur Pascal*). It is also apparent in the general movement of the book: in each of the chapters and subsections—which can be read without reference to the others—my trajectory is identical, moving through the descriptive toward the speculative. Due allowance being made, the overall structure I have adopted is not unlike that of the *Rougon-Macquart*, itself composed of individual novels which are both connected to and independent from the other novels in the series: what the family is to the *Rougon-Macquart*, the crowd is to this book. In short, in my perspective the crowd is not a strandlike theme which can or should be detached from the fabric of the text, but an Ariadne's thread drawing one deeper into the maze, a structuring theme which engages all of Zola's fiction. When studied in the light of current critical methodologies and epistemological preoccupations, Zola's crowds are the royal way to an understanding of some of the fundamental questions which obsessed Zola (as well, of course, as his contemporaries Darwin, Nietzsche, and Freud). And these are the *anxieties* of origin and difference.

These two words—among the few in the critical lexicon to resonate with equal intensity on both sides of the Atlantic—are to be taken in their widest acceptations. Zola's obsession with origins is inscribed at all levels of his text: it can easily be apprehended in his lifelong interest in theories of heredity, in the dynastic design of his three novelistic cycles, in the title of his "masterpiece," *Germinal*. Now, taking the individual/crowd relationship as it is repeatedly manifested in Zola's fiction as my starting point, I have been able to arrive at a deeper level, the basic layer of the

xi

palimpsest, Zola's *myth* of origins; and this myth turns out to be, not surprisingly, a myth of the origins of (his) writing. But to speak of Zola's myth of origins is at the same time to speak of his myth of originality. For, as Edward Said has remarked, "Beginning is *making* or *producing* difference."[1] The inseparability of the inaugural gesture and the "anxiety of influence," to borrow Harold Bloom's phrase, is poignantly patent in that remarkable prolegomenon to the *Rougon-Macquart*, Zola's notes to himself on the "Differences between Balzac and Me."[2] Indeed, over the years Zola's notes reveal a twofold preoccupation with difference: on the one hand, the initial necessity to distinguish text from intertext; on the other, the constant effort to ensure difference within repetition, that is, between his own texts.[3] But to study Zola's crowd-fictions is to be confronted with the problem of difference writ large, as Zola manipulates huge armies of characters to body forth the shaky differences between male and female, friend and foe, the living and the dead.

If *Zola's Crowds* had a subtitle, it would be "Zola and the Romantic Heritage," for the drama played out in Zola's crowd-fictions is his anguished and I think largely unsuccessful attempt to assume and/or liquidate his debt to romanticism. In his own words, "I hate romanticism for the false education it gave me; I am caught in it and it makes me wild."[4] In this connection it would be well to recall that while the Romantics were the first to situate the modern, post-1789 crowd at the center of the nineteenth-century literary imagination, at the same time they assigned the individual and individuality a prominence they have never recovered since (or should I say, from). Zola's ambivalence reflects this inherited double-bind: the crowd as *topos,* individuality as *ethos.* And, as Zola remarked, "Heredity, like gravity, has its laws."[5]

The anxieties of origin and difference are, of course, a shared neurosis, common to both author and critic. As I begin, I too must authorize my project by articulating the difference(s) between my approach and that of my predecessors. Their books too are about but not on Zola's crowds, but not in the same sense as mine: for while no book on Zola does not at some point touch on Zola's crowds, not a single one is exclusively devoted to the subject. This remark applies to both traditional and more recent studies of Zola, though the hypothesis I have formulated to explain this paradoxical situation is aimed particularly at an earlier generation of critics, the one whose analyses engendered my own, by default. These critics—and they include those who describe themselves or are described as Marxists—share certain aesthetic and ideological assumptions which effectively prevented them from dealing with the subject at length. And these assumptions can be reduced to the following: the proper subject of the novel is the individual, writing about crowds is

not as good (read: great) as writing about individuals, hence Zola's undisputed achievement is ultimately secondary or second-rate. I would term this the compensatory theory: Zola (over-)compensated for his congenital ineptitude at creating "well-rounded" protagonists by creating impressive crowds. Or, in the words of one representative critic, "I know of no other novelist who displayed such skill at making a virtue of necessity."[6]

As long as the hegemony of the French "psychological" novel and the criticism that existed to reinforce it held sway, no book could be written on or about Zola's crowds. One could argue that to implicitly equate psychology in the novel with a "love story" between a man and a woman, as this critical tradition has, is to reduce rather drastically psychology's (not to mention eroticism's) sphere of action. But this argument has a serious drawback: it seems to suggest that turned away at the door, Zola should come in through the window, that is, as a group psychologist. If auxiliary disciplines are to be brought to bear on Zola's texts—and I think they are—sociology seems to me to be the most sterile, the least pertinent. Not that Zola's talents as a crowd psychologist are negligible; they easily rival those of his eminent scientific contemporaries, Gustave Le Bon and Gabriel Tarde. No, it is the whole notion of psychology, individual or group, that is quite simply beside the point. If today it is, perhaps for the first time, possible to entitle a book *Zola's Crowds*, it is not only because questions of value have been evacuated from practical criticism, but because an *aesthetic* of the novel grounded in the belief in a strong, unified, and unifying central subject (a "hero") has given way to a *poetics* of the novel founded on the structural analysis of myth, which decomposes characters into bundles of qualifications and functions, thereby blurring the hard and fast distinctions between crowd and individual.[7]

Written in the heyday/wake of structuralism and poststructuralism, this study draws on structural semantics and anthropology as well as psychoanalysis for its guiding concepts and working vocabulary. This eclecticism or, to adopt Lévi-Strauss's term, *bricolage* is risky; to juxtapose those who would structure and those who would deconstruct, to deny the relevance of psychology to the novel while giving the unconscious full play, to promote a synchronic view of Zola while flirting with diachrony —these are contradictions one cannot assume lightly or innocently. In retrospect it seems to me that the critical strategy I devised as I advanced was designed to allay my anxiety of origins (which is to say originality); by multiplying affiliations, superimposing borrowings, decentering the starting point, the notion of an absolute origin, the hold of one spiritual father is (de)negated. In conclusion then, this text is theoretical, but only

in the etymological sense: *theōria*, "a looking at." The lenses change, but the focus remains somewhat obsessively the same. Miming the mythical thought patterns operative in Zola's works, each chapter—indeed, the entire book—builds toward one conclusion: the inevitability of mediation.

Note on Abbreviations and Translations

The following abbreviations have been used in the text and notes for works by Zola:

French Texts

Lebl *OC*	*Oeuvres complètes,* ed. Maurice Leblond
Mitt *OC*	*Oeuvres complètes,* ed. Henri Mitterand
R-M	*Les Rougon-Macquart,* ed. Henri Mitterand

English Translations

D	*La Débâcle,* trans. Leonard Tancock
G	*Germinal,* trans. L. W. Tancock
K	*The Kill,* trans. A Teixeira de Maltos
N	*Nana,* trans. George Holden
TR	*Thérèse Raquin,* trans. Leonard Tancock

Details of publication for all these volumes can be found in the Bibliography.

Translations from Zola's works and from French critical studies are my own when not otherwise indicated. For Zola, the French text as well as volume and page references are incorporated in the body of the text where length permits; for longer quotations, this material can be found in the notes.

Note on Abbreviations and Translations

Part I

Chapter 1

The Founding Myth

On y déchiffre encor ces quelques lettres: —Sacre;—
Texte obscur et tronqué, reste du mot Massacre.

Victor Hugo, "On loge à la nuit," Châtiments

At least ever since Flaubert exclaimed in one of his letters, "Nana verges on the mythic without ceasing to be realistic,"[1] much has been written about Zola and his myths, whether they be the Nietzschean myth of Eternal Return, the syncretic "prophetic myths," or the Freudian Oedipal myth.[2] In a sense, the combined effort of the best Zola scholars resembles a vast intellectual rescue operation, somewhat similar to the one carried out previously for Balzac (with Baudelaire playing Flaubert's initiatory role): by firmly establishing Zola's mythopoeic credentials, or Balzac's status as a "visionary," the critics have afforded them entry into sanctuaries from which their professions of realism and naturalism had hitherto barred them. Over the years (since about 1950), the relentless probing into the unconscious wellsprings of Zola's writings has nearly erased the stigma of his positivism and even led to a revalorization of his scientific theories. But at the same time, this revisionist approach has opened up a veritable Pandora's box of questions: do the myths mentioned above—the cyclical, the Oedipal—adequately account for the majority of Zola's images and narrative structures? do they exhaust the mythic resources of his texts? are there not aspects of Zola's fiction which, even while participating in the above, point to yet other forms of mythical organization? Coming at the subject by way of Zola's crowds and in the

3

light of recent structural analyses of myth, it became apparent to me that there were indeed other mythical readings possible. Or to put it another way: there is another possible reading of the two myths mentioned above, one which connects them, viewing them as components of what Northrop Frye has termed "a central unifying myth."[3] The possibility of formulating such a concept is inherent in the description of myth which Lévi-Strauss gives in the opening pages of his *Introduction to a Science of Mythology* (*Mythologiques*). The frontiers between myths are, he emphasizes, hazy: one myth leads to another. Any attempt at airtight classifications violates the very Protean nature of myth: "Myths, like rites, are 'interminable.'"[4] If practiced as a literal anamorphosis of its subject matter, the analysis of myth runs the danger of becoming, in a Freudian sense, "interminable." Yet, despite these discouraging prospects, one must begin; the starting point should be the myth which contains (virtually) all its transformations. Such a "founding myth" appears encoded in the first chapter of *La Fortune des Rougon,* the novel which Zola clearly subtitled "by its scientific title: *The Origins.*"[5]

My initial hypothesis is that Zola's crowd-fictions are archetypal narratives, that is, imitations "of generic and recurrent action or ritual."[6] They are *mythoi.* Frye's adoption of the original Aristotelian term for plot, *mythos,* serves to underscore the difference between the general and the specifically literary acceptation of the word *myth:* "In literary criticism myth ultimately means *mythos,* a structural organizing principle of literary form."[7] It is in this strict literary sense that I will speak of Zola's founding myth, a myth which, as Frye's work amply demonstrates, is in no way specific to Zola. Indeed this myth(os) is so fundamental, so all-pervasive, that traces of the ritual it imitates are to be found in all four of Frye's archetypal narratives to a greater or lesser degree—in descending order, (1) tragedy, (2) irony, (3) comedy, (4) romance. Zola's founding myth is the ritual slaying or expulsion of the scapegoat, or *pharmakos;* according to Frye's taxonomy, Zola's crowd-fictions come under the rubric *"mythos of winter: irony,"* irony being a degraded form of tragedy—synonymous with realist or naturalist fiction—and featuring in the place of the super-human (divine or royal) tragic victim an eminently human one, an everyman.

Now Frye's system, correlating as it does *mythoi* and seasons, is based largely and very explicitly on Frazer's *Golden Bough.* Let us recall that Frazer's point of departure is the brutal slaying of the King of the Wood at Nemi and that, after having investigated numerous analogous ritual slayings in a great variety of cultures, he concludes that the King of the Wood is only one of the many god-men slain in order to ensure renewed and continued fertility in their respective societies. In Frazer's perspective the victim of the ritual slaying is first and foremost either a god or a

representative of a god associated with vegetation; his model sacrifice is essentially agrarian in nature and propitiatory in function. It is only in certain specific instances, particularly in ancient Greece and Rome, that the ritual slaying of the divine king and the "periodic expulsion of evils"[8] are joined together in a single ceremony, in the spirit of killing two birds with one stone, or making one victim serve two functions. This theory of the transformation of the propitiatory sacrifice into the expiatory presupposes the priority of the deity of vegetation as victim:

> If we ask why a dying god should be chosen to take upon himself and carry away the sins and sorrows of the people, it may be suggested that in the practice of using the divinity as scapegoat we have a combination of two customs which were at one time distinct and independent. On the one hand we have seen that it has been customary to kill the human or animal god in order to save his divine life from being weakened by the inroads of age. On the other hand we have seen that it has been customary to have a general expulsion of evils and sins once a year. Now, if it occurred to people to combine these two customs, the result would be the employment of the dying god as a scapegoat. He was killed not originally to take away sins, but to save the divine life from the degeneracy of age; but, since he had to be killed at any rate, people may have thought they might as well seize the opportunity to lay upon him the burden of their sufferings and sins, in order that he might bear it away with him to the unknown world beyond the grave.[9]

The upshot of all this is that any myth criticism derived from Frazer—e.g., Frye's—will make rather short shrift of the pharmakos. Given my initial hypothesis—namely, that the founding myth of Zola's crowd-fictions is based on the ritual slaying or expulsion of the pharmakos—a theoretical model of this kind of sacrifice would be preferable to the Frazerian model, which has served so many Anglo-Saxon critics so well for so long. Such a model is provided in a recent work by René Girard, *Violence and the Sacred.* For Girard, the pharmakos ritual is no afterthought; it is primordial: it is the hidden central mechanism upon which all religious practices are based. According to this theory—whose anthropological validity I am incompetent to judge, but whose relevance to my corpus is indisputable—the pharmakos ritual involves the necessary, unavoidable, and hitherto elided connection of violence and the sacred: "Religion invariably strives to subdue violence, to keep it from running wild."[10]

If we attempt to reconstruct the stages of the transformation of violence into the single source of morality and religion, as set out by Girard, we arrive at the following hypothetical chronology. The first stage consists of an unspecified, unlimited period of time during which sacrifice, whether animal or human, functions as an efficacious means of catharsis for a collectivity mined from within by conflict and pent-up

aggression. In order for this catharsis, this restoration of peace and harmony, to take place, the victim must be drawn from among the marginal members of society—slave, stranger, uninitiated adolescent—or from the category of the nonhuman; the victim's death must not be cause for renewed violence in the form of revenge.

The second stage, by far the most important in this scheme, consists of the breakdown of this sacrificial system. The attention Girard brings to bear on this phase of the sacrificial cycle constitutes (in my opinion) his major contribution to a better understanding of the pharmakos ritual and how it informs certain literary works. It is instructive to compare Girard and Roger Caillois on this point. In Caillois's work, *Man and the Sacred,* there is no satisfying explanation given for the passage from the "sacred as respect" to the "sacred as transgression,"[11] that is, from an order based on a network of prohibitions to a disorder marked by the violation of all these prohibitions—the chaos of the festival. The festival—the equivalent in Caillois's system to the ritual sacrifice in Girard's[12]—simply occurs when nature is run-down and in need of a lift:

> Time erodes dams, and the functioning of a mechanism wears away and soils its parts. Man grows old and dies, renewed, it is true, in his descendants. Nature at the approach of winter loses its fertility and seems to die. It is necessary to recreate the world, to rejuvenate the system. Taboos can only prevent its accidental end. They are incapable of saving it from its inevitable destruction, from its beautiful death. They slow its decline, without being able to stop it. The moment comes when rebuilding is necessary. A positive act must assure a new stability to the order. A facsimile of creation is needed to restore nature and society. That is what the festival provides.[13]

In sharp contrast to this vague, neo-Frazerian account of events, Girard offers a rigorous structuralist analysis of this crucial stage. In effect, he turns Caillois's logic on its head: what the one perceives as effects the other reveals as causes. Thus, the disintegration of the *differences* that underlie the social order, a typical "effect" of ancient festivals (e.g., the Roman Saturnalia with its social and sexual role reversals), are shown by Girard to be symptomatic of a presacrificial climate: "The sacrificial crisis can be defined, therefore, as a crisis of distinctions—that is, a crisis affecting the cultural order. This cultural order is nothing more than a regulated system of distinctions, in which the differences among individuals are used to establish their 'identity' and their mutual relationships" (Girard, *Violence,* p. 49).

The examples Girard gives of "differential breakdowns" are numerous and drawn from a wide variety of sources; they range from the birth of twins—much feared in primitive societies—to the proliferation of doubles in certain literary works such as *Oedipus the King* and *The Bacchae,* from parricide to incest:

Parricide represents the establishment of violent reciprocity between father and son, the reduction of the paternal relationship to "fraternal" revenge.

Incest is also a form of violence, an extreme form, and it plays in consequence an extreme role in the destruction of differences. It destroys that other crucial family distinction, that between the mother and her children. (Girard, *Violence*, p. 74)

It is then in response to this crisis, this threat of cultural self-destruction, that the mechanism of the surrogate victim ("victime émissaire") comes into play. The workings of this mechanism are observable in *Oedipus the King*, where Oedipus's crimes both mark the breakdown of difference and institute a new difference, that which separates the criminal from the community and designates him as the scapegoat for a sick society. However—and this is the crux of Girard's demonstration —Oedipus is not in (textual) fact essentially different from his doubles Creon, Tiresias, and Laius, who all share his quick temper, his propensity to violence: "In the myth, the fearful transgression of a single individual is substituted for the universal onslaught of reciprocal violence. Although Oedipus is not guilty in the modern sense of the term, he is nonetheless responsible for the ills that have befallen his people. He has become a prime example of the human scapegoat" (Girard, *Violence*, p. 77).

The expulsion, whether by exile or death, of the surrogate victim, unanimously carried out by the community, ushers in the final phase of the sacrificial cycle: a new era of peace and harmony. The surrogate victim is a human lightning rod, drawing all the fire which imperils the survival of the city. The passage from chaos to order, the metamorphosis of reciprocal violence into unilateral violence, the substitution of a single victim for the multiple enemy, constitutes the keystone or pivot of Girard's system. Once again a brief comparison between Caillois and Girard is illuminating: carried to its logical extreme, Caillois's theory culminates in the equation of ancient festivals with modern warfare, war being described either as "a black festival" or "a Goddess of tragic fertility."[14] In other words, mass murder regenerates society. In contradistinction to this fascist mythology/ideology, Girard's mechanism uses a minimum of bloodshed to put an end to or avoid a major bloodletting: by virtue of its economy, this proto-Christian system offers the more "elegant" solution to the as yet unsolved problem of internecine violence.

Rituals—from initiation rites to the spectacular sacrifices of the African kings—are nothing more or rather less than reenactments of the "original, spontaneous 'lynching'" (Girard, *Violence*, p. 95). Perhaps the most controversial aspect of Girard's argument is his insistence that at some point in this cyclical process there was a primordial murder, a unique victim, a first time: "Even if innumerable intermediary stages exist between the spontaneous outbursts of violence and its religious

imitations, even if it is only these imitations that come to our notice, I want to affirm that these imitations had their origin in a real event" (ibid., p. 309).

When it comes to rehabilitating the Freud of *Totem and Taboo* and affirming the existence of an absolute origin of the sacrificial ritual, we must part company with Girard and take up again with Frye, for in his words, "The critic...is concerned only with the ritual or dream patterns which are actually in what he is studying, however they got there."[15] The question of whether or not there *really* was a first time, a primal murder, is not pertinent to my inquiry; when I speak of a "first victim," I will mean within the spatio-temporal limits of my corpus. At the end of this section I will return to and dwell on the more difficult and far-reaching issue being raised and skirted here: the very viability of the whole notion of an absolute origin. But, differing for the moment the articulation of Girard and Derrida, one might say of Girard's book what Lévi-Strauss says of his own *Mythologiques:* "It follows that this book on myths is itself a kind of myth."[16]

La Fortune des Rougon

To examine a work of art from the perspective of the surrogate victim and its attendant mechanism is to consider it in terms of collective violence, to attempt to discover what the work omits as much, if not more, as what it includes.

René Girard, Violence and the Sacred

All myths, according to Mircea Eliade, are concerned with beginnings: "It is always therefore the story of a 'creation': one recounts how something was produced, came into being." And all origin myths are patterned on and refer back to the macro-origin myth of the creation of the universe: "The creation of the World being *the* creation par excellence, cosmogonies become exemplary models for all kinds of creations." Thus many "ritual genealogical chants" begin with a cosmogony.[17] *La Fortune des Rougon,* the first of the *Rougon-Macquart* series, is no exception to this rule: this modern—which is to say bourgeois—genealogical chant features a two-tiered structure, as cosmogony (Chapter I) precedes/prefaces genealogy (Chapter II). In the place where primitive chants rehearse the story of the Cosmos, however, Zola inscribes the story of the Aire Saint-Mittre. An anomolous cosmogony to be sure: for what we have here is not a creation *ex nihilo,* but rather a creation which presupposes destruction, instead of an origin myth, a myth of transformation. And a very

significant form of transformation: the de-secration of consecrated ground. For, let us recall, the *aire* Saint-Mittre was once the *cimetière* Saint-Mittre. The holy ground of the cemetery, explicitly placed under the patronage of a local saint (*Mittre* ≃ *mitre* = *miter*), is, as the novel opens, a profane vacant lot, camping ground for passing gypsies, sawyard for local cartwrights, and playground for neighborhood children.

However anomalous this origin myth, however unorthodox this cosmogony, the mythic status of the initial pages of *La Fortune des Rougon* is indisputable. Even before we begin to read the novel proper, we are as it were alerted by Zola's preface to the mythic nature of what is to follow; for as a comparison of Zola's "scientific" subtitle, *The Origins,* with Darwin's title *The Origin of Species,* demonstrates, the very plural of the origins belies Zola's claim to scientificity. Then, as we begin to read the text, other indices appear, in particular the striking imprecision and vagueness of the temporal indications. There is a curious and marked progression from an obscure point in the past—a "pre-text"—to a clearly specified moment in the present; we seem to emerge slowly from the realm of legend, "formerly" ("anciennement"), into an era of clocks and calendars: "One Sunday evening, at about seven o'clock...in the early part of December, 1851" ("Un dimanche soir, vers sept heures...dans les premiers jours de décembre 1851" [*R-M,* 1: 9]). The main temporal indications allow us to reconstruct the following sequence:

1. A century of use as a cemetery: "The ground glutted with corpses for over a century" ("La terre, que l'on gorgeait de cadavres depuis plus d'un siècle" [*R-M,* 1: 5]).

2. Abandonment for an unspecified number of years: "In 1851 the old men of Plassans could still recall having seen the walls of this cemetery, which had been closed for years" ("Les vieux de Plassans, en 1851, se souvenaient encore d'avoir vu debout les murs de ce cimetière, qui était resté fermé pendant des années" [ibid.]).

3. The transfer of the remains from the old cemetery to the new: "Around that time the town thought of turning this communal property to account" ("Vers ce temps, la ville songea à tirer parti de ce bien communal" [p. 6]); "only the old men, seated on the beams while warming themselves in the setting sun, sometimes still speak among themselves of the bones they once saw carted through the streets of Plassans by the legendary tumbril" ("il n'y a que les vieux, assis sur les poutres et se chauffant au soleil couchant, qui parfois parlent encore entre eux des os qu'ils ont vu jadis charrier dans les rues de Plassans, par le tombereau légendaire" [p. 9]).

4. The second period of abandonment for an unspecified number of years: "For several years the plot of land once occupied by the Saint-

Mittre cemetery remained an object of terror" ("pendant plusieurs années le terrain de l'ancien cimetière Saint-Mittre resta un objet d'épouvante" [p. 6]).

5. The resurgence of the area, renamed *aire* Saint-Mittre: "And, gradually, with the years, people grew accustomed to this empty spot" ("Et, peu à peu, les années aidant, on s'habitua à ce coin vide" [p. 7]).

6. Thirty years or more of its current appearance and function: "These occurences go back a long time. For more than thirty years the Aire Saint-Mittre has had a special character" ("Ces faits datent de loin. Depuis plus de trente ans, l'aire Saint-Mittre a une physionomie particulière" [ibid.]).

7. The unspecified present of the narration: "It is still today" ("Elle est encore aujourd'hui" [ibid.]).

The remoteness in time of the central event—the transfer of the remains from one cemetery to the other—is reinforced by the age of those who recount it, the "elders" of Plassans. In Zola's fictional universe, the always problematical distinction between myth and history seems to rest on the same criteria as that of the Trobriand islanders studied by Malinowski:

> Whenever they speak of some event in the past, they distinguish whether it happened within their own memory or that of their fathers or not. But, once beyond this line of demarcation, all the past events are placed by them on one plane, and there are no gradations of "long ago" and "very long ago." Any idea of epochs in time is absent from their mind: the past is one vast storehouse of events, and the line between myth and history does not coincide with any division into definite and distinct periods of time.[18]

Indeed, a recurrent character in Zola's novels is the ancestor-witness, the grandfather or grandmother who provides the only link between an undifferentiated past and the immediate present: tante Dide in *La Fortune des Rougon*, Bonnemort in *Germinal*, Fouan in *La Terre*, Jérôme Qurignon in *Travail*. Myth, as opposed to history, is transmitted orally.

The genesis of the Aire Saint-Mittre is then a mimesis of myth, or "mytho-mimetic." By combining two devices—the age of the informants and the accumulation of temporal lacunae—Zola transforms the relatively commonplace events of local history into the stuff of myth. The actual facts surrounding the deconsecration of the cemetery are prosaic, but when their narration is distorted by a series of what Gérard Genette terms "explicit ellipses"[19] and delegated in part to only moderately "reliable" narrators, they become enigmatic. In keeping with nineteenth-century narrative conventions, Zola, like Balzac before him, begins his novel by what Roland Barthes calls "the proposal of the enigma" and its concomitant, "the *avoided (or suspended) answer*,"[20] for one enigma always

leads to another, maintaining the reader's interest until the final solution (generally synchronic with the closure[21]). From the outset the origin myth of the Aire Saint-Mittre is subsumed to a "hermeneutic code."[22] The reader asks, Why is the chronicle of the rise of the Rougon-Macquart preceded by an account of how the Aire Saint-Mittre got its name? What is the underlying connection between these two seemingly unrelated stories? And further: What are we doing in this vacant lot which Zola describes as an "impasse," a dead end? To measure the incongruity of this point of departure, we need only compare the first pages of *La Fortune des Rougon* with those of Stendhal's *Le Rouge et le noir* (*The Red and the Black*). In the latter a knowledgeable and attentive tour guide takes the reader on a visit of Verrières's scenic vistas, whereas in the former we are unceremoniously exiled, as it were, outside the city limits in an ex-centric, a-topic place where we sense that something is being kept from us. When we learn from manuscript evidence that the idea of making the Aire Saint-Mittre into a former cemetery, of endowing it with a past history, was a last-minute "inspiration" of the author's, our questions grow more insistent: why have added a historical dimension only to cancel it out by the devices mentioned above? Only a close, even microscopic, reading of the text can contribute to the elucidation of the "mystery of the Aire Saint-Mittre."

A seemingly innocent detail provides us with our first clue. Zola remarks almost in passing, in a verbless aside, that the transfer of the remains from the old cemetery to the new is carried out without cere-mony: "Not in the least a religious ceremony, just a slow and brutal cartage" ("Pas la moindre cérémonie religieuse; un charroi lent et brutal" [*R-M*, 1: 6]). The emphasis here is on the loss of ritual; the transformation accounted for by our myth is the passage from an older, religious era to a new, nonreligious one. Now, if one recalls that one of the major enter-prises of the French Revolution was the secularization of church property, one might emit the hypothesis that the myth of the Aire Saint-Mittre is nothing less than a transposition of the French Revolution. This apparently far-fetched hypothesis gains in plausibility if one considers two factors, one outside the text, one within it. First the external evidence: as Zola stresses in his preliminary notes ("Notes sur la marche générale de l'oeuvre"), the story of the Rougon-Macquart is rooted in the history of nineteenth-century France, a history which begins with the Revolution: "My novel would have been impossible before 89" ("Mon roman eût été impossible avant 89" [*R-M*, 5: 1738]). And yet, for all the historical flashbacks in the novel, the date 1789 is never mentioned, the Revolution, glossed over: the very events which made the novel possible are con-spicuous by their absence.

Is this absence total? I think not: not only does the myth of the Aire

Saint-Mittre appear to be a transposition of the history of France before and after 1789, but the life story of tante Dide, the "founding mother" of the Rougon-Macquart, presents some rather interesting parallels with the unmentioned (unmentionable?) events. If we attempt to reconstruct the precise chronology of tante Dide's personal history—a chronology as scrambled as that of the Aire Saint-Mittre—we arrive at a discovery quickly confirmed by the "Arbre Généalogique": "Adélaïde FOUQUE ...takes a lover, Macquart, in 1789" ("Adélaïde FOUQUE...prend un amant Macquart, en 1789" [R-M, 5: 1738]).[23] Mere coincidence? Again, I think not. It seems difficult not to see in this intersection of personal history and the history of France a (hidden) meaning, an oblique allusion to the interpenetration of sex and politics. What more apt representative of the newly enfranchised lower classes than Macquart the poacher, "a man of ill fame, usually referred to as 'that beggar Macquart'" ("un homme mal famé, que l'on désignait d'habitude sous cette locution: 'ce gueux de Macquart'" [R-M, 1: 42])?

This external evidence of the hidden presence of the French Revolution seems to be corroborated by a piece of internal evidence. In describing the relocation of the cemetery, Zola emphasizes not only the lack of religious ceremony, but also the grisly mode of transportation: "The worst thing was that this tumbril had to cross the whole of the length of Plassans, and with every jolt the poorly paved streets caused it to scatter bone fragments and handfuls of rich soil" ("Le pis était que ce tombereau devait traverser Plassans dans toute sa longueur, et que le mauvais pavé des rues lui faisait semer, à chaque cahot, des fragments d'os et des poignées de terre grasse" [R-M, 1: 6]). The sinister passage of the "legendary tumbril" calls to mind descriptions of the tumbrils carrying their cargo of victims to be guillotined.

While it would be tempting but futile to speculate on Zola's reasons for presenting the French Revolution by indirection, in the somewhat caricatural and unrecognizable form of its strictly local and personal consequences, we are now in a position to answer the question posed earlier regarding the link between "cosmogony" and "genealogy": both the Aire Saint-Mittre and the Rougon fortune are by-products of the tremendous sociopolitical upheaval caused by the Revolution. We might schematize this interrelation as shown in Table 1.

This reading of our myth as a myth of Revolution is incomplete, however, because it applies only to the diachronic, syntagmatic level of the text. It fails to take into account what Lévi-Strauss identifies as "the specific character of mythological time, which...is both reversible and non-reversible, synchronic and diachronic."[24] We must now consider the synchronic dimension, which is to say the one where redundancy becomes the significant factor; for, again quoting Lévi-Strauss, "The function of

Table 1

	History	
	Before 1789	After 1789
Saint-Mittre	cemetery (sacred)	aire (profane)
Rougon-Macquart	peasantry	bourgeoisie

repetition is to render the structure of the myth apparent."[25] It is this structure we will now attempt to uncover.

Given what we already know about our myth-text, we may posit at the outset the basic binary opposition

LIFE vs. DEATH

This initial and fundamental opposition is first qualified as follows:

$$\frac{\text{Life}}{\text{Death}} \simeq \frac{\text{Pear trees}}{\text{Corpses}}$$

In other words, the opposition between life and death is *mediated* by a complex term, *fertility:* "This rich soil, which the gravediggers could not sink their spades into without unearthing some shred of human flesh, was extraordinarily fertile" ("Ce sol gras, dans lequel les fossoyeurs ne pouvaient plus donner un coup de bêche sans arracher quelque lambeau humain, eut une fertilité formidable" [*R-M*, 1: 5]).

This excessive fertility is reiterated in another code (human vs. vegetal) by the excessive voluptuousness of the cemetery: "One can sense faint stirrings of the hot, hazy breath of voluptuous death rising from the old graves heated up by the glaring sun" ("On y sent courir ces souffles chauds et vagues des voluptés de la mort qui sortent des vieilles tombes chauffées par les grands soleils" [*R-M*, 1: 8-9]). The corpses buried in the cemetery generate both trees and love, the love of young Miette and Silvère: "With their lively imaginations, they would tell each other that in a way their love had grown like a fine, hardy, and thick-leaved plant in this compost, this patch of earth fertilized by death" ("Vaguement, avec leur imagination vive, ils se disaient que leur amour avait poussé, comme une belle plante robuste et grasse, dans ce terreau, dans ce coin de terre fertilisé par la mort" [*R-M*, 1: 206]). Just as the trees recycle the corpses' material substance, the young lovers reincarnate their spirits. Viewed in a structuralist perspective, the notion of a great Life/Death/Life cycle—possibly Zola's most persistent leitmotiv—can be seen as a typical instance of a basic process of mythical thought, thereby further confirming the mythical status of our text: "Mythical thought always works from the awareness of oppositions towards their progressive mediation."[26]

A second qualification of the initial opposition brings us closer to what I believe to be the deep structure, the *invariant*, of this text. In an interesting example of what one might call the intersection of synchrony and diachrony, the Revolution (mediating historical term) provokes a series of reversals on the ahistorical level. What is *below* is unearthed: "The soil was excavated several meters down, and the bones which the earth was willing to surrender were piled up in a corner" ("Le sol fut fouillé à plusieurs mètres, et l'on amoncela, dans un coin, les ossements que la terre voulut bien rendre" [*R-M*, 1: 6]). What is *above* is torn down: "The weeds and the pear trees were uprooted" ("On arracha les herbes et les poiriers" [ibid.]). This gives rise to a new set of oppositions, which represents a simple inversion of the first one:

$$\frac{\text{Trees (vegetal} + \text{vertical)}}{\text{Corpses (human} + \text{horizontal)}} \simeq \frac{\text{Gypsies (human} + \text{vertical)}}{\text{Beams (vegetal} + \text{horizontal)}}$$

The reversal consists in an exchange of constituent semantic units. What is crucial in this equivalence is the relationship which it establishes between elements of the text that appear superficially unrelated, namely, pear trees $\simeq$ gypsies. In order to bring out their common constituent units, or semes, let us place the two passages side by side:

> One of the *strangest* features of the field at that time were pear trees with twisted branches and *monstrous* knots; no housewife in Plassans would have wanted to pick its *enormous* fruit. In town people grimaced with *disgust* when speaking of this fruit.

> The final touch contributing to the *peculiar* aspect of this out-of-the-way spot is that, in keeping with time-honored custom, passing gypsies have elected domicile there…one can always find some *strange* looking band there, some pack of wild men and dreadfully desiccated women, among which groups of beautiful children are to be seen rolling on the ground. These people live *without shame, in the open air,* publicly: boiling their pots, eating nameless things, laying out their tattered old clothes, sleeping, fighting, kissing, reeking of filth and poverty.[27]

The common semes should now be apparent: both the pear trees and the gypsies are *extra-ordinary;* both are somehow *scandalous* and inspire feelings of *disgust* on the part of the community. Zola's idiosyncratic identification of gypsies and pear trees renews a literary association that became cliché in nineteenth-century France, that of gypsies and nature. In a certain nineteenth-century mythology, gypsies occupy the same place as the eighteenth century's noble savages: they are the privileged representatives of unrepressed instinctual life.[28]

Before exploring still further the outrageousness of the pear trees and the gypsies, let us note that the connection between an overdeveloped

nature and an underdeveloped man is reiterated throughout *La Fortune des Rougon*. Thus, in the course of the first chapter, an implicit comparison is made between the giant elms which will be cut down by the municipality and the heroic insurrectionists who will be decimated by the army:

> In 1851 the road to Nice...was lined with century-old *giant* elms, *grandiose* ruins still full of *vigor*, which the tidy town municipality replaced several years ago by small plane trees.

> Leading the way came *great* strapping fellows, stubborn men who seemed to have the *strength* of Hercules and the naïve faith of *giants*.[29]

(Ironically, these giants are professional woodcutters!)

Farther along in the novel, the connection between the trees and the people is made quite explicit, in the scene where the "liberty tree" ("arbre de la liberté"), symbol of the hopes raised among the working-class citizens of Plassans by the revolution of 1848, is torn down, to the delight of Félicité Rougon and her conservative entourage:

> This tree, a young poplar brought from the banks of the Viorne river, had gradually withered, to the great despair of the republican workers who would come every Sunday to check the disease's progress, unable to understand the causes of this slow death....Once the tree was dead, the municipality declared that the dignity of the Republic necessitated its removal.... All the members of the "yellow salon" had gone to the windows. When the poplar cracked with a hollow sound and crashed down in the darkness with the tragic strength of a stricken hero, Félicité felt called upon to wave a white handkerchief.[30]

Returning to our original equivalence, pear trees ≃ gypsies, we can now see that it is in fact only a fragment of a longer chain of equivalences: corpses ≃ pear trees ≃ gypsies ≃ the people. These four links in the chain share a common seme—they are scandalous—and thus, a similar fate—they must be eliminated. The invariant of our myth is clear: burial, felling, exile, execution, are but variants of the same basic repression invariant, with its concomitant, the return of the repressed. Beginning with the burial of the dead, there is a constant alternation of *repression/ return of the repressed:*

> burial of the dead / growth of the pear trees
> transfer of the bones / scattering of the bones
> cutting down of the pear trees / camping out of the gypsies

The letting out of the former cemetery to cartwrights is highly significant: the sawmill represents the town officials' determined effort to submit nature to culture. The spatial reorganization spells out this message unmistakably:

Mornings and afternoons, warmed by the sun, the entire area swarms with people, and *above* all this tumult, *above* the young scamps playing among the pieces of wood and the gypsies lighting the fires under their kettles, the gaunt silhouette of the sawyer perched on his beam stands out against the open sky, going to and fro with the regular movements of a pendulum, as if to order the intense new life which has grown up in this former field of eternal repose.[31]

Once we have established beyond a reasonable doubt that there is more to this cemetery than meets the eye, that there is something hidden here which the municipality would very much like to keep out of sight, our next question must be, What is the *secret* of the cemetery/Aire Saint-Mittre? I use the word *secret* advisedly, because in terms of frequency alone, it is the key word of the novel. There are two main zones of secrecy. First, there is the one surrounding tante Dide, her affair with Macquart, and her periodic fits of catatonia: "The house in the Impasse Saint-Mittre remained hermetically sealed and kept its secrets" ("Le logis de l'impasse Saint-Mittre resta hermétiquement clos et garda ses secrets" [*R-M*, 1: 45]); "These secret dramas which recurred every month, this old woman as rigid as a corpse and this child bending over her, watching for signs of a return to life" ("Ces drames secrets, qui revenaient chaque mois, cette vieille femme rigide comme un cadavre et cet enfant penché sur elle, épiant en silence le retour de la vie" [p. 137]). Second, there is the one surrounding the political activities of factions on both sides of the barricades: "The priests—and they are numerous—set the tone for local politics: subterranean mines, underhand blows, skillful but timid tactics ....These secret struggles..." ("Les prêtres, très nombreux, donnent le ton à la politique de l'endroit; ce sont des mines souterraines, des coups dans l'ombre, une tactique savante et peureuse....Ces luttes secrètes..." [*R-M*, 1: 73]); "But the neighboring towns...have long been stirred up by secret societies" ("Mais les villes voisines...sont travaillées depuis longtemps par des sociétés secrètes" [p. 98]). In this novel everyone has something to hide, and each secret engenders another. For example, Pierre Rougon hides from his wife, Félicité, that their son Eugène is a secret agent of Louis-Napoléon's; however, once she discovers this secret, she keeps her discovery a secret from her husband. Or: Eugène's secret → Pierre's secret → Félicité's secret. This proliferation begins with the secret of the Aire Saint-Mittre.

To progress in our detective work, let us be guided by Jacques Lacan's remark in the "Seminar on 'The Purloined Letter'": "What is hidden is never but what is *missing from its place.*"[32] For there is in the Aire Saint-Mittre just such a misplaced object:

In a corner there was an old tombstone, which had been overlooked when

the old cemetery was moved, and which, set on edge and slightly aslant, formed a sort of raised bench. The rain had worn away its border, and the moss was slowly consuming it. Nevertheless, in the moonlight one might still have been able to make out this fragment of an epitaph, engraved on the base of the stone: *Here lies...Marie...died....*Time had erased the rest.[33]

This tombstone constitutes the true center of the novel. The young lovers use it as their meeting place and speculate on who Marie was. Miette, whose own name is encoded in the French text ("worn away" ≃ "émietté"), evinces a particularly morbid fascination with this tombstone bearing (doubly) her name:

> One evening a strange fancy came over her: she wanted Silvère to turn over the stone in order to see what lay beneath. He refused to do so as though it were a sacrilege, and his refusal fostered Miette's reverie about the dear spirit who bore her name. She insisted that she had died at her age, thirteen, in the midst of a romance. She felt pity for the very stone which she stepped over so nimbly, where they had so often sat, a stone chilled by death but warmed by their love. She would add: "You'll see; it will bring us bad luck. If you were to die, *I* would come here to die, and I would want this block to be rolled over my body.[34]

Miette's premonitions will prove correct and her wish, be fulfilled, only in reverse: it is she who will die first, struck down by a bullet at the massacre of Saint-Roure, and it is Silvère who will return to be executed on the fateful spot: "The child's skull burst open like a ripe pomegranate; his face fell down on the block, his lips pressed against the spot worn by Miette's feet" ("Le crâne de l'enfant éclata come une grenade mûre; sa face retomba sur le bloc, les lèvres collées à l'endroit usé par les pieds de Miette" [*R-M*, 1: 314]). Thus, the tombstone serves explicitly, in a murder, as a sacrificial altar: Silvère is the privileged representative of all the victims in the book—M. Peirotte, Miette, as well as the anonymous victims of the ambush at the Hôtel-de-Ville. Silvère is privileged because he alone of all the victims is a member of the Rougon-Macquart family, and as Girard points out, in order to guarantee a revenge-proof victim, the surrogate victim is often chosen from among close family members. While the "reciprocal violence" which precedes the sacrifice of the scapegoat may claim multiple victims, there is only one victim whose death puts an end to the cycle of violence. The ultimate form of sacrifice is the sacrifice of a family member, and no one is more aware of this than the author of these pompous remarks of Pierre Rougon's: "'I will do my duty, gentlemen. I swore I would save this town from anarchy and I will, should it require acting as the executioner of my closest kin.' He sounded like an old Roman sacrificing his family on the altar of patriotism" ("'J'accomplirai mon devoir, messieurs. J'ai juré de sauver la ville de

l'anarchie, et je la sauverai, dussé-je être le bourreau de mon plus proche parent.' On eût dit un vieux Romain sacrifiant sa famille sur l'autel de la patrie" [*R-M*, 1: 228]).

The fortune of the Rougons springs from the blood of these victims: "Blood is a good fertilizer. It would be a fine thing if the Rougons, like certain illustrious families, went back to a massacre" ("Le sang est un bon engrais. Il sera beau que les Rougon, comme certaines familles illustres, datent d'un massacre" [*R-M*, 1: 98]). The origins of the Rougons reproduce in microcosm the origins of the Second Empire. The question becomes inescapable: is this founding massacre the first, the absolute origin, or does it in turn reduplicate a previous massacre? To borrow Girard's terms, is Silvère a "ritual victim" (one of a series) or the original (single) "surrogate victim"?

To ask this question is to raise the troublesome question of the mysterious origin of the "curse" of the Rougon-Macquart family, alluded to in the preface to *La Fortune des Rougon*, as "a *first* organic lesion" ("une *première* lésion organique" [*R-M*, 1: 3]). Recently, critics such as Jean Borie, Gilles Deleuze, and Michel Serres have argued that terms drawn from the paradigm of the "crack" ("fêlure") are to be taken metaphorically, as transpositions into a biological code of a metaphysical void or a ritual crime.[35] As Borie remarks, nowhere does Zola spell out the nature of the crime that started it all: "Never, not even in *Le Docteur Pascal* when he summarizes and reviews the entire cycle, does Zola name that initial crime which will bring down its curse upon the family. At most we might note that the first novel of the series recounts the *murder of a child.*"[36] Borie is much "warmer" in his observation than he may know. The child referred to is, of course, Silvère, but just as Silvère's murder reiterates, completes Miette's, can we not, must we not infer that the Miette/Silvère murder reiterates that of Marie, buried under the forgotten tombstone? The forgetting of this precious piece of evidence by the vigilant municipality provides the answer to the questions we have raised: the secret of the Aire Saint-Mittre lies hidden in the tomb of the unknown victim, its "Purloined Letter"-like prominence guaranteeing its invisibility. Marie is then (within the *Rougon-Macquart*) the original surrogate victim:

> The role of the surrogate victim can be ascertained, I believe, even on a spatial plane. There is good reason to think that it has imposed its image on the very structures of some communities, at those special locations forming the center of the community, sites generally dedicated to the spirit of collective unity and whose true nature is sometimes brought to light through archeological investigation.
>
> In Greece these sites include the tombs of heroes, the omphalos, the stone of the agora and, finally, that perfect symbol of the polis, Hestia, the common

hearth. Louis Gernet's essay on these sites leaves this reader at least with the overwhelming conviction that these are places where the surrogate victim met his death or where he was believed to have died.[37]

Just as, in *A la recherche du temps perdu*, all of Combray springs full-blown from the narrator's teacup, it would not be any exaggeration to affirm that all of the *Rougon-Macquart* rests on this moss-eaten stone.[38] Marie's tombstone is the center around which the entire imaginary topography of the cycle is organized and, what is more, the convergence point of the origins of the Aire Saint-Mittre and the family Rougon-Macquart. Everything about this marker designates it as emblematic: the origins of the Rougon-Macquart are encoded in a half-erased message, at the same time revealed and concealed, thus literally indecipherable. The textual fabric of *La Fortune des Rougon* is shot through with holes: the well where Miette and Silvère first meet and fall in love is already a grave; indeed, there is throughout the novel an emphasis on the word *hole* (*trou*)—comparable in frequency to the word *secret*, suggesting that the two are somehow linked—which brings us, like the lovers, relentlessly back to the tombstone. This hole, these blanks, introduce a radical discontinuity into the story of the Rougon-Macquart; when we hypothesize, or even dream, that Marie stands for the original human scapegoat, we are driven by the same *horror vacui* as that which Zola attributes to Docteur Pascal, who, in the final novel of the series, struggles in the face of family opposition and death to leave behind him a document with no lacunae, a seamless genealogy.

The tomb/stone is the crack ("fêlure") through which the reader is allowed, or even invited, to participate, to write his own story. And yet, just as Silvère refuses to overturn the tombstone, to violate the grave, alleging that such an act would be sacrilegious, the reader/critic refuses to violate the text, which inspires in him a sense of the "sacred as respect." Yet the reluctant or pious reader/critic would do well to remember that while Silvère refuses to violate Marie's tomb, elsewhere in the novel he does commit an analogous sacrilege. I am referring to his opening of the door—boarded up many years earlier by tante Dide, after her lover Macquart's death—connecting the Jas Meiffren and the Impasse Saint-Mittre. When tante Dide discovers the gaping door, she experiences Silvère's gesture as a profanation: "And, to her amazement, a sense of revulsion flared up in her against the sacrilegious hand which had, after violating this threshold, left behind it the gaping whiteness of an open tomb" ("Et, dans son étonnement, montait sourdement une révolte contre la main sacrilège qui, après avoir violé ce seuil, avait laissé derrière elle la trouée blanche comme une tombe ouverte" [*R-M*, 1: 188]). This profanation sets a precedent; we are asked to follow Silvère's example, to

look for the keys that will unlock the metaphoric doors to the novel and the cycle beyond it.

To read a text in the perspective of the surrogate victim and collective violence is, as Girard states in our epigraph, to explore its omissions, to expose its ellipses and enigmas, to explode its silences. But this disrespectful reading, this desecration, is, paradoxically, the necessary preliminary to (re)discovering the origins of the sacred: violence. Needless to say, the blanks in the message cannot be filled in with random associations; the reader's participation is strictly controlled by the context, both immediate (*La Fortune des Rougon*) and extended (the *Rougon-Macquart* and the rest of the Zola canon). If we affirm that the origins of the *Rougon-Macquart* are steeped in sacrificial blood, it is because—as I hope to demonstrate in what follows—their power is consolidated by the constant reiteration of the original sacrifice. In other words, I posit that before the opening of the *Rougon-Macquart*, there occurred an act of collective violence against an "innocent" individual, and that this individual/crowd relationship will recur throughout the *Rougon-Macquart*, as well as in some of the later novels. Zola's crowd-fictions return repeatedly to the scene of the crime; they constitute a series of variants on their own genesis, the ritualization of the founding myth. That the "original" event is relegated to a pre- or extra-text seems to indicate Zola's recognition that the ultimate origins are unknowable, truly mythical.

Nevertheless, what Zola's own pre-texts—in particular *Thérèse Raquin*—do suggest is that murder and artistic creation are somehow linked. Only after Thérèse and Laurent have murdered her husband, Camille, does Laurent's talent as a painter emerge:

> In the life of terror he was living his mind was delivered from reason and could rise to the ecstasy of genius. The quasi-moral disease or neurosis which had disturbed his whole being had developed in him a strangely lucid artistic sense. Since he had killed a man his flesh was, as it were, appeased, and his distracted mind seemed limitless; and in this sudden broadening of his thought there floated before him exquisite creations and poetic visions. (*TR*, pp. 195-96)[39]

There is a catch to this new-found genius: Laurent is condemned to always repeat the same image, paint the same portrait; Camille's features have contaminated his every model: "Back came the drowned man always and always, whether as angel, virgin, warrior, child, or ruffian" (*TR*, p. 198; "Toujours, toujours le noyé renaissait, il était tour à tour ange, vierge, guerrier, enfant et bandit" [Mitt *OC*, 1: 630]). This compulsion to repeat the image of death—albeit in varied disguises—is described by Zola as a form of demonic possession, indeed as an *unconscious* mechanism: "His fingers had this inescapable involuntary power of continuously

reproducing Camille's portrait" (*TR*, p. 199; "Ses doigts avaient la faculté fatale et inconsciente de reproduire sans cesse le portrait de Camille" [Mitt *OC*, 1: 631]). The founding myth thus carries with it an artistic curse: the eternal return of certain motifs. Zola's crowd-fictions are an invaluable corpus in which to study the strategies for variations, for escaping the dangers inherent in ritual: the loss of effectiveness resulting from a breakdown of differences between successive works of fiction by a single author.[40]

Le Ventre de Paris

The specter of a dead woman haunts the *Rougon-Macquart*. The model established in *La Fortune des Rougon* of a double death, one occurring in a remote past, the other, in the course of the novel, sets a precedent for the entire series. The figure of the dead lady ("la dame morte") crops up in novels as dissimilar in all other respects as *La Faute de l'abbé Mouret* and *Au bonheur des dames*. Thus Albine, like Miette, displays a morbid fascination with the legend of a dead lady who once lived in le Paradou, who died in Albine's room, and who is buried under a tree reputed to bring both ecstasy and death, the Tree of Knowledge in this new Eden:

> "A long, long time ago Le Paradou belonged to a very rich lord who came there to shut himself up with a very beautiful lady....

> "When the lord went away, his hair was white. He had all the openings barricaded, so that his lady would not be disturbed...The lady had died in this chamber."[41]

Albine's identification with the dead woman, like Miette's, will prove fatal: Albine will commit suicide in the very room where the other woman is said to have died. Both are victims of the death-dealing tree. The place occupied by this legend in Zola's imagination is attested to by a "mise en abyme" we find in *Le Docteur Pascal*, where Clotilde is haunted not only by Albine's tragic end but also by that of the original "dame morte," rumored to have been Pascal's only and very chaste love. But because in *Le Docteur Pascal* everything that was negatively valorized in the early works is positively valorized, Clotilde survives her double (necrophilic) identification.

In *Au bonheur des dames*, we have yet another variant on this structure. The dead woman is Mme Hédouin, Octave Mouret's first wife, whose death occurs in a parenthesis between *Pot-Bouille* and *Au bonheur des dames*. This unnatural demise is explicitly linked with Octave Mouret's rise. Mme Hédouin's blood stains the cornerstone of his empire, the department store bearing the ironic name Au Bonheur des dames: "It

was the dead woman, the one the neighborhood accused him of having killed in order to found his establishment on the blood from her limbs" ("C'était la dame morte, celle que le quartier l'accusait d'avoir tuée, pour fonder la maison sur le sang de ses membres" [R-M, 3: 503]). The dead woman has two doubles—Geneviève Baudu and her cousin, Denise Baudu, the negative and the positive. (This split is a compromise solution, an indication of Zola's midcareer passage from one system of valorization to another.) Geneviève, like Mme Hédouin, will die a victim of Mouret's empire-building. Her funeral procession rallies all the small shopkeepers put out of business by the encroachment of the department store: "It was an obsession; the young girl's piteous body was carried around the department store like that of the first victim fallen in battle in times of revolution" ("C'était une obsession, ce pauvre corps de jeune fille était promené autour du grand magasin, comme la première victime tombée sous les balles, en temps de révolution" [R-M, 3: 742]). Let us note in passing the association of the "première victime" and revolution, which seems to lend more weight to our hypothetical reconstruction of the founding myth.

If Geneviève is Mme Hédouin's negative double, then Denise is the positive one. Denise's connections with both Geneviève and Mme Hédouin are made quite explicit. The identity/opposition with Geneviève turns on their outstanding common physical attribute—their hair. Whereas Geneviève's thick, dark hair robs her of her lifeblood, Denise's blond mane becomes quite literally her crowning glory: "While her [Geneviève's] black hair, heavy with passion, seemed to have grown thicker still and hungrily devoured her poor face" ("Tandis que ses cheveux noirs, lourds de passion, semblaient s'être encore épaissis et mangeaient de leur vie vorace son pauvre visage . . ." [R-M, 3: 737]); "As for him, he looked at her and smiled: with her plain and unadorned silk dress, her one luxury was her regal blond mane" ("Lui, la regardait en souriant, dans sa robe de soie toute simple, sans un bijou, n'ayant que le luxe de sa royale chevelure blonde" [R-M, 3: 645]). If Denise's marriage is contrasted with Geneviève's broken engagement, it is likened to Mme Hédouin's earlier marriage with Mouret: "And it was like a resurrection; he found in Denise the good sense and the solid poise of the one he had lost" ("Et c'était comme une résurrection, il retrouvait chez Denise le bon sens, le juste équilibre de celle qu'il avait perdue" [R-M, 3: 724-25]).

One novel stands out, however, as determined by the link between the original victim, the dead woman, and the surrogate victim, in this instance a man. That novel is Le Ventre de Paris, Zola's "sacrificial novel" par excellence, in that the sacrificial ritual is coextensive with the main plot, saturates (which is not to say exhausts) the text.

The original victim is "la dame en rose," the anonymous female

cadaver which haunts Florent, the protagonist of the novel. The lady's kinship with Miette is evident: both are young women shot in a battle between revolutionaries and the forces of order; both die with their eyes open; both become the object of a necrophilic cult on the part of their surviving male companion:

> On top of him lay a young woman with a pink hat, whose shawl slipped, exposing a finely pleated chemisette. Above her bosom, in the chemisette, two bullets had entered; and, when he gently pushed the young woman away in order to free his legs, two thin streams of blood trickled from the holes onto his hands. He then leapt up and went off, hatless, his hands wet. Until evening he roamed about, bewildered, still seeing the young woman lying across his legs with her ashen face, her big blue eyes open, her pained expression, her astonishment at having died there and so quickly. He was shy; at thirty he did not dare look women in the face, and yet this woman's face was with him for life, in his memory and his heart. It was as though he had lost a woman of his own.[42]

The blood which flows from the dead woman's wounds onto Florent's hands will mark him for life. This metonymic guilt by association, this mystic marriage, will cause Florent to be arrested and exiled to Cayenne, from which he will escape, only to be recaptured and redeported. Once Florent has come into contact with the "bad blood" of revolutionary violence—just as Silvère does in his fatal encounter with the gendarme Rengade[43]—only a new sacrifice, a ritual sacrifice, can rid the community of the contagion he carries. Sacrifice is founded on the ambivalent nature of blood: "Blood serves to illustrate the point that the same substance can stain or cleanse, contaminate or purify, drive men to fury and murder or appease their anger and restore them to life" (Girard, *Violence*, p. 37).

"Good blood" must root out the bad. The opposition between good and bad blood is developed in the book through two "relays." First, there is the long description of the making of blood sausage (*boudin*), with its emphasis on the quality of the pig's blood. Two details link and oppose the dead woman's blood and the pig's: whereas Florent can never wash out the "damned spot" which stains his hands, Auguste, the expert young butcher, can plunge his hands into the animal blood with impunity: "For a moment he remained with his hand in the air, complacent, languid; the hand which lived in buckets of blood was all pink with bright fingernails sticking out of the white sleeve" ("Il resta un instant la main en l'air, complaisamment, l'attitude molle; cette main qui vivait dans des seaux de sang était toute rose, avec des ongles vifs, au bout de la manche blanche" [*R-M*, 1: 684]). Further, the same word ("filet") is used to describe the trickle of blood from wounds to hand as from jug to pot: "Auguste fetched the two jugs. And slowly he poured the blood into the kettle in thin red streams" ("Auguste apporta les deux brocs. Et, lente-

ment, il versa le sang dans la marmite, par minces filet rouges" [*R-M*, 1: 689]).

The second relay is Marjolin, who functions as a substitute victim for Florent. Lisa Quenu takes out on the "innocent" child the aggressive impulses she feels against her brother-in-law, Florent. Her gesture of violence has unmistakable connotations, for she imitates a stockyard butcher: "She raised her arm as she had seen them do in the slaughter-house, tightened her beautiful woman's fist, and knocked Marjolin out with one blow right between the eyes. He collapsed, smashing his head against the edge of a butcher's block" ("Elle leva le bras, comme elle avait vu faire aux abattoirs, serra son poing de belle femme, assomma Marjolin d'un seul coup, entre les deux yeux. Il s'affaissa, sa tête se fendit contre l'angle d'une pierre d'abatage" [*R-M*, 1: 795]).

Despite certain circumstantial similarities between Silvère's execution and Marjolin's injury, and despite the fact that Florent is ultimately deported and not executed, Florent and not Marjolin is the surrogate victim in *Le Ventre de Paris*. Sacrifice does not, let us recall, necessarily take the form of a bloody ritual murder; Silvère's gory death is the exception rather than the rule in Zola's sacrificial novels. What informs the structure of these novels are the *preliminaries* to sacrifice, persecution rather than execution or expulsion. Bloodletting is only one of the two possible outcomes and is, of course, strictly synchronous with closure, whereas persecution is a long, linear process which allows, as we shall see, of many variations.

In *Le Ventre de Paris*, we may say without exaggeration that the plot turns entirely on the ups and downs of Florent's relationship with the people of les Halles, that is, a clearly defined collectivity. As in so many of Zola's novels, the first chapter recounts the arrival of a stranger in a community: cf. Gervaise (*L'Assommoir*), l'abbé Faujas (*La Conquête de Plassans*), Etienne (*Germinal*), and others.[44] Florent is an outsider who suddenly appears in the midst of a tightly knit community. But, at the same time, Florent is an insider: he is related to two members in good standing of this community, his half-brother, Quenu, and his sister-in-law, Lisa. By his ambiguous position, half insider, half outsider, Florent fulfills the first prerequisite for a surrogate victim: "If the victim is to polarize the aggressive tendencies of the community and effect their transfer to himself, continuity must be maintained. There must be a 'metonymic' relationship between members of the community and ritual victims. There must also be discontinuity. The victim must be neither too familiar to the community nor too foreign to it" (Girard, *Violence*, p. 271). Due to the peculiar nature of his blood-relationship to Quenu and Lisa, Florent fulfills yet another prerequisite; he is doubly determined as brother-in-law, the ritual victim par excellence: "The brother-in-law, then, becomes the sacrificial substitute for the brother as hostile object . . . .

And this structure reminds us once more of Greek tragedy, which abounds in enemy brothers and enemy brothers-in-law" (ibid., p. 279).

Florent seems like a walking sacrificial encyclopedia: his hands are tainted with "bad blood"; in prison he has consumed "impure" foods; he stands in the perfect ambiguous position vis-à-vis the community of les Halles; he is a stranger in his own family—in short, he is a black sheep ready for the kill. But, for all his *potential* as a victim, Florent might not be called upon to function as a human scapegoat if the community were not in need of one. He is, so to speak, the right man in the right place at the right time: for a character's potential as victim to be actualized, he or she must be placed in a community in crisis. Les Halles is such a community, the theater for all sorts of petty rivalries. The crisis, a veritable "crisis of distinctions," is symbolized by the specular relationship of Lisa Quenu and Louise Méhudin—"la belle Normande"—who are clearly designated as what Girard terms "mimetic doubles":

> Having lived in the same house, rue Pirouette, the two women were intimate friends, bound together by a touch of rivalry which made each one be continually preoccupied with the other. In the neighborhood people said "la belle Normande" just as they said "la belle Lisa." They were thus paired and compared, forced to keep up their renowned beauty. By leaning forward a little, the pork-butcher could, from her counter, see the fishmonger amidst her salmons and turbots in the shop across the way. Each woman kept a sharp watch on the other.[45]

Florent's arrival on the scene will cause a definite escalation in the hostilities, with Florent functioning as a pawn, an innocent victim of an undeclared war. The battleground for the conflict is at first the fishmarket, where Florent, at Lisa's urging, has accepted a job as inspector. For Lisa to pressure Florent into taking this job is tantamount to throwing him to the sharks, for the fishmarket is the Méhudins' undisputed territory, and they are out to "get" Lisa: "The first weeks Florent spent at the fishmarket were very rough. He found the Méhudins to be openly hostile to him, and this brought him into conflict with the entire market. La belle Normande meant to wreak vengeance on la belle Lisa and the latter's cousin was *a ready victim.*" ("Les premières semaines que Florent passa au pavillon de la marée furent très pénibles. Il avait trouvé dans les Méhudin une hostilité ouverte qui le mit en lutte avec le marché entier. La belle Normande entendait se venger de la belle Lisa, et le cousin était *une victime toute trouvée*" [R-M, 1: 713-14]).

Let us note in passing that as the Méhudins go, so goes the entire market: persecution by one family is equivalent to persecution by a collectivity. The first stage of Florent's relationship to the crowd is thus one of relentless persecution engineered by the Méhudins; Florent feels himself to be the victim of "the Méhudin conspiracy" ("la conspiration des Méhudin" [R-M, 1: 717]). At the very point in the narrative when this

persecution has reached epidemic proportions and Florent is thinking of quitting, a slow rapprochement with the Méhudin family begins to take place: first, through Claire, la belle Normande's somewhat eccentric sister, who is revolted by the treatment inflicted on Florent, then, through Muche, la belle Normande's illegitimate son, whom Florent befriends and tutors. This brings us to the second stage of Florent's relationship with the crowd: protection by the Méhudins can be equated with acceptance by the entire market. "There was peace. La belle Normande even took Florent under her wing. Moreover, the inspector was finally becoming accepted" ("Ce fut la paix. La belle Normande prit même Florent sous sa protection. L'inspecteur finissait, d'ailleurs, par être accepté" [R-M, 1: 727]).

Inevitably, this adoption of Florent by the Méhudins inaugurates a new round of "reciprocal violence" between the rival women. The fight for Florent, the pawn mechanism, is a classical instance of a situation Girard has analyzed under the heading "mimetic desire"—that is, a desire fueled by rivalry, a desire that consists in desiring the Object the Other desires: *"The subject desires the object because the rival desires it"* (Girard, *Violence*, p. 145). The more closely two subjects resemble each other—and this is what occurs in the case of doubles—the more heated is this kind of contest. Lack of significant difference, contrary to popular belief, breeds violence, not peace and harmony. The object of the convergent desire of doubles is a hyperbolical instance of mimetic desire. Florent draws all his value from the triangular configuration of which he is the least essential part; he is desirable to la belle Normande only because she thinks he is desired by la belle Lisa, and vice versa:

> The rivalry between la belle Lisa and la belle Normande then became fierce. La belle Normande was convinced that she had stolen her enemy's lover, and la belle Lisa was furious at that nonentity who would end up getting them into trouble by attracting that humbug Florent over to her side.

> But the two women's true victim was Florent. Fundamentally he alone had them up in arms; they fought only over him.[46]

The final, most dramatic stage consists in the union of all the warring doubles in the community against the common enemy. This final permutation, this alliance of factions heretofore divided—the Méhudins, the Quenu-Gradelles, the entire neighborhood—is predicted by Claude Lantier, the observer in the novel. (There are, in effect, two observers: Mlle Saget, the busybody/observer, is but a caricature, a double, of Claude, the artist/observer. Both are essentially voyeurs who carry around complete files on their neighbors in their heads). Claude's prediction is allegorized as the battle between the Thin and the Fat ("les Maigres et les Gras"):

And you! you are an astonishing Thin Man, the king of the Thin People, on my word of honor....As a rule, you see, a Fat Man holds a Thin Man in abomination. Consequently, he feels the need to put him out of his sight, with a bite or a kick. That's why, in your place, I would take precautions. The Quenus are Fat People, the Méhudins are Fat People—in short, you're surrounded by Fat People. If I were you, I would be worried.[47]

This Manichean allegory is remarkable, for it contains Zola's most explicit *theory* of sacrifice, including a precise allusion to the original crime, the first time: "'For sure,' he said, 'Cain was a Fat Man and Abel, a Thin one. Ever since *the first murder*, the big eaters have sucked the blood of the small eaters—It's a chain orgy, from the weakest to the strongest, each one swallowing his neighbor and being swallowed in turn" ("—Pour sûr, dit-il, Caïn était un gras et Abel un Maigre [*sic*]. Depuis *le premier meurtre*, ce sont toujours les grosses faims qui ont sucé le sang des petits mangeurs... C'est une continuelle ripaille, du plus faible au plus fort, chacun avalant son voisin et se trouvant avalé à son tour" [*R-M*, 1: 805]).

Zola's reading of the Biblical text is doubly revealing: first, it separates him from the Romantics, whose well-known fascination with Cain is exemplified, in France, by Baudelaire's *Abel et Caïn*. As this excerpt from Baudelaire shows, Zola's paradigm—Abel ("Thin) / Cain ("Fat")—runs counter to tradition:

> Race of Abel, eat, sleep and drink;
> God smiles on you approvingly.
>
> Race of Cain, in filth and stink
> Grovel and die, miserably.
> ....
>
> Race of Cain, within your gut
> Howls hunger like an ancient cur.
>
> Race of Abel, your innards take
> Warmth from the patriarchal hearth.[48]

Second, Zola's correlation of the first murder with the setting in motion of a nutritional cycle of violence—a dog-eats-dog world—is a characteristic (mis)reading or interpretation: the single cathartic sacrificial murder is transformed into a biologically determined serial carnage. What we have here is the story of Cain and Abel as retold by Darwin. If we superimpose (to borrow a term and a practice from Charles Mauron) on our text two others on the same subject, Zola's distortion becomes clear. Whether negatively valorized, as in his very early short story "Le Sang" ("Blood"), or positively valorized, as in *Au bonheur des dames*, whether equated with the Fall or with Progress, the nutritional chain is a parody of ritual sacrifice:

At the victim's cry, I saw the creatures scatter, driven by the wind of terror....

Then the eternal flight passed before me. The sparrow hawk swooped down on the swallow, the swallow in flight snapped at the gnat, the gnat settled on the corpse. From the worm on up to the lion, all beings felt threatened. The world bit its tail and devoured itself eternally.

That night Denise did not sleep a wink. A fit of insomnia, shot through with nightmares, made her twist and turn under the covers. It seemed to her that she was very little, and she burst into tears at the far end of their garden at Valognes on seeing the warblers eat the spiders, who in turn ate the flies. Was it then necessarily so: death fertilizing the world, the struggle for life causing all beings to spring from the charnel house of eternal destruction? ...Yes, it was blood's due: every revolution had to have its martyrs; one went forward only over the bodies of the dead.[49]

In *Le Ventre de Paris,* there is no such wise, "adult" acceptance of the necessity of sacrifice, no such resigned sanction of a Darwinistic survival of the fittest; rather, the last words of the novel—and they are Claude's exclamation "Honest folk! What scoundrels" ("Quels gredins que les honnêtes gens" [*R-M*, 1: 895])—deplore the triumph of the "Fat." The last stage of Florent's relationship with the crowd illustrates perfectly the mechanism of the union of warring doubles against a single victim. Whereas at first Florent is the object of partial, fragmented hostilities, in the end he reaches the apotheosis of persecution, the unconcerted unanimity of an entire community against one of its members. This spontaneous unanimity is revealed to Lisa when she finally decides to go to the Palais de Justice to denounce Florent's subversive political activities, only to learn that there already exists a bulging file on Florent, made up of duplicate accusations from independent (and mostly anonymous) sources. Then it is Florent's turn to become aware, belatedly, of his status as public enemy number one: "He saw Auguste's livid face again, the lowered eyes of the fishwives; he remembered the words of Mother Méhudin, la Normande's silence, the empty pork-butchery; and he said to himself that les Halles had collaborated, the entire neighborhood was turning him in" ("Il revoyait la face blême d'Auguste, les nez baissés des poissonnières; il se rappelait les paroles de la mère Méhudin, le silence de la Normande, la charcuterie vide; et il se disait que les Halles étaient complices, que c'était le quartier entier qui le livrait" [*R-M*, 1: 888]). In a passage quoted above, Claude had observed that there were two ways of disposing of superfluous "maigres": "à coups de dents" ("with a bite") or "à coups de pieds" ("with a kick"), which, transcoded into the sacrificial system, reads murder or exile. Florent is condemned to the latter; he is the victim of a bloodless sacrifice, but a sacrifice just the same, as evidenced by the after-effects.

Florent's presence in the community, like Oedipus's in Thebes, is

linked to illness, pestilential air. When Quenu complains of feeling unwell and in need of a doctor, Lisa answers: "There is no need for a doctor....It will pass. You see, there's an ill wind blowing just now. Everyone in the neighborhood is sick" ("Il n'y a pas besoin de médecin....Ça passera... Vois-tu, c'est un mauvais air qui souffle en ce moment. Tout le monde est malade dans le quartier" [R-M, 1: 854]). The expulsion of the supposed source of contagion—the carrier, as it were—thus restores not only peace and harmony, but above all health: "Once again the pork-butchery exuded health, a kind of greasy health" ("La charcuterie suait de nouveau la santé, une santé grasse" [R-M, 1: 895]).

In discussing Florent's qualifications as a victim, I have purposely made no mention of what might seem to be the most blatant: his subversive political activities. Certainly on the superficial level, on the level of rationalization, Lisa betrays her brother-in-law because he threatens the status quo by his projects for a revolution in Paris. Florent is a troublemaker who must be eliminated; contaminated by the bad blood of a revolutionary martyr, he seeks to spread the contagion by "reddening" the whole neighborhood. When Lisa goes up to inspect Florent's room, she is horrified to find its virginal whiteness sullied by the red paraphernalia of the coming insurrection. She is literally afraid to touch the inanimate objects, as though they could harm her:

> The childlike daintiness of the bed was sullied by a bundle of red sashes which hung down to the ground. Over the chimney, amidst the gilt boxes and old pomade jars, red arm bands trailed, along with packets of cockades which seemed to spread like enormous drops of blood....Lisa walked around, inspecting the guidons, the arm bands, the sashes, without touching anything, as though she were afraid those frightful rags would burn her.[50]

The association of bad blood and fire, the notion of an inflammable cloth stained with blood, goes back at least to the robe impregnated with the centaur Nessus's blood which Dejanira offers to Herakles. Given the "chemistry" of the Rougon-Macquart, Lisa's fears are well-founded, for as several of Zola's finest critics—I am referring to Michel Butor, F. W. J. Hemmings, and Michel Serres—have conclusively shown, Zola suffered from an acute "Joan of Arc complex," to borrow Serres' expression.[51] Indeed, as Serres argues, the genealogy = holocaust equation is encoded in Zola's onomastic system: "Red, Rougon. The family of fire."[52]

Lisa's fears are echoed not only by her neighbors, but even by members of Parliament, where the trumped-up story of a "Halles plot" ("le complot des Halles") brings together the opposing parties—final proof, on the macrocosmic level of the body politic, of the unifying function of the surrogate victim: "At the Legislative Assembly the agitation was so great that the center and the right forgot all about the unfortunate law on senatorial annuities which had divided them for a

moment, and made it up by voting, with an overwhelming majority, an unpopular taxation project. In the wave of panic that swept over the city, even the working-class districts went along without protest."[53]

Despite their importance in the unfolding of the plot, the political issues must be seen for what they are: a variable, a historically determined aspect of Zola's reactivation of a mythical model. Florent's revolutionary activities are an obfuscation, a sugar-coating of the horrifying reality of ritual sacrifice. Like Oedipus's crimes, Florent's serve a double function: they both mark a breakdown in the differences that structure the society he invades, and designate him as different and hence a perfect scapegoat. The revolutionary is to Zola's post-1789 (and 1848 and 1871) society what the parricide and the perpetrator of incest are to archaic societies: by the very nature of his actions, he seeks to subvert the differences that define bourgeois society, namely, the differences between the classes, the "Thin" and the "Fat"; by his very espousal of the ideology of non-difference, the revolutionary protagonist distinguishes himself from other characters who are in every other way his doubles.

Indeed, close attention must be paid to the system of doubles which informs the structure of the novel and which makes of it *the* sacrificial novel. Let us recall that in order for the sacrificial substitution, or "metonymic" shifting, to function effectively, the victim must be both within and without the community, both identical to all its members and a monstrous exception. *Le Ventre de Paris* offers a textbook-case for the study of doubles; from the minor characters to the main protagonists, everyone finds himself confronted with a mirror image, accompanied by a familiar shadow; "la belle Normande" / "la belle Lisa", Claude Lantier / Mlle Saget, are some of the obvious pairings I have already mentioned. One could add many more, but one extreme example should suffice to drive the point home: it is the doubly determined pairing of Auguste and Augustine, who are not only horizontal doubles of each other, as their names indicate — "they had had the same godfather; they bore the same given name" ("ils avaient eu le même parrain, ils portaient le même prénom" [*R-M*, 1: 660]) — but also vertical doubles of Lisa and Quenu: "Auguste was a pallid Quenu; Augustine, an immature Lisa" ("Auguste était un Quenu blême; Augustine, une Lisa pas mûre" [ibid.]). Or:

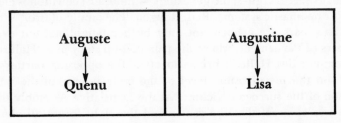

Figure 1

Florent is no exception to the rule. On the contrary, he holds a plurality of substitutive functions. He doubles for his mother as his brother's keeper; he takes on the identity of his nominal double, Florent Laquerrière; finally, he takes over from Verlaque as inspector of the fish market. But beyond these obvious doublings, there lie the deeper identities, two in particular. In the first place, there is his identity with Claude, which supports my argument that the actual content of Florent's political beliefs is, ultimately, irrelevant:

> "And may I be frank? Well! if I like *you*, it's because you seem to me to practice politics exactly the way I practice painting. It's titillation, my dear fellow."
> And, as Florent objected: "Come now! you are an artist in your own way; you're a political dreamer.... In short, you are titillating yourself with your ideas of truth and justice. The proof is that your ideas, just as my sketches, terrify the bourgeoisie."[54]

The artist and the revolutionary are thus explicitly linked. Both share a penchant for self-gratification; both elicit the same response from the bourgeoisie. Inevitably, in *L'Oeuvre*, Claude will suffer the same fate as Florent: his suicide, caused by the Philistines' mocking repudiation of his art, is a variant on Florent's expulsion, a non-Christian, not to say atheistic form of self-sacrifice. The equation of the artist and the revolutionary can be interpreted in two ways: as emphasizing the revolutionary aspect of modern art or as emphasizing the aesthetic aspect of revolution. As is so frequently the case with Zola, his ideological position is difficult to locate; the line between reaction and revolution is sometimes a thin one.

This ambiguity obtains in what is perhaps the deepest identity of all, surely the most essential, for without it there would be no story: the identity/rivalry between Lisa and Florent. Florent's pathetic status as victim should not blind us to his less attractive qualities as Lisa's double. Though at opposite ends of the sacrificial axis, both are part of the same semantic network; both are referred to as "sacred": "Florent became sacred" ("Florent devint sacré" [*R-M*, 1: 662]); "and standing there holding the burning candle with the beautiful and calm face of a sacred cow, she looked at Florent with satisfaction" ("Et elle, debout, le bougeoir allumé, regardait Florent d'un air satisfait, avec sa belle face tranquille de vache sacrée" [*R-M*, 1: 695]). Both share a similar longing for the sleep of forgetfulness and escape:

> Moreover, the books spoke only of rebellion, exciting his pride, while he felt a pressing need for peace and forgetfulness. To rock himself to sleep, to dream that he was perfectly happy and that the world was going to become so ...he planned moral measures, humanitarian bills which would have transformed this city of pain into a city of bliss.

She was but a dutiful Macquart, reasonable and logical in her craving for well-being, having understood that the best way to go to sleep warm and happy is still to make one's own bed of bliss.[55]

But, above all, despite the sharp contrast between Florent's humanitarian ideal of a *"city* of bliss" and Lisa's purely selfish dream of a *"bed* of bliss," both share the hunger for power which motivates so many of Zola's characters. For all Florent's innocence and altruism, he is a rival worthy of Lisa—but rival for what or for whom? one might well ask. For Quenu. Just as Florent is a pawn in the feud that pits la belle Normande against Lisa, Quenu is a pawn in the struggle that pits Lisa against Florent.

When Florent replaces his mother as Quenu's guardian, he revels in the new-found joys of immaculate fatherhood. He raises Quenu in an overprotective, mother-hen fashion, treating him not just as a child, but worse yet, as a girl, thus combining babying with emasculation: "At eighteen he still treated him like a young lady in need of a dowry" ("A dix-huit ans, il le traitait encore en demoiselle qu'il faut doter" [R-M, 1: 642]). Later on in the novel, Florent reenacts the same scenario with Muche, la belle Normande's little boy: "It seemed to him that his brother Quenu was becoming smaller, that they both still lived in his big room on the rue Royer-Collard. His great pleasure, his secret dream, was to live always in the company of a youth who would not grow up and to whom he would devote himself, instructing him constantly, and in whose innocence he would love mankind."[56]

This remarkable fantasy—the hyperbole of the Giant/Dwarf relationship adumbrated in Zola's early works and first described by John Lapp[57]—confirms the strong homosexual component in Florent's makeup, manifested repeatedly in the course of the narrative by his horror of all women, with the notable and significant exceptions of the maternal and masculine Mme François, and the anonymous and unthreatening dead woman. Indeed, Florent seems a model of male homosexuality, as described by Freud in his article "Certain Neurotic Mechanisms in Jealousy, Paranoia, and Homosexuality": Florent's "object-choice" is a perfect instance of sibling rivalry transformed into love (resented male sibling → adored male love-object). This reversal or transformation is a direct consequence of a fixation on the mother, as this sentence from *Le Ventre* makes abundantly clear: "They loved each other in the mother they shared" ("ils s'aimaient dans leur mère commune" [R-M, 1: 644]). Furthermore, Florent's confusion of love for a young boy (literally, pederasty) with his love for mankind-in-him is in keeping with Freud's observation that homosexualism and social feelings are often closely linked, precisely because of the homosexual's early conversion of the

rival into a love-object. This conversion makes him less apt to view his fellow men as potential sexual rivals and more apt to view them as "brothers": "In the light of psychoanalysis we are accustomed to regard social feelings as a sublimation of homosexual attitudes towards objects. In the homosexuals with marked social interests, it would seem that the detachment of social feelings from object-choice has not been fully carried through."[58]

For Zola, as for Freud, his contemporary, the fraternal relationship is an integral part of the founding myth. In *La Fortune des Rougon*, Antoine Macquart narrowly escapes an ambush laid for him by his half-brother Pierre Rougon, and while Antoine survives this attempted re-enactment of the "first murder," Pierre, the legitimate son, does succeed in despoiling the bastard-brother of his share in the family fortune. For both Zola and Freud, homosexualism is the only alternative to sibling rivalry and fratricide; thus, in *Totem and Taboo*, when the band of brothers united to kill the primal father, Freud hypothesizes that their possibly divisive sexual rivalry was held in check by their "homosexual feelings and acts."[59] The importance of Florent's homosexuality cannot be over-emphasized: it functions in conjunction with his political activities, for both threaten the differences which structure bourgeois society, and both mark Florent as "different."

If we superimpose *Le Ventre de Paris* on "Jacques Damour," the homosexual aspect becomes flagrant. In "Jacques Damour," we have a strikingly similar story: a deported revolutionary (a Communard) returns home after years in exile only to find his *wife* remarried. In the column where we would place Quenu, we how find Félicie. Once we have estab-lished the unmistakable connection between *Le Ventre de Paris* and "Jacques Damour" (down to Félicie's marrying a flourishing butcher by the fitting name of Sagnard), it becomes possible to link *Le Ventre* to the important subgroup of Zola's novels featuring a common plot structure already familiar to readers of Balzac's *Le Colonel Chabert:* the return of the first lover/husband from exile/death to find his former mistress/wife with another man. In its most explicit elaboration, *Madeleine Férat*, we have, as Borie has shown, the familiar, familial triangle of the Oedipus complex. What we seem to find, then, in these novels, as in so many plays by Racine, is a plot that hinges on the return of the "father"; but whereas in Racine's theater the father's return restores order—see, for example, the role of Theseus in *Phèdre*—in Zola's fiction, it threatens disintegration. If one were to list the novels featuring an intruder figure, Table 2 would comprise several other examples, for, as Philippe Hamon has noted, the intruder is a typical character ("personnage-type") in Zola's fiction.[60] But by limiting our examples to the works that adhere to the complete schema outlined above, we arrive at this table. (This plot

structure tends to fade out in Zola's later production, though traces of it persist well into *La Bête humaine,* to cite but one such case.)

Table 2

Work	Intruder	Couple
Les Mystères de Marseille (1867)	Philippe	Fine and Marius
Madeleine Férat (1868)	Jacques	Madeleine and Guillaume
Le Ventre de Paris (1873)	Florent	Lisa and Quenu
L'Assommoir (1877)	Lantier	Gervaise and Coupeau
Jacques Damour (1880)	Jacques	Félicie and Sagnard

Le Ventre de Paris is clearly an anomolous variant in this series, in that Florent's homosexuality short-circuits the conventional triangle: unlike all the other father/intruders, he desires to reclaim the *man* in the couple. From this crucial variation, others follow: whereas in all the other instances, one of the two male rivals abdicates (again: shades of *Chabert*), thereby avoiding any direct conflict, in *Le Ventre* there is an intense power-struggle for an unmediated relationship with Quenu: both Lisa and Florent are uncompromising and inflexible. The significance of Lisa's ultimate triumph in this battle of wills is at least twofold: not only are the structuring differences preserved on both the political and the sexual levels, but also the superiority of women is affirmed, the myth of the phallic mother preserved. Lisa, of course, does not act alone; she is part of a matriarchy that runs and rules les Halles. Of all the warring doubles that unite to expel Florent, perhaps the most important are the two systems of justice at work in the novel: the female sacrificial system and the male penal system. We find in Zola's version of the reenactment of the founding myth a confirmation of the phenomenon postulated by Girard with reference to the all-female, blood-thirsty crowd in *The Bacchae:* "a mythological substitution of women for men in regard to violence" (Girard, *Violence,* p. 139). Once again, the verification—were it possible—of the reality that myth distorts is not a pressing task. More urgent is to pose the question, What purpose do these distortions serve? If, in the founding myth, male violence is projected onto women, then it would appear that the founding myth cannot be separated from myths about the origins of sexual difference.

Chapter 2

The Founding Myth:
Structure and Variations

One never leaves Saint-Mittre.

Michel Serres, *Zola*

Le Ventre de Paris provides a prototype for all of Zola's subsequent sacrificial novels, which is to say his crowd-fictions. The several stages of Florent's "progress"—nonacceptance/acceptance/rejection—constitute narrative segments, action blocks which Zola will use to build his other novels centered on the individual/crowd relationship (hereafter abbreviated as the I/C relationship). While not endless, the variations possible along the syntagmatic axis of the plot line are sufficiently diversified to maintain reader interest from novel to novel. Zola was nothing if not a superb craftsman, an ingenious and instinctive structuralist. Generally he favors two devices: rearranging the *order* of the segments and/or modulating their *duration*.[1] Thus, in *Son Excellence Eugène Rougon*, the I/C relationship is reduced to a basic paradigm, in power/out of power, which corresponds to Florent's acceptance/rejection + exile, the initial and final segments of *Le Ventre* being exile, a sort of "degree zero" in the I/C relationship. A breakdown of the chapters of *Son Excellence* in terms of this paradigm produces the following configuration:

> chapter I: in power
> chapters II-VIII: out of power
> chapters IX-XIII: in power
> chapter XIV: in power

35

Though both *Le Ventre* and *Son Excellence* are cyclical novels, the in/out or—as Henri Mitterand would have it—up/down[2] structure of *Son Excellence* produces a narrative of a very different shape from that of *Le Ventre*, with its emphasis on Florent's linear progression. The difference between the two novels is perhaps most evident in Zola's handling of duration. The intervening "out" segment which occurs between chapters XIII and XIV is compressed to the point of ellipsis. Eugène's three years of wandering in the political desert (to adapt André Malraux's phrase with reference to De Gaule's "traversée du désert") are covered in three or four words: "three years later . . ." ("trois ans plus tard . . ."). The lessons or examples of Stendhal and Flaubert, the prime nineteenth-century French practitioners of the art of ellipsis, were not lost on Zola; while he stopped short of Flaubert's audacious ellipsis in the next-to-last chapter of *L'Education sentimentale*—"years passed"[3]—in works as similarly structured as *Son Excellence* and *Nana*, he used ellipsis to great advantage.

Nonetheless, in terms of the founding myth and the sacrificial novels it informs, variations along the paradigmatic axis are of far greater interest than those projected along the syntagmatic axis, simply because the former are more specific to our corpus than the latter. I will focus on two modes of paradigmatic variation: *disjunction* and *hyperbolization*. I define *disjunction* as the splitting up of the ritual victim into two distinct characters, one character corresponding to the "up," or acceptance, phase, the other, to the "down," or rejection, phase. *Hyperbolization* is the process whereby the affect of a narrative sequence is raised to its maximum intensity: e.g., acceptance becomes apotheosis.

Disjunction

In little more than a decade—between *Sémantique structurale* (1966) and *Maupassant: La Sémiotique du texte* (1976)—A. J. Greimas has reshaped or (re)structured our thinking about characters, forcing us (at least in our descriptions) to go beyond our anthropomorphism, our one-to-one identifications with heroes and heroines. He has accomplished (not singlehandedly, of course) this "Copernican revolution" by setting up a hierarchy going from the "actor" (the individual, individuated character as he appears on the surface of the text—e.g. Silvère, Florent), to the "actant" (a metatextual, metalinguistic construct based on the functions characters perform—e.g. the Subject, the Object). Midway between these two poles lies the so-called thematic role, that is, the role played by "typical characters" such as a doctor or, in another sphere, a father, each of which comes equipped with a socially coded narrative program.[4] The question

of where the ritual victim—or, as I prefer to call him, pharmakos (to avoid the confusion caused by the word *victim*)—fits on this scale is not as gratuitous as might at first appear, for to attempt to situate the pharmakos in Greimas's hierarchy is to refine the rather simple model we have worked with thus far, to go beyond the level of the actor. It would appear from what we have seen of and said about Florent that the pharmakos is coextensive with a single thematic role (victim), hence with a single actor. But if we go on to consider other pharmakoi in Zola's novels—such as Eugène (*Son Excellence Eugène Rougon*), Etienne (*Germinal*), Saccard (*L'Argent*), and Luc (*Travail*)—the falseness of this assumption becomes apparent, for in all these examples, the pharmakos plays not one but two equally important and complementary roles: he is *both victim and leader* (though, of course, never simultaneously). This double role—or, in Greimasian terms, "syncretism"—is, in fact, foreshadowed by Florent's leading role in planning the insurrection. Now, if the pharmakos syncretizes two distinct thematic roles, with two distinct narrative programs, if follows that the pharmakos is not necessarily coextensive with a single actor; each role may be assigned to a separate character. This always virtual disjunction occurs in two novels written almost thirty years apart, *La Conquête de Plassans* (1874) and *Vérité* (1902), two novels which share another distinguishing feature, the dubious distinction of being among the most neglected by readers and critics alike. Before going on to consider these cases running counter to the norm, let me summarize these methodological preliminaries. I will classify Zola's pharmakos as a thematic role with at least two peculiarities: this role always subsumes two others, and, perhaps more troubling, this role is always metatextual and thus on a higher level of abstraction than the usual thematic role. Without wanting to contribute to the inflation of metalanguage rampant in structuralist criticism, I would propose the notion of a "metathematic role" to cover this and analogous cases.

La Conquête de Plassans

To the extent that all the novels we are studying are "conquest novels," *La Conquête de Plassans* is, as evidenced by the title, the purest of the series. It is the story of l'abbé Faujas, a secret agent sent down from Paris by mysterious, hidden powers of the Second Empire to conquer Plassans. Just as, in *Le Ventre de Paris,* there is a constant, painful accumulation of events leading up to Florent's expulsion, *La Conquête de Plassans* is entirely taken up with the complex intrigues and strategies culminating in the triumphant execution of Faujas's mission. Faujas's passage from

nonacceptance to conquest is rendered by two symmetrical descriptions; the first describes Faujas's entrance into Félicité Rougon's "green salon" *before* his conquest; the second, *after*:

> Meanwhile, in *passing* through the salon, the priest had created a stir. One young woman, who had raised her head suddenly, even suppressed a gesture of terror on seeing that black mass before her. The impression made was unfavorable: he was *too big*, too broad-shouldered; his face was too hard, his hands, too thick. In the garish light of the chandelier his *cassock* appeared *so pitiful* that the ladies felt somehow ashamed to see such a poorly dressed abbot. They raised their fans and began to whisper again, pretending to turn their backs. Raising their eyebrows, the men exchanged meaningful glances.

> Just as Plassans's society was crowding into the Rougons' green salon, abbot Faujas *appeared* on the threshold. He was *magnificent*, tall, rosy, dressed in a *fine cassock* which shone like satin....About him there were the sounds of a flattering ovation, the fluttering of enchanted women....The mayor, the justice of the peace, even M. de Bourdeu—all shook hands with him vigorously.[5]

The transformation is extraordinary, total. Point by point all the aspects of the abbot's appearance which were negatively valorized in the first passage are positively valorized in the second: yet, aside from his new cassock, nothing tangible has changed. The abbot's recent successes have altered others' perceptions of his person: thus, instead of being perceived as excessively tall ("trop grand"), he appears as the hyperbole of grandeur ("superbe"); instead of making a furtive entrance ("passage"), he makes a dramatic one ("parut"); and instead of being eyed with suspicion, he is welcomed enthusiastically.

But *La Conquête de Plassans* is not only the story of Abbot Faujas's rise from rags to riches, from obscurity to prominence; it is also and no less the story of François Mouret, who goes from complacent bourgeois to institutionalized madman. Step by step these two actors will follow parallel but reverse courses; thus, if Faujas's basic paradigm is nonacceptance/conquest, Mouret's is acceptance/exile. Indeed, as Faujas and his locust-like swarm of hungry relatives invade the Mouret household, Mouret is supplanted as master of the family, disposessed as owner of the house. The two characters are mutually exclusive—they cannot coexist peacefully—and this is the fundamental structural principle in the novel. As Faujas gains in popularity, Mouret declines: the torch of persecution is passed from one pariah to the other. Whereas at first, when Mouret is in the dominant position, Faujas is the object of the townspeople's ridicule, later, when their positions are reversed, Mouret becomes the laughing-stock of Plassans:

> Serge, in turn, told them that several times while returning home from

school, he had followed Abbot Faujas, who was coming back from Saint-Saturnin. He would cross the streets without speaking to anyone; he seemed not to know a living soul and to be somewhat ashamed of the covert derision he felt around him.

· At the end of the Cours Sauvaire, when Mouret went by the Youth Club, he once again met with the muffled laughter which had accompanied him ever since he had set foot in the street.[6]

The analogy between the two scenes is reinforced by the intangible, amorphous nature of the rejection. The two actors are, on this level, doubles; and doubles, as we know from our examination of *Le Ventre de Paris*, spell trouble.

In fact, it would be very easy to demonstrate the profound similarities between the social structures of the communities represented in *Le Ventre* and *La Conquête*, which account for their common need for a pharmakos. Just as in *Le Ventre*, we had the rivalry of the mimetic doubles Lisa and la belle Normande, in *La Conquête*, we have the rivalry of the two mimetic political factions: the legitimists and the supporters of the Second Empire. And like Florent, caught in the cross fire between the two women, Mouret, the republican, is used as a pawn in a larger political struggle. The sociopolitical situation is transposed into a topographical code, as Mouret confides to the abbot in the very beginning:

Imagine that rightly or wrongly I am considered to be a republican.... Well! I have here on my right, at the Rastoils, the flower of the legitimists, and there on my left, at the subprefect's, the bigwigs of the Empire. Isn't it ludicrous? my poor old garden, which is so peaceful, my little haven of happiness, between these two enemy camps. I am always afraid that they will throw stones at each other over my walls.... You realize that their stones could land in my garden.[7]

Mouret's fears, like those of so many of Zola's characters, will be partially realized. There will be stone throwing, indeed stoning, and he will be the target, not by accident, but by express intent, as a result of the mechanism which transforms reciprocal violence into cathartic, unanimous violence against a single scapegoat. At the height of Faujas's success, the two rival factions will come together under his authority: "The great triumph of the day consummated the merging of the two groups into one" ("Le grand triomphe de la journée achevait de fondre les deux groupes en un seul" [*R-M*, 1: 1153]). Consequently, Mouret will be locked up in the local madhouse, les Tulettes.[8]

On the basis of what I have said so far, it would appear that Mouret and Faujas are two totally distinct characters and that, were it not for my superimposing *La Conquête* on *Germinal*, *L'Argent*, and so on, I would have no grounds for stating that they constitute a single thematic role.

But the novel's ending should serve as strong evidence in support of this contention, for if in life Faujas and Mouret are mutually exclusive, in death they are inextricably intertwined. Complementary actors, doubles, cannot outlive each other, so it is not surprising to find that in the end Faujas and Mouret perish together in the fire that Mouret, escaped from les Tulettes, has set to his own home. In this final, very melodramatic scene, the doubles are literally fused into one, into the pharmakos they constitute, and this despite Mme Faujas's heroic effort to save her son by carrying him out of the burning building on her back:

> But just as she was about to come down, the madman, whom she had not seen, jumped on Abbot Faujas and wrenched him from her shoulders. His plaintive wail culminated in a howl, while a fit kept him writhing at the edge of the staircase. He battered the priest, scratched and strangled him.
> "Marthe! Marthe!" he screamed.
> And with the body he rolled down the flaming steps, while Mme Faujas, who had dug her teeth into his throat, drank his blood.[9]

The fact that Mme Faujas participates in this infernal copulation does not alter the basic situation, for she clearly functions throughout the novel as an aspect, an adjunct, of her son, and not as an autonomous character with an independent will.

Vérité

Vérité, the most autobiographical of Zola's later works, is a thinly disguised fictional account of the Dreyfus affair. Here, the distance between history and myth has shrunk to a minimum, and what is more, "individual myth" and historical reality coincide. If the faithful transposition of the actual events dictated the disjunction of the leader (Zola) and the victim (Dreyfus), this disjunction had been, as I am attempting to demonstrate, long since adumbrated in Zola's writings, his art criticism as well as his fiction.

Two actors share the role of pharmakos: Simon, the Jewish schoolteacher accused of raping and killing his own beloved nephew,[10] and Marc, his gentile colleague, who devotes his life to winning a reversal of Simon's condemnation. Simon is the ritual pariah, the Jew who has for centuries served as the prime scapegoat for all the disorders affecting the dominant Christian societies in which he lives: "And so, fed on the tales of the Petit Beaumontais, still shaken by the horror of the crime, the crowd uttered a cry as soon as it caught sight of the schoolmaster, the cursed Jew, the infant-killer, who needed their virgin blood still sanctified by the host to perform his evil deeds."[11]

Simon's story can be broken down into the following segments: rejec-

tion/exile/rejection/exile/apotheosis. The greater part of the novel deals with the periods of Simon's exile, confirming the pattern already observed in *La Conquête:* the victim and the leader cannot coexist. Let us note that the leader/victim relationship is reversed here: whereas Faujas leads the persecution of Mouret, Marc is Simon's most ardent defender. Thus, when disjunction of the leader and the victim occurs, their relationship can be either one of persecution or protection. Though both protection and persecution leader/victim relationships signify the necessary absence of one of the two actors (generally the victim), the actualization of one rather than the other will determine very dissimilar novelistic structures. The persecution relationship—leader (Faujas) persecutes victim (Mouret) —generates, as we have seen, two parallel but reverse sequences; not so the protection relationship. In *Vérité*, Simon's physical exile is closely duplicated by Marc's spiritual exile in the form of his gradual ostracism by the community and his estrangement from his family. In other words, protection of the victim by the leader results not only in parallel, but in mimetic sequences. Compare the home of the Lehmann-Simons during Simon's exile and Marc's schoolhouse quarters, abandoned by his wife: "It would soon be ten years since the Lehmanns, execrated by the public, had retired into their humid and deathlike little house" ("Depuis dix ans bientôt, les Lehmann, sous l'exécration publique, vivaient dans l'ombre de leur petite maison humide et comme morte" [Mitt *OC*, 8: 1225]); "The house was dead; the absent one had taken away life, warmth, and light" ("Le logis était mort, l'absente avait emporté la vie, la chaleur et la lumière" [p. 1258]).

Consider the constantly reiterated depictions of both Marc and Simon as Christian martyrs, indeed Christ-figures. (It should be pointed out that Zola's virulent anticlerical diatribes in *Vérité* and elsewhere are matched in passion and intensity only by his deep immersion in Christian mythology. Just as in *Lourdes,* Zola attacks the rampant commercialization of the Church, in *Vérité,* he decries the nefarious role played by the Jesuits in education, but for the early Christian martyrs, for the true visionaries like Bernadette, he has the admiration that only imitation can adequately bespeak.) But whereas Simon is described as "the crucified Jew who agonized down there" ("le juif crucifié, qui agonisait là-bas" [Mitt *OC*, 8: 1225]), Marc is given the far more glamourous role of redeemer; whereas Simon is an unwilling victim, constantly protesting his innocence, Marc's leadership takes the form of voluntary self-sacrifice. Marc does not merely submit to the crowd's abuse: he welcomes it. For him, as for Rousseau, persecution is the proof of innocence: "All that his fellow citizens hurled at him that was foul and bitter, he returned in kindness, goodness, and sacrifice. Tenderly he strove to make the children better than their fathers; he sowed the abominable present with the seeds

of the happy future, redeeming the crimes of others at the cost of his own personal happiness."[12]

In the end, after their separate but equal trials and tribulations, Simon and Marc will be united in a moment of triumph, of unanimous acclamation by the newly educated and repentant crowd:

> Meanwhile, Marc having gone to meet Simon and David, whom Delbos had overtaken, the four men found themselves together for a moment on the very threshold of the house. There was a heightening of joyous passion, a veritable ecstasy of cries and gestures, on seeing them all four thus side by side, arm in arm, the three heroic defenders and the innocent man they had saved from the direst tortures.
>
> With a great leap, Simon fell on Marc's neck, and Marc returned his embrace. Both men were sobbing.[13]

We have here the positive version of the Faujas-Mouret death scene, down to the point of fusion, the neck. Zola's well-known "neck fixation" follows, over the years, the same path as so many of his other obsessions, the path of edulcoration. A hug replaces strangulation; a reciprocal gesture of love replaces a nonreciprocal chain of gestures of hate (Mme Faujas biting Mouret while the latter gets a stranglehold on Faujas).

Given the close resemblance between the leader and the victim even in the face of disjunction, one might well ask, What distinctive features designate the leader actor? what constitutes the specificity of the leader function? If Marc and Simon are both ostracised by the community, only to be united in triumph at the end, how are they different? Beyond the two crucial oppositions implicit in what precedes—leader : victim : : present : absent : : active : passive—are there others? The answer can be only partial at this point, to be completed in the subsequent section on hyperbolization, for what distinguishes the leader actor (or the leader role of the syncretic leader/victim figure like Etienne) is the hyperbolization of the acceptance segment into *conversion*.

Conversion is suprasegmental: it subordinates alternating segments of acceptance and rejection; it relies on an extreme distortion of duration (hence the Methusalah-like old age of Zola's "apostles," hence the very length of his "gospels"). *Vérité* is the ultimate conversion novel; Marc, the most evangelical of the Froment brothers. The pages of this lengthy work are largely taken up with an account of Marc's half-century-long struggle to raise the masses from their long sleep of ignorance, to convert the crowd to his progressive vision of the world. The stages of this long quest for truth are dramatized by three visits to three representative families—the Bongards (peasants), the Doloirs (workers), and the Savins (bureaucrats). The first round of visits takes place at the time of Simon's condemnation; the second, fifteen years later, at the time of his retrial;

the third, forty years after the first, just prior to Simon's triumphant return. Let us compare Marc's thoughts after the initial and final rounds:

> These people were France—the great crowd, ponderous and inert; there were doubtless many good people in it, but like a mass of lead, it riveted the nation to the ground, incapable as it was of a better life, of being free, just, happy, since it was ignorant and poisoned.

> This was what he had wanted; his design was being carried out: the deliverance of a people through primary education, all citizens pulled out of the inequity in which they wallowed, the stupid herd at last become capable of truth and justice.[14]

The reincarnation of the Poet-Magus as a primary-school teacher bears witness to Zola's immense debt to Romantic I/C clichés in general, and to Hugo's in particular. Zola was never closer to Hugo than in this hymn to secular education, to the enlightenment of the benighted masses. In the words of Victor Brombert: "He had been brutally unfair to Hugo—but owed him far more than he would ever dare acknowledge: a taste for grandiose visions, sympathy for the 'people,' a tendency to self-dramatization and self-glorification, and, above all, that inner conviction that the poet is prophet, *vates*, seer, a fierce magus, a voice that announces the truth."[15]

Along with the basic vision of the writer as leader of the crowd came a network of images, a series of *topoi*. The raising of the masses from darkness to light along the vertical axis, an insistent motif in Hugo, is perhaps the best known of these clichés: as we shall see in the next section, the pivotal scene in *Germinal* (IV, vii)—Etienne's address to the miners—is an expansion of this matrix structure. But there are other image clusters. In *Les Misérables,* we find this striking passage—the sentence in italics could serve as an epigraph to *Vérité*—where the I/C relationship is transposed into a nutritional code. And, of course, both the title *Germinal* and the family name of Zola's apostles, Froment ("wheat"), share a common seme: nourishment.

> Intellectual and moral growth is no less indispensable than material improvement. To know is a sacrament, to think is the prime necessity, *truth is nourishment as well as grain [froment]*. A reason which fasts from science and wisdom grows thin. Let us enter equal complaint against stomachs and minds which do not eat. If there is anything more heart-breaking than a body perishing for lack of bread, it is a soul which is dying from hunger for the light.[16]

The interplay between the nutritional and light codes is nowhere more evident than in the final sentence, which brings them together in a rhetorical figure.

But for all his immense and unacknowledged debt to Hugo (the "bad father" in Zola's literary Oedipal drama), and despite his reinvestment of some of the most hackneyed imagery in the Romantic repertoire, Zola infused the Poet-Seer-Schoolteacher / Crowd-Blind Man-Child relationship with obsessive imagery unmistakably his own. Thus, Marc sees his role not so much as torchbearer, but rather as faith-healer. The crowd's ignorance takes the very Zola-esque form of paralysis (is, as it were, transposed into a medical code). The educator's mission is one of reeducation, of making the blind see, the halt walk unaided — in short, of performing a miracle. As Borie writes, "The theme of the miracle meets with a surprising acceptance on the part of that 'rationalist' Zola. We can admire the consistency of these works and decide that *Lourdes* occupies a necessary place within them . . . the entire second half of Zola's works hinges on a resurrection."[17]

Such is the consistency of Zola's production that we find the image of the paralyzed crowd in Zola's earliest crowd-fiction, "Celle qui m'aime." The first-person narrator wanders about a fairground on the outskirts of Paris, mingling with the crowd, yet already and at the same time standing apart as an observer. Among his observations is the following:

> There hovers above the crowd an indefinable anguish, an immeasurable sadness, as though terror and pity rose from the multitude. I have never found myself at a great concourse of people without experiencing a vague uneasiness. It seems to me that a dreadful disaster threatens these assemblages, that a single bolt of lightning in the midst of their excited gestures and voices could easily paralyze these men, silencing them forever.[18]

If we superimpose this text on the passage from *Vérité* quoted above ("These people were France . . ."), some revealing variations stand out: what is felt to be a potential disaster in this early text, becomes a painful *fait accompli* in the later one. What applies to the crowd in the short story applies to France in the novel. The confrontation of these two texts leads me to venture a hypothesis: what is given as a fear in "Celle qui m'aime" is in fact (or also) a wish, for if the exceptional individual is to manifest himself, he must be needed; the crowd must be paralyzed before it can be made to walk again. Further, if the crowd can be stilled by a single bolt of lightning, then a "miracle" can restore it to life. This hypothesis gains in plausibility if we consider an external, that is, biographical, datum: Zola's intense phobia of the crowd, which can be traced back to a traumatic childhood experience, as told to/by Dr. Toulouse: "Being caught in the crush of a mid-Lenten crowd once brought on in M. Zola an anxiety attack with symptoms of what appeared to be angina pectoris."[19] If, as I suspect and am suggesting, the "vague uneasiness" of the narrator of "Celle qui m'aime" is related to Zola's anxiety attack, then it would

appear that the narrator fears not for the crowd, but for himself. By transferring, not to say projecting, the suffocating effects of the phobia onto the crowd, Zola "saves" himself while preparing to save others.

The analogy between the two texts continues: in both, potential paralysis—future or metaphoric—is contrasted with actual, literal paralysis. Immediately after his expression of uneasiness, the narrator of "Celle qui m'aime" sees the following sight: "I gradually slackened my pace, looking at this heartrending gaiety. At the foot of a tree, in the bright yellow glare of the Chinese lanterns, there stood an old beggar, his body stiffened and horribly twisted by paralysis. Fresh-faced and blushing young girls passed by, laughing at this hideous sight."[20] It would seem that by juxtaposing the projected general paralysis and the present individual case of the beggar, by reducing an apocalyptic vision to the dimensions of a cliché—Beauty and Beast—Zola is attempting to reassure both himself and the reader, to minimize the impact of the "cathartic" experience. In *Vérité*, the paralytic is the Savins's son, Achille, whom Marc, completing his final round of visits, finds confined to an armchair. By inserting the figure of the paralytic at this precise point in the narrative syntagm, Zola seems to be saying: though much progress has been made, though Marc has delivered the people from the bonds of ignorance, there is still an irreducible sum of pain in the world. There are those Marc cannot help; the omnipotence fantasy which colors the early part of the story has been played out. In the last analysis, Marc recognizes that he is not God: "Children, children, you must not make me into a god. You know the churches are being closed.... I am nothing but a hard-working laborer who has done his day's work" ("Mes enfants, mes enfants, il ne faut pas faire de moi un dieu. Vous savez qu'on ferme les églises... Je ne suis qu'un ouvrier laborieux qui a fait sa journée" [Mitt *OC*, 8: 1488]).

The leader remains an apostle, and the apostle's task is to make new converts. Conversion is, as we have seen, a diachronic process, involving generations of men. But synchrony precedes diachrony, so to speak. Before conversion can affect large crowds, there must be a first convert. This privileged character is Mignot, Marc's assistant:

> A remarkable moral phenomenon had occurred, that kind of slow action of a master on his disciple, who at first rebels, then is brought round and absorbed. Certainly no one in the past would have suspected that Mignot had the makings of the hero he was becoming today. He had acted very shadily during the affair, accusing Simon, concerned above all with not being implicated....And then Marc had come, and in this tragic story, he had turned out to be the man with the intelligence and the will to influence Mignot's conscience, to beautify it and raise it up to the level of truth and justice. Thus, the lesson was perfectly clear, even luminous, and unquestion-

able: the example and the teachings of a single hero were enough to make other heroes rise up from the dark and shadowy heart of the average crowd.[21]

The master/disciple relationship between Marc and Mignot could serve to illustrate the theories of group formation Freud sets forth in *Group Psychology and the Analysis of the Ego*. Schematizing his intricate analyses, one might say that Freud distinguishes two complementary processes in group formation, which we can distribute along two axes. On the vertical axis we would place the relationship between each individual member of the group and the leader; on the horizontal, the relationship between the members. The first of these two relationships is compared by Freud to two states: love and hypnosis. The hypnosis analogy is particularly relevant to our master/disciple configuration: "The hypnotic relation is . . . a group formation with two members. . . . Out of the complicated fabric of the group it isolates one element for us—the behaviour of the individual to the leader."[22]

In this vertical relationship, "the object has been put in the place of the ego ideal."[23] The word *absorbed* in the Zola text refers to this process of assimilation, or better, substitution: the idealization of the object (Marc, the leader) is achieved at the expense of the subject's identity, involving a relinquishment of the subject's own ego-ideal (Mignot's personal ambitions). Once this group of two has been formed, the horizontal relationship between Mignot and Marc's other disciples can develop. Nevertheless, vertical substitution and horizontal identification do not adequately account for the situation described in our text. In *Vérité*, we find a confirmation of Freud's analysis of the Church: "Every Christian loves Christ as his ideal and feels himself united with all other Christians by the tie of identification. But the Church requires more of him. He has also to identify himself with Christ and love all other Christians as Christ loved them."[24] In other words, in the Church, the vertical relationship is both hierarchical and nonhierarchical, both one of substitution and identification. This is exactly what occurs in *Vérité*—further confirmation of Zola's immersion in Christian mythology. Mignot's absorption by Marc does not simply signify a loss of identity for Mignot; it also means his taking on Marc's heroism. Mignot is first a disciple, then a master in his own right. Each new convert becomes a new apostle: the leader's combination of pedagogy and demagogy ensures his posterity.

To summarize our findings: the disjunction of the pharmakos—split into two separate actors, the leader and the victim—generates not only two different narrative sequences but also, ultimately, two different outcomes: either the leader persecutes the victim, and both die, or the leader protects the victim, and both live.

As we turn from instances of actual disjunction to a case of nonactua-

lized but virtual disjunction—Etienne in *Germinal*—the question becomes, Inasmuch as the coexistence, the syncretism, of the leader and the victim provides the pharmakos with a life insurance policy, what form does the reenactment of the founding sacrifice take? In other words, inasmuch as the combined leader-victim is, because of his leadership qualities, invulnerable, what can the crowd do to him which would in any way reduplicate the original event?

Hyperbolization

Variations in the order of narrative segments along the syntagmatic axis, disjunction of character-actors performing complementary functions —these are the province of structural analysis. But as we have already observed, in some instances these structural variations are supplemented by an affective variation, an occurence I have termed hyperbolization. Hyperbolization consists in the heightening, the highlighting, of certain scenes. Not only is excessive duration a sign of hyperbolization; so, too, is the recurrence of this scene in many texts. Hyperbolization takes us from the relative security of structural analysis to the relative insecurity of psycho- or text analysis, from the near-infinite play of permutation to the monotony of compulsive repetition. Hyperbolization invites speculation on the why's rather than formalizations of the how's: why does Zola dwell with particular intensity on two diametrically opposed but equally obsessive moments—the apotheosis of the leader and the lapidation of the victim? why is the pharmakos so highly polarized a thematic role? *Germinal* is the ideal text for the study of these questions, for in no other novel is the dialectic of the I/C relationship so central, so thoroughly explored. In a letter to his friend Henri Céard, Zola writes, apropos of *Germinal*: "My subject was the reciprocal action and reaction of the individual and the crowd."[25] I will focus here on the two hyperbolized moments in the I/C relationship as represented in *Germinal*: the highest point in Etienne's fortunes, the meeting at the Plan-des-Dames, and the lowest, his lapidation.

Apotheosis

In *Germinal,* the conversion segment (itself already a hyperbolization of the acceptance segment) culminates in a strategically placed central scene: the night meeting of the miners in a forest clearing called the Plan-des-Dames. This scene, coextensive with a chapter, recapitulates and brings to a climax the entire conversion segment—that is, Etienne's

gradual emergence as the leader of the miners' political action—through an intensification of symbolic modulations of light, a play of chiaroscuro.

From the outset, Etienne is distinguished from the miners on the semantic axis of absence of color. Whereas the miners, represented by the Maheu family, are characterized by their "anaemic pallor" (G, p. 30), Etienne is described as "very dark" (G, p. 20). The excessive pallor vs. excessive darkness opposition corresponds to a whole series of oppositions set up in the very first chapter of the novel:

$$\frac{\text{Etienne}}{\text{Maheu}} \simeq \frac{\text{Outsider}}{\text{Insider}} \simeq \frac{\text{South}}{\text{North}} \simeq \frac{\text{Swarthiness}}{\text{Anaemia}}$$

While the achromatic semantic axis remains intact and active throughout *Germinal*,[26] in the course of the conversion segment, the physical opposition is reversed on the spiritual plane. In keeping with a cliché paradox, the dark-complected Etienne becomes, through his revolutionary teachings, the bearer of light, Lucifer: "He talked on and on, like one possessed. Suddenly the closed horizon burst asunder as he spoke, and there opened a gap of light in the dark existence of these poor folk" (G, p. 168; "D'une voix ardente, il parlait sans fin. C'était, brusquement, l'horizon fermé qui éclatait, une trouée de lumière s'ouvrait dans la vie sombre de ces pauvres gens" [R-M, 3: 1278]).

In the Plan-des-Dames scene, oppositions along the vertical axis reinforce those along the achromatic axis. At first, Etienne is separated from the crowd by a difference in levels: he stands above the miners, addressing them from the double vantage point of a hill and a tree trunk. Yet, though quite literally superior to the crowd, Etienne is hardly visible: "Etienne stood still for a moment on his log. The moon was still too low on the horizon, and only lit the topmost branches, so that the crowd, which had gradually calmed down into complete silence, was still lost in shadow. He too looked black and stood out above the crowd at the top of the slope like a dark pillar" (G, p. 272).[27] This situation corresponds to the initial stage of Etienne's conversion sequence: his natural intellectual superiority sets him apart from his fellow workers, but his ignorance in sociopolitical matters is almost as great as theirs. Gradually, however, through his program of self-education (Etienne incarnates yet another typical character in Zola, the autodidact) the innate differences are confirmed by acquired ones. The second stage of the conversion sequence is symbolized in the Plan-des-Dames scene by Etienne's sudden illumination, light supplementing height as a distinctive feature: "Just then the moon rose clear of the topmost branches and lit him up. When the crowd, still in darkness, saw his figure standing out white, distributing fortunes with open hands, they burst out again into prolonged applause" (G, p. 275; "A ce moment, la lune, qui montait de l'horizon, glissant des

hautes branches, l'éclaira. Lorsque la foule, encore dans l'ombre, l'aperçut ainsi, blanc de lumière, distribuant la fortune de ses mains, elle applaudit de nouveau, d'un battement prolongé" [*R-M*, 3: 1379]).

Finally, when Etienne's proseletyzing has attained its maximal effectiveness, the differences are seemingly abolished as the miners follow their leader out of the dungeon of ignorance into the light of awareness and hope: "Acclamations roared towards him from the depths of the forest. By now the moon lit up the whole clearing and picked out the isolated points in the sea of heads" (*G*, p. 276; "Une acclamation roula jusqu'à lui, du fond de la forêt. La lune, maintenant, blanchissait toute la clairière, découpait en arêtes vives la houle des têtes" [*R-M*, 3: 1380]). This is the moment of Etienne's apotheosis—the word occurs in the text—and the scene is supercharged with religious analogies. The very excessive quality of Zola's language underscores the grim irony of these analogies, points up the discrepancy between the miners and the early Christian martyrs to whom they are compared: "They were uplifted in a religious ecstasy, like the feverish hope of the early Christians expecting the coming reign of justice" (*G*, p. 276; "Une exaltation religieuse les soulevait de terre, la fièvre d'espoir des premiers chrétiens de l'Eglise, attendant le règne prochain de la justice" [*R-M*, 3: 1380]). Throughout the work there is an abundance of religious imagery, imagery typical of its age by its syncretism: Zola draws equally from the Judaeo-Christian and the pagan codes. Etienne is sometimes described as an "apostle bringing the gospel of truth" (*G*, p. 273; "l'apôtre apportant la vérité" [*R-M*, 3: 1378]) and sometimes as an oracle: "The evening conversations became oracles which he delivered" (*G*, p. 221; "Dans les coversations du soir, il rendait des oracles" [*R-M*, 3: 1328]).

In what concerns the I/C relationship, religious syncretism confirms the main protagonists' functional syncretism. In the pagan code, Etienne is *turannos-pharmakos;* in the Christian, he is Christ. The time has come to take a longer look at the leader figure and recognize him for what he is, perhaps the supreme incarnation of Baudelaire's *Homme-Dieu* ("Man-God"). Under the apostolic mask, at the moment of apotheosis, the true nature of the leader stands revealed: he is no mere apostle, but the son of God himself. At least on two occasions in the course of the novel, there are oblique references to Etienne's special status. First, in a rare moment of self-doubt, Etienne wonders if he is not a false Messiah: "And so in his more self-critical moments [he] had had doubts about his mission and feared that he might not after all be the man the world was waiting for" (*G*, p. 222; "Aussi, à certaines heures de bon sens, éprouvait-il une inquiétude sur sa mission, la peur de n'être point l'homme attendu" [*R-M*, 3: 1328]). Then, in a very different context, Etienne succumbs to the pleadings of Mouquette, "a girl who worshipped him like a holy

image" (*G*, p. 261; "cette fille qui l'adorait comme un Jésus" [*R-M*, 3: 1366]).

The point I am trying to make is that whether decoded in a pagan or a Christian perspective, Etienne's relationship to the crowd oscillates between two extremes, ranging from the omnipotence of the Man-God to the impotence of the lowliest member of the community, the false prophet. The moment of apotheosis is the moment of omnipotence: "Etienne was tasting the heady wine of popularity. This was power that he was holding in his hands, materialized in the three thousand breasts whose hearts were beating at his bidding" (*G*, pp. 276-77; "Etienne goûtait l'ivresse de sa popularité. C'était son pouvoir qu'il tenait, comme matérialisé, dans ces trois mille poitrines dont il faisait d'un mot battre les coeurs" [*R-M*, 3: 1381]).

To revel in total power over one's fellow men, to achieve godlike supremacy, are, at least in Western literature, inevitable preludes to a fall; the transformation of the leader into the victim results from the leader's *hubris*. And Etienne definitely indulges in the sin of pride; he is, as Zola's choice of words makes clear, "drunk" with power, intoxicated with success: "He tasted the joys of satisfied vanity and drank the heady wine of growing popularity—it filled him with pride to think that, young as he was, and so recently only an unskilled labourer, he was now at the head of others and in a position to command, and this encouraged still more his dreams of the coming revolution in which he was destined to play a part" (*G*, pp. 171-72).[28]

At this juncture we must refine our original sacrificial model, for one can hardly consider the leader at the moment of apotheosis simply a pharmakos; and furthermore, one can hardly minimize the difference between the punishment inflicted on him—lapidation—and sacrifice, though both fulfill the same purpose. The leader and his fate call to mind another ancient Greek ritual, one very closely related to the sacrifice of the pharmakos—the ostracism of the *isotheos*, that is, the God-like member of the community:

> Through the ostracized person, the city expels that within it which is too lofty and incarnates the evil that can befall it from above. Through the *pharmakós*, the city expels its lowest element, which embodies the evil threatening it from below. By means of this double and complementary rejection, the city thus defines itself in relation to a beyond and a beneath. It takes the measure of what is properly human, as opposed to divine and heroic on the one hand, and bestial and monstrous on the other.[29]

The passage from apotheosis to lapidation is heavily overdetermined: Etienne is expelled from the community not only because of his natural superiority and his will to power, but also because of the essential

ambiguity of (his) political leadership. In order to elucidate the nature of this ambiguity, let us retrace very briefly the evolution of criticism dealing with Zola's revolutionary characters. At a time when qualification rather than function was held to be the prime, indeed the only criterion for setting up taxonomies, Peter Hambly proposed the following troika typology: "In *La Fortune des Rougon,* three kinds of republicans are brought face to face: the dreamer, the egoist, and the scientist. Generally speaking, the psychological infrastructure of all the militants in the cycle can more or less be assimilated to one of these types or a combination of these characteristics."[30]

Dismissing altogether the "savant" type as nonactive in the revolution, Aimé Guedj argued, in "Les Révolutionnaires de Zola," that the apparent binary opposition between the "good" revolutionary (the "dreamer") and the "bad" (the "egoist") is neutralized, rendered inoperative, if one judges the characters not in terms of their intentions but in terms of their effects on their followers: "The Manichaean opposition of the 'good' and the 'bad' revolutionaries, which is so prevalent in the Rougon cycle, is but a stage in the dialectics of the type. Silvère and Florent point to Etienne, Etienne to Pluchart, Pluchart to Macquart and Chouteau, *antithetical but complementary* representations of one and the same destiny."[31]

Guedj's analysis can easily be reformulated in the terminology I am using here: by his emphasis on the identical *roles* attributed to two distinct character types, Guedj is corroborating my description of the sacrificial thematic role as double, the sum of two complementary but antithetical functions. The notion of narrative roles is of prime importance here; to borrow Claude Bremond's neologism, Etienne's role is that of "influencer." Now, according to Bremond, there are two types of influencers: "The motives aroused by the influencer may be either well-founded (promise real satisfactions or dissatisfactions) or ill-founded (promise illusory satisfactions or dissatisfactions). The influencer who arouses well-founded motives in his partner plays the role of a *truth-bearer* [*révélateur*]; the one who arouses ill founded motives, that of *deceiver* [*trompeur*]."[32] To classify Etienne as either a truth-bearer or a deceiver is to relapse into the Manichaean fallacy. In order to do justice to the complexity of Etienne's role, we must follow in Bremond's footsteps as he brings in another set of variables: "If he is in good faith, the *voluntary* informer takes on the role of *voluntary truth-bearer;* but if he himself is laboring under a delusion, then he tends at the same time to play the part of an *involuntary deceiver.*"[33]

So long as Etienne's promises to the miners seem realizable, his leadership goes unchallenged; but when events belie his promises, revealing their emptiness, the miners turn away from and ultimately against

him. The apotheosis of the voluntary truth-bearer gives way to the lapidation of the involuntary deceiver. The leader's fall results neither from the "ingratitude of the mob" (G, p. 277), nor from the leader's duplicity, but rather from the encounter of the ambiguous leader with the ambiguous crowd. What Guedj and Bremond both fail to consider is the other party in the influence game—the influenced, the "patient." The crowd in *Germinal* is not monolithic, not passive putty in the hands of an omnipotent leader. The crowd, when aroused, has a mind of its own and, it is my contention, one very similar to that of the leader-victim: the crowd is the mirror image of its supposed master. This means, among other things, that the crowd is no more Manichaean than the pharmakos; the opposition *good crowd* (nonviolent) vs. *bad crowd* (violent) is as much of an oversimplification as the *good leader* vs. *bad leader* opposition rejected earlier. Like Etienne, the crowd is double: on the one hand, it is willingly deceived; on the other, unwillingly deceptive. Just as Etienne appears to be the Messiah, the crowd appear to be Christian martyrs, but just as the Messiah turns out to be a false prophet, the martyrs turn into lions. The next step is inevitable: the lions turn on their tamer.

Lapidation

Symmetry is not the least of the factors contributing to Etienne's downfall. According to the law that governs the structure of many of Zola's novels, what goes up must come down. Almost point by point, Etienne's lapidation scene parodies his apotheosis; we might speak here of a "negative" symmetry. Two examples: just as in the forest episode, Etienne's triumph spells the defeat of Rasseneur, his political rival, in the lapidation scene Etienne's humiliation marks Rasseneur's return to power. The Etienne-Rasseneur disjunction is nothing but a projection into two distinct actors of Etienne's virtual internal split. Indeed, the Plan-des-Dames chapter contains the paradigm we have been studying (apotheosis/lapidation), linking as it does Etienne's apotheosis with Rasseneur's lapidation: "He was a fallen idol the very sight of whom annoyed his former supporters....In the end they threw bits of frozen moss at him" (G, p. 277; "C'était une idole renversée dont la vue seule fâchait ses anciens fidèles....On finit par lui jeter des poignées de mousse gelée" [R-M, 3: 1381]). The entire syntagmatic development of the novel between IV, vii, and VII, i, consists of the events leading up to the exchange of roles by the actors in this scenario.

On the linguistic level, negative symmetry takes the form of an almost word-by-word repetition of the passage quoted above describing Etienne's feeling of omnipotence; however, the tenses have changed from

the past to the pluperfect, emphasizing the contrast between then and now:

> He recalled how under the beech-trees he had heard three thousand hearts beating in time with his own. On that night he had grasped popularity with both hands, these people had belonged to him and he knew he was their master. At that time he had been drunk with grandiose visions....All over now! This was the awakening, to find himself miserable and ostracized—his own people had driven him off with brickbats. (*G*, p. 424)[34]

From dreams of glory, Etienne has awakened to a reality of infamy; from the positive cynosure of the crowd, he has become a negative pole of attraction, the surrogate victim, the single object of an entire community's rage and frustration. We recognize the characteristic phenomenon of reciprocal hostilities, or rivalries, transformed into unanimous, unifying hostility as la Pierronne (as appropriate or "motivated" a name for a stone-thrower as "Etienne"—see St. Stephen—is for a victim of lapidation) sides with her former critics against Etienne, though she personally has reaped nothing but gains from the strike: "But she sided with her neighbours so as to get back in their favour" (*G*, p. 422; "Mais elle se mettait avec les voisines, dans l'idée de se réconcilier" [*R-M*, 3: 1519]). We recognize also the rationalizations that obscure the community's need to restore order through an act of collective violence: "He was now the exploiter, the murderer, the sole cause of all their woe" (*G*, p. 423; "C'était lui, l'exploiteur, l'assassin, la cause unique de leur malheur" [*R-M*, 3: 1519]). What is less familiar, within our frame of reference, is the particular form of aggression directed against Etienne: he is driven out of town "with brickbats."

The range of possible forms of collective violence against the scapegoat is, admittedly, not very extensive; however, it is surely remarkable that within this already limited gamut, Zola invariably selects the same mode: lapidation. A combination of an intracorpus comparison of the four major lapidation scenes in Zola's novels—Mouret's in *La Conquête de Plassans,* Etienne's in *Germinal,* Claude's in *L'Oeuvre,* Luc's in *Travail* —and an extracorpus confrontation with Hugo's poem "Le Lapidé" should allow us to pinpoint the distinctive features of Zola's recurrent fantasy of a man's being stoned.

Before considering the three lapidation scenes as yet unexamined serially, it should be noted that all four are inserted into the narrative syntagm at a common point: they are all preceded by a conquest episode (potential or realized) and followed by imprisonment (voluntary or involuntary). Thus, after his lapidation, Mouret is locked up in the asylum at les Tulettes; Etienne's lapidation is a prelude to his entrapment in the flooded mine; Claude's, to his self-imposed exile from Paris. The

lapidation/enclosure sequence persists in *Travail*, where Luc locks himself in after his lapidation by the citizens of Beauclair: "That evening Luc locked himself in, wanting to be alone in the lodge he still lived in. . . . During his rare moments of weakness, he preferred to shut himself up completely; he would drain the cup of sorrow to the dregs only to reappear fully recovered and strong. He had therefore locked all the windows and doors and given strict orders that no one be admitted."[35]

What I have referred to as the lapidation scene in *La Conquête de Plassans* appears so only retroactively, when superimposed on subsequent variants. It is not otherwise readily identifiable as a reenactment of the ritual sacrifice because it is artfully camouflaged by the use of irony: Zola's first full-length lapidation scene is a grotesque parody of Calvary. To begin with, François Mouret, the scapegoat, is a ridiculous, pathetic figure, somewhat on the same order as Gide's hapless victim in *Les Caves du Vatican*, Amédée Fleurissoire. His ordeal begins innocently enough as he sets out on his weekly Sunday walk through town. No sooner has he crossed the threshold, however, than he becomes aware that things are not as usual; his appearance seems to create a stir wherever he goes:

> One Sunday, as he was stepping out the door, he saw Rose on the sidewalk of the rue Balande, chatting animatedly with M. Rastoil's maid. On seeing him the two cooks fell silent. . . . When he had arrived at the place de la Sous-Préfecture, he turned his head and saw them still standing in the same spot. . . .
>
> . . . In his wake he left a trail of excitement; groups formed, the sound of voices rose, mixed with derisive laughter. . . .
>
> . . . Having arrived at the market, he hesitated for a moment, then plunged resolutely into the midst of the women selling vegetables. But there, the sight of him produced a veritable revolution.[36]

Throughout this scene (which culminates in his lapidation by a gang of children), Mouret's attitude hovers between a sense that he is indeed the unfortunate object of all this attention and an equally strong sense that it must be his imagination:

> "I am walking too fast; they are laughing at me," thought Mouret.
>
> He kept on quickening his pace, in an attempt to escape, utterly unable to believe that he was creating such an uproar.
>
> It seemed to him that the shopkeepers of the Rue de la Banne, the women of the market, the pedestrians along the Promenade, the young gentlemen of the Circle, the Rougons, the Condamins, all Plassans with its muffled laughter rumbled behind his back, down the steep slope.[37]

This oscillation between awareness and denial contributes to creating in the mind of the reader a very real doubt as to whether Mouret is mad

or not: is he suffering from a delusion of persecution or is his persecution real? Are the townspeople all really laughing at him, or is he simply imagining that he is the center of everyone's attention? Is Mouret "disturbed" or the victim of a concerted plot to rid the town of an undesirable citizen, precisely by driving him crazy? In short, where does one, indeed *can* one, draw the line between the scapegoat and the paranoiac? From the outset, the two seem inseparable, indistinguishable. Thus, Oedipus accuses both Tiresias and Creon of hatching plots to drive him out of Thebes:

> For God's sake, tell me what you saw in me,
> what cowardice or what stupidity,
> that made you lay a plot like this against me?
> Did you imagine I should not observe
> the crafty scheme that stole upon me or
> seeing it, take no means to counter it?[38]

In contemporary fiction, such as Dostoievsky's *Double*, Kafka's *Trial*, Camus' *L'Etranger*, or Saul Bellow's *Victim*, the pharmakos is a cog in a large and impersonal bureaucracy, a middle-level white-collar worker aimlessly pushing a pencil in an office. As the pharmakos trades his robes for a business suit—that is, becomes a bourgeois—the problem of distinguishing the mythic function from social pathology becomes very nearly insoluble. Rousseau is in this respect, as in so many others, the pivotal, exemplary figure: the convergence of imaginary and real persecution is nowhere more evident than in his autobiographical writings. The lapidation of a paranoiac is an event which dramatizes the imbrication of delusion and reality.

The figure of Mouret belongs to this great tradition. The value of the specific terms in which the problem is formulated in *La Conquête* can best be appreciated if one compares it to a short story entitled "Histoire d'un fou" ("The Story of a Madman"), whose similarities with *La Conquête* have long been acknowledged.[39] In this early novella (1868), a bourgeois property owner named Maurin (→ Mouret) is the victim of a plot concocted by his young wife Henriette and her doctor-lover. In order to rid themselves of the obstacle to their love affair, they decide to make it look as though Maurin is crazy, thereby substituting—in the words of Freud's "psychotic Dr. Schreber"—"soul murder" for actual murder: "The lovers shrank from committing a murder. They could not strike such a lamb; besides, they were afraid of being caught and having their heads chopped off" ("Les amants reculèrent devant un meurtre. Ils ne pouvaient frapper un pareil mouton; puis ils craignaient d'être pris et d'avoir le cou tranché" [*R-M*, 1: 1641]).[40] The lovers' playacting ("comédie") succeeds so well that not only is Maurin locked up, but in the end, he has become truly insane.

The main difference between "Histoire d'un fou" and *La Conquête* is

that in the short story the author's point of view is made explicit in the opening paragraph, obviating any doubt or ambiguity from the outset: Maurin *is* driven crazy, his persecution is all too real, and furthermore, his case is not unique:

> Of late there has been a great deal of interest in lunatics. It would seem that there have been some startling confinements; men of sound mind were allegedly bound hand and foot and thrown into padded cells for having committed the sole crime of getting in the way of certain people. I think an investigation was ordered. Heaven preserve me from delving into these infamies; but I can safely tell the story of a madman, which current concerns have just recalled to mind.[41]

Like Florent, Maurin is the scapegoat of a self-contained community within Paris. The unanimity of Montmartre against Maurin takes the same form as that of les Halles against Florent: multiple and independent denunciations to the police. The choice of these two comparable neighborhoods is significant; the expulsion of the scapegoat must be a community event: "When Henriette and her lover saw that their stratagem had succeeded and that it was time for the finale, they informed the police commissioner, who had long since been informed by public rumor" ("Lorsque Henriette et son amant virent que la comédie avait réussi, et qu'il était temps de lui donner un dénouement, ils prévinrent le commissaire de police, lequel d'ailleurs était averti depuis longtemps par la rumeur publique" [*R-M*, 1: 1643]). The identity between Florent and Maurin extends to the circumstances surrounding their "capture." Both are victims of elaborately laid traps; both are carted off in a hansom cab: "One fine day, after a dreadful scene which Henriette had played with professional artistry, Maurin was put into a hansom cab on some pretense or other, and taken to Charenton" ("Un beau jour, à la suite d'une scène épouvantable qu'Henriette avait jouée en artiste consommée, Maurin fut mis dans un fiacre, sous un prétexte quelconque, et conduit à Charenton" [ibid.]).

We might summarize Maurin's connection with a whole cast of characters shown in Table 3. Mouret is a member of this extended family of intruder figures, a direct descendant of Maurin's, but the absence of any direct intervention by the author in the lapidation scene invests Mouret with a special status; our adoption of (restriction to) the victim's point of view gives us a new perspective on the familiar scenario of ritual sacrifice. The doubt and malaise we experience on reading the lapidation scene in *La Conquête* results from Zola's translation into action (*faire*) of what is said (*dire*) in "Histoire d'un fou." And that *dire* is "there is nothing that looks more like a madman than a man of sound mind; everything depends on how you view and judge his actions" ("rien ne ressemble plus

à un fou qu'un homme sain d'esprit; tout dépend de la façon dont on regarde et dont on juge ses actes" [*R-M*, 1: 1643]).

Table 3

Work	Character	Fate
Thérèse Raquin	Camille	murder
"Histoire d'un fou"	Maurin	internment
Le Ventre de Paris	Florent	exile
"La Mort d'O. Bécaille"	Olivier Bécaille	burial alive

The lapidation scene in *La Conquête* is then a fiction of epistemology, calling into question as it does the very principles of realism and naturalism: the belief in a scientific objectivity, the fetishization of the eye as organ of observation. To affirm or to demonstrate that it is impossible to distinguish sanity from insanity is, for a novelist whose protestations of positivism are an artistic credo, an extraordinary admission of failure. For—as "La Mort d'Olivier Bécaille" makes clear—carried to its logical conclusion, the lack of objective criteria for distinguishing binary opposites can prove fatal. Thus, in the short story bearing his name, Olivier Bécaille is buried alive because of the failure of a doctor (privileged representative of Science in Zola's fiction) to distinguish between life and death. This borderline case takes a nineteenth-century *topos*, inherited from Gothic fiction—the entombment of a live man—and places it in service of a critique of the realist and naturalist's most cherished ideological assumptions. Finally, what is at stake in Mouret's lapidation scene is *observation, its limits and its dangers.*

If realism and naturalism consisted merely in the accumulation of details destined to produce a realistic effect ("un effet de réel"), there would be nothing problematic about nineteenth-century French fiction. But the great novels of that century are not catalogues of clothes or inventories of furniture; no matter how extravagant the author's mimetic ambition, mimesis is always selective. Let us recall, at this point, Zola's famous description of his *modus percipiendi:* "I am afflicted with an overdeveloped sense of true-to-life details, shooting to the stars on the springboard of exact observation. Truth soars instantaneously to the heights of symbolism" ("J'ai l'hypertrophie du détail vrai, le saut dans les étoiles sur le tremlin de l'observation exacte. La vérité monte d'un coup d'aile jusqu'au symbole").[42]

The passage from detail to symbol, that is, from observation to *interpretation* (and that is the key word), is not as strictly controlled by "truth" as Zola would have us believe, or wants himself to believe. This

statement begs the question. What makes one detail *truer* than another? Who decides on the truth quotient and quality of the observation? The appeal to truth—a magic word in Zola's vocabulary—cannot conceal the difficulty and the danger inherent in the leap from observation to interpretation, for in that brief interval between the springboard and the stars there is ample room for the observer to introduce his ideology and even pathology. As long as realistic and naturalistic fiction are viewed as essentially "obsessional"—that is anaphoric—they are eminently reassuring and nonproblematic, a perfect foil for modern and postmodern fiction ("les textes de la modernité"), but if one becomes aware of their "paranoid trends," they become strange and disquieting. At a time when nosological systems are under attack from within the clinical establishment, the recourse to such labels needs to be explained and justified, for it poses two problems. First, can one link a style of writing to what has been termed a "neurotic style"?[43] Second, if so, what are the arguments in favor of linking paranoia and realistic-naturalistic fiction?

In answer to the first question I would like to quote a celebrated and somewhat lengthy passage from Freud, where he attempts to relate the principal neuroses to the principal cultural productions:

> Psycho-analytic work upon patients itself pointed persistently in the direction of this new task, for it was obvious that the forms assumed by the different neuroses echoed the most highly admired productions of our culture. Thus hysterics are undoubtedly imaginative artists, even if they express their phantasies *mimetically* in the main and without considering their intelligibility to other people; the ceremonials and prohibitions of obsessional neurotics drive us to suppose that they have created a private religion of their own; and the delusions of paranoics have an unpalatable external similarity and internal kinship to the systems of our philosophers. It is impossible to escape the conclusion that these patients are, in an *asocial* fashion, making the very attempts at solving their conflicts and appeasing their pressing needs which, when those attempts are carried out in a fashion that is acceptable to the majority, are known as poetry, religion and philosophy.[44]

Freud opens the door to other attempts at correlating forms of neurosis with forms of cultural production, without at the same time following slavishly in the master's giant footsteps. Thus I would concur with Sarah Kofman when she writes: "So, several aspects of a work of art might call to mind the other illnesses, in particular paranoia."[45] For me the analogy between certain types of fiction and paranoia is based on their common preoccupation with the interpretation of signs. The specific relevance of paranoia to the study of literature is that paranoia is the model, the extreme limit, the "unpalatable" caricature of all systems of interpretation and all systematic interpretation. Being a kind of hyper-semiology—I am referring here to that form of paranoia known in France

as *délire d'interprétation* ("delusion of reference")—paranoia cannot but bear certain illuminating resemblances to any hermeneutic, psychoanalysis and literary criticism included. Freud was the first to acknowledge the paranoid trends in the theory and practice of psychoanalysis. Thus in *The Psychopathology of Everyday Life* (a title which could serve as a subtitle to many of Zola's novels), he develops at some length the analogy between the paranoid and the psychoanalytic interpretations of reality, both of which attribute meaning to details generally considered insignificant. Thus at the end of *The Psychotic Doctor Schreber*, he draws our attention to the similarity between his theory of paranoia and Schreber's delusion, and in his article "Construction in Analysis," he remarks: "The delusions of patients appear to me to be the equivalents of the constructions which we build up in the course of an analytic treatment —attempts at explanation and cure."[46]

My concern, then, is fiction as interpretation / interpretation as fiction. When I say that Zola's (or Balzac's or Stendhal's) fiction contains elements of paranoia, I am not speaking as a lay literary analyst, but as a literary critic who borrows from the vocabulary of psychoanalysis rather than applying its grid(s) on the text. Zola's fiction is "paranoid" not because it presents persecution or represents madness, but because in a scene such as the one under discussion, it presents and represents a hermeneutic crisis. The literariness of madness is not the representation of *madness in the text* (thematic approach), but rather of the *madness of the text* (linguistic approach).

Let us now return to our two texts and reconsider them in the light of the above remarks. In "Histoire d'un fou," Zola provides several examples of insignificant details interpreted by members of the community to signify Maurin's insanity. One in particular will retain our attention because it will be taken up, expanded, and transformed in *La Conquête:* "People related strange incidents in hushed tones. One woman said that on a rainy day she had met Maurin hatless on the place du Panthéon. It was true: the poor man's hat had been blown off by a gust of wind" ("On racontait à voix basse des faits inouïs. Une femme disait avoir rencontré Maurin sans chapeau sur la place du Panthéon, par un jour de pluie. C'était vrai: le chapeau du bonhomme avait été emporté par un coup de vent" [*R-M,* 1: 1643]).

The vestmental code is so highly privileged in bourgeois and petit bourgeois society that the slightest infraction is susceptible to the most extreme attention: see the description of the cousin Pons's anachronistic attire in the opening pages of Balzac's *Le Cousin Pons* or the description of Charles Bovary's extraordinary hat in chapter I of *Madame Bovary*. In *La Conquête,* the preoccupation with vestmental infractions is common to both author and character. Indeed, at first it is Mouret who is constantly

checking over his clothes to locate the signal for all the commotion, taking it for granted that an out-of-place handkerchief or an old-fashioned jacket or a donkey's tail pinned on his back would disrupt the ordinary Sunday routine of a sleepy provincial town:

> On seeing him the two cooks fell silent. They scrutinized him with such strange expressions on their faces that he checked to see if his handkerchief were hanging out of one of his back pockets.
>
> Feeling intimidated, Mouret did not dare turn around again; while not entirely sure that people were talking about him, he was seized with a vague sense of anxiety. He walked faster, letting his arms swing freely. He was sorry he had worn his old frock coat, a hazel frock coat which was no longer in fashion.
>
> He removed his hat and looked at it, afraid that some boy had thrown a handful of plaster at him; but he had neither a kite nor a donkey's tail hanging down his back. This inspection allayed his fears.[47]

Then, just when Mouret has satisfied himself that everything is in order with his outward appearance, he becomes the object of the highly suspicious scrutiny of a group of rentiers—his former cronies—sunning themselves on a bench in the center of town. This bench rapidly turns into a jurors' bench as one of the rentiers discovers the sought-after clue, the unmistakable proof of Mouret's suspected insanity:

> A former hatter from the outskirts of town, who had inspected Mouret from the knot in his tie down to the last button on his frock coat, had finally become engrossed in the spectacle of his shoes. The left shoelace happened to be untied, a fact which seemed outrageous to the hatter; he nudged his neighbors, winking in the direction of the drooping shoelace. Soon everyone on the bench had eyes only for the shoelace. That was the limit. All the gentlemen shrugged their shoulders, showing that they had given up all hope.[48]

Coming at this point in our analysis, this passage takes on its full significance. Here, social satire and literary parody converge; by exaggerating the disproportion between the detail (the untied shoelace) and the interpretation (madness) it grounds, Zola calls into question not only bourgeois value systems (Barthes's "système de la mode"), but also the basic assumptions of realist and naturalist fiction. This passage calls to mind Stendhal's succinct indictment of the seminary mentality in *Le Rouge et le noir:* "In Seminaries, there is a way of eating a boiled egg which reveals the progress one has made in the godly life."[49] Furthermore, in this pivotal passage, hermeneutics is shown even as it is being shown up, so to speak: while maintaining a safe ironic distance between himself and the "interpretant"[50]—"a fact which seemed outrageous *to the hatter*"

—the author reveals here some of the secrets of his trade. His decoding apparatus turns out, not surprisingly, to be strikingly similar to the one used by the analyst in decoding dream language. In order to justify this claim, let us return to our superimposition of "Histoire d'un fou" on *La Conquête*, for the transformations that the pre-text undergoes are highly significant: Maurin's missing hat becomes Mouret's untied shoelace, but a trace of the hat persists in the shape of the hatter. What do these repetitions and differences mean? Why the persistence of the hat? How does a missing hat turn into an untied shoelace? And what logic determines the association missing hat = untied shoelace = insanity?

If we consider the following remarks by Freud in *The Interpretation of Dreams*, the connection between the hat and insanity on the one hand and the reiteration of the hat motif on the other becomes intelligible: "In view of the part played by jokes, quotations, songs and proverbs in the mental life of educated people, it would fully agree with our expectations if disguises of such kinds were used with extreme frequency for representing dream-thoughts."[51] What we have in our two passages is a literal, pictorial representation of the familiar French expression "travailler du chapeau," to be as crazy or mad as a hatter. In the first version we have the (missing) hat; in the second, the hatter, or the "travailleur du chapeau." The transformation of the hat into its binary opposite along the vertical axis, the shoelace, is a typical instance of reversal. In *La Conquête*, the vertical axis is the semantic axis of mental health; thus M. de Condamin says of Mouret: "He is cracked from top to bottom, that joker" ("Il est fêlé du haut en bas, ce farceur-là" [*R-M*, 1: 1127]). One might add that the vertical axis also structures Mouret's "subversive" (republican) political activities: before his commitment to les Tulettes, Mouret threatens to have a shoemaker elected; after his commitment, the republicans nominate a hatter.

Now if the reader has followed me thus far and has granted me the possibility and the interest of reading *one* passage in *La Conquête* as a "dream-text," of practicing oneirocriticism, I would ask him to go a step further with me and consider the entire lapidation scene as a dream, in fact a dream which Freud analyzes under the heading "Typical Dreams." Because these dreams are "typical"—that is, refer to universal infantile wishes—they play an important part in literature that presupposes a sort of collective unconscious; or, because material from these dreams appears so often in literature, they are typical. However circular Freud's argumentation, the pertinence of this category of dreams to literature is undeniable:

> There can be no doubt that the connection between our typical dreams and fairy tales and the material of other kinds of creative writings are neither few

nor accidental. It sometimes happens that the sharp eye of a creative writer has an analytic realization of the process of transformation of which he is habitually no more than the tool. If so, he may follow the process in a reverse direction and so trace back the imaginative writing to a dream. (*Interpretation of Dreams*, 4: 246)

If we consider the reiterated motif in the lapidation scene—the preoccupation with a vestmental lack—it becomes possible to see it as a variant of the genre Freud terms "Embarassing Dreams of Being Naked" (ibid., pp. 242-48).[52] One might object that Mouret is not actually naked, but as Freud points out, anticipating this objection, "In the case of a man who has worn the Emperor's uniform, nakedness is often replaced by some breach of the dress regulations" (p. 242). The revealing indication that there is more to the dream than meets the eye is the strength of the dreamers's reaction: "As a rule the defect in the dreamer's toilet is not so grave as to appear to justify the shame to which it gives rise" (ibid.). According to Freud, the wish expressed in this dream is to return to the childhood paradise where, as in the Garden of Eden, there was no shame in nakedness: "Thus dreams of being naked are dreams of exhibiting" (p. 245).

At this point another objection arises: there is no evidence in the text of Mouret's conscious or unconscious desire to exhibit himself. And this objection is valid if we confine ourselves to the text of *La Conquête*. The technique of superimposition, however, presupposes the constant interplay of all an author's texts, considering each individual text as a fragment of a whole, extrapolating from Freud's contention: "The content of all dreams that occur during the night forms part of the same whole" (*Interpretation of Dreams*, 4: 333). Thus *L'Oeuvre* provides the evidence missing in *La Conquête*. The shameful wish that brings on lapidation is here writ large; it is literally an *exhibition:* Claude's participation in the Salon des Refusés. My joining together of these two fragments which had been so artfully sundered, though highly productive or instructive, should not be (mis)taken for a minimization of the essential fact of their separation, for as Freud goes on to say, immediately after the sentence quoted above, "The fact of their being divided into several sections, as well as the grouping and number of those sections—all this has a meaning" (pp. 333-34). On the most obvious level, the separation of the punishment from the wish functions as an effective obstacle to a correct interpretation: what is hidden in *La Conquête* (the exhibition) is explicit in *L'Oeuvre*, but conversely, what is explicit in *La Conquête* (the lapidation) is hidden in *L'Oeuvre*. In *La Conquête*, the parody of Calvary culminates in a fitting parody of lapidation; instead of being assaulted, as is Etienne, by grown men hurling bricks, Mouret is pelted by a rotten orange thrown by the smallest of the children pursuing him: "To ward off sudden blows the

youngsters formed a circle and shouted in triumph, while the smallest one stepped forward solemnly and threw the rotten orange at him. It landed on his left eye" ("Les gamins, craignant les ruades, firent le cercle en poussant des cris de triomphe; tandis que le tout petit, s'avançant gravement, lui jeta l'orange pourrie, qui s'écrasa sur son oeil gauche" [*R-M*, 1: 1121]).

In *L'Oeuvre*, the lapidation is entirely figurative: it consists in the laughter and jeers with which the uncomprehending spectators greet Claude's revolutionary painting *Plein Air*. That laughter and jeers are weapons in the lapidation arsenal can be shown in two ways. First, in a section of his piece on Manet, "Le Public," in *Salons*, Zola equates laughter with lapidation, children with the crowd. The relevant section ends on the following allegorical note:

> And this is how a gang of urchins met Edouard Manet in the street one day and created the disturbance which stopped me, a curious and disinterested passerby. I drew up my report as well as I could, laying the blame on the urchins, trying to tear the artist from their hands and take him to a safe place. There were policemen there—excuse me, I meant to say art critics —who assured me that this man was being lapidated because he had irreverently defiled the temple of Beauty.[53]

Second, the function of laughter and jeers as variants of lapidation is revealed by the persistence, the insistence of the semantic field of lapidation, minus the kernel word. In the four scenes under consideration, lapidation generates a semantic network which includes two invariant expressions drawn from the hunting code: *meute* ("pack") and *derrière son dos* ("behind his back"). In Zola's idiolect and private mythology, sacrifice and the hunt are intimately linked; the lapidation scenes are all sacrificial hunts,[54] manhunts in which the pursuers are portrayed as hunting dogs. The following excerpts are in chronological order (*La Conquête, Germinal, L'Oeuvre*):

> They [the youngsters] jumped sideways, laughing and yelling, running away *on all fours*. Feeling ridiculous, Mouret blushed deeply....What frightened him most was the thought of crossing the place de la Sous-Préfecture and passing under the Rougons' windows with this train of young good-for-nothings growing audibly larger and bolder *behind his back*.
> ...The children stamped their feet, slid on the angular paving stones and roared like a *pack of hounds* let loose in the quiet neighborhood.

> Soon it became a headlong flight, every household booed him as he went by, they *dogged* his steps....He rushed away from the village, pale and terrified, with the yelling crowd *at his heels*. (*G*, p. 423)

> Starting from the gallery where he had been jeered, they pursued him like a

pack of hounds baying at his heels, first on the Champs-Elysées, then along the Seine, and even now at home.[55]

The sacrificial hunt imagery, muted in *La Conquête,* becomes strident in *Travail,* as evidenced by the proliferation of allusions to the canine pursuers:

If he fell, the *pack* would attack him, and he would be devoured.

Ah! climbing the rue de Brias with that growing band of enemies *at his heels*. . . .he felt [the whole town] behind this band *barking at his heels.*

He sensed the galloping crowd coming closer; he faced it one last time, when he felt on his neck the hot breath of the *pack* pursuing him.[56]

Whereas in the earliest version of this scene or scenario, the persecution is so subtly presented as to be called into doubt, in *Travail*—the ultimate reworking of the material—the Christian symbolism is so overworked as to leave little to the imagination. The word *Calvary,* nowhere to be found in the first three texts, is reiterated here; Luc's status as a saint, already indicated by his name, is reinforced, confirmed by the stigmata lapidation produces: "Finally a pebble struck him and lacerated his right ear, while another hit him in the left hand, cutting his palm like a knife. And blood flowed, falling in large drops."[57]

Luc's lapidation is the hyperbole of a hyperbole—the lapidation scene itself. The progression from *La Conquête* to *Travail* seems to confirm Freud's final remarks in the passage I have been weaving into the text (quoting it in the appropriate separate sections): "In interpreting dreams consisting of several main sections or, in general, dreams occurring during the same night, the possibility should not be overlooked that separate and successive dreams of this kind may have the same meaning. . . .If so, *the first of these homologous dreams to occur is often the more distorted and timid, while the succeeding one will be more confident and distinct"* (*Interpretation of Dreams,* 4: 334; emphasis added).

Yet, the specificity of Zola's lapidation scenario does not lie in the manifest message so confidently and distinctly proclaimed in *Travail,* for it is identical to the message expressed by Hugo in his poem "Le Lapidé" (the person stoned or "the lapidated prophet"). The notion of the superior man (translate: genius) put to death by the ignorant mob is *the* Romantic version of the sacrificial ritual: Hugo's poem is hardly an isolated example in a literature which boasts such works as Hugo's own *William Shakespeare,* Vigny's *Chatterton,* and Baudelaire's "Albatross," a representative but very partial selection from this veritable martyrology. The figure of the magus-as-martyr is an integral part of Zola's Romantic heritage:

He had made himself the apostle of tomorrow's society of solidarity and fraternity. . . . He had given an example, the Crêcherie where the City of the

Future was in the making, and where a maximum of justice and happiness reigned. And that was enough to make the whole town view him as a malefactor.[58]

> The people are too humble, the priest is too haughty
> To let a passerby shout at it long
> That one must help the meek and bless the innocent,
> That one must fear the augur and his maple sceptre,
> But that truth above all is venerable,
> And that the sons of Adam must tell each other
> That the question is to be just and not to be happy.
> This man was sublime and pure in his prayers;
> That is why, I say, he lies here under these stones.[59]

Nor, we are bound to note, does the specificity of Zola's lapidation scenario consist in his imagery, for we find in Hugo's poem a similar use of hunting imagery; the magus or magus symbol (e.g., the Albatross or the wolf in Vigny's "La Mort du loup") is always also a prey. This is God's reply to the poet-narrator's questioning of the wise man's lapidation:

> "And," continued the boundless Spirit, "listen further.
> When, like hunters leading with their horns
> Their pack into the ominous forest of darkness,
> The nations, driving ahead of them those funereal curs,
> Hatred, Ignorance, Envy, Pride, Rebellion,
> Hunted down my prophet like a lion..."[60]

What remains then, once we have decanted the clichés of latter-day Romanticism? What remains is the original dream which has simply borrowed the ready-made scenario, lapidation, as Zola's culturally determined, personally resonant vehicle for bodying forth an essential aspect of this "typical dream," one I have not mentioned so far, its anxiety-producing component: "Its essence [in its typical form] lies in a distressing feeling in the nature of shame and in the fact that one wishes to hide one's nakedness, as a rule by locomotion, but finds one is unable to do so" (Freud, *Interpretation of Dreams,* 4: 242). The inhibition of movement features prominently in Zola's lapidation scenes; unlike Hugo's victim, a corpse, Zola's are vulnerable living men desperately attempting to flee their persecutors.

The assimilation of lapidation to paralysis by virtue of their common component—the inhibition of the subject's movements—allows us to link up two extraordinarily rich thematic networks: on the one hand, the "epidemic" of a polymorphous paralysis; on the other, the almost equally prevalent motif of the hunt. Taken together they account for a preponderance of Zola's obsessive imagery. As made available to us in the lapidation scenes, Zola's work appears, on one level, as a constant

reworking of a typical dream, one involving the conflict between a power-ful wish to exhibit and an equally strong wish to conceal, for, as Freud points out, "The sensation of the inhibition of a movement represents a *conflict of will*" (*Interpretation of Dreams*, 4: 337).

This "typical" conflict between exhibition and concealment takes on special significance when the "dreamer" is a writer and one whose artistic credo, reiterated *ad nauseam*, is impersonality, pseudoscientific objectivity. The complete elimination of all traces of the Romantics' bathetic lyricism — that is the goal Zola sets for himself in his theoretical writings and for his artist-characters in *L'Oeuvre*. Not the least of Zola's animus toward Hugo is directed against what he perceives as Hugo's personality cult.[61] For Zola the theoretician, as for Pascal the theologian, "the *I* is hateful."[62] Nonetheless, much modern Zola criticism has sought to define the contra-dictions between his theory and his practice, to amplify the dissonance between *Le Roman expérimental* and the fiction, to dramatize "the never quite resolved struggle, in the name of objectivity, to submerge his own person, the I of the narrator, in the character-receptor through whose consciousness the world of *conte* or novel comes into being."[63] The divine indifference and invisibility of the omniscient narrator did not come naturally to the author of *Mes Haines* and *J'accuse*. We can only speculate on the reasons for Zola's fervent espousal of an aesthetic of impersonality: possibly it was the conjunction of a historical reaction against the excesses of Romanticism with a personal fear of exposure.

Perhaps one of the hardiest myths about Zola, one which he ac-credited energetically and which has gained wide currency in recent years, is the myth of transparency.[64] Like Rousseau, Zola aspired to live in a glass house; thus, prefacing Dr. Toulouse's document baring the most intimate details about his psychophysiology, Zola proclaims: "My brain is like a glass skull: I opened it to all and am not afraid that all may read in it."[65] Not for him the prison house of language; in his article on Stendhal, he outlines his linguistic ideal: "A clear language, something like a glass house displaying the ideas within."[66] But all the windows in Zola's house of fiction — and there are many — draw our attention away from what I would call Zola's cryptophilia, his love of secrecy. From the founding myth to its reenactment in the lapidation scene, the conflict between exposure and concealment rages; transparency — like imperson-ality — is not a given, but a goal. The internment of tante Dide, which occurs in a parenthesis or ellipsis between *La Fortune* and *La Conquête*, and which cannot be dated with any degree of certainty,[67] is an integral part of the founding myth; the connection between lapidation and enclosure is hardly gratuitous. The victim — whether incarnated as a retired shopkeeper, an unsuccessful painter, a revolutionary organizer, or a prophetic social engineer — is first and last a madman, subject to fits

and in need of constant supervision. But, just as Mouret escapes from les Tulettes and sets his house on fire, the secret(s) Zola fears to expose / wishes to exhibit will out.

The Founding Myth: Encore

Un livre est un grand cimetière où sur la plupart des tombes on ne peut lire les noms effacés.
Marcel Proust, A la recherche du temps perdu

From the first pages of *La Fortune des Rougon* to the last pages of *Le Docteur Pascal*, the desire for expression and publication is held in check by an equally strong desire for suppression and destruction. Thus, in *L'Argent*, the dying socialist theoretician, Sigismond Busch, haunted by the fear that his brother will destroy his papers, his lifework, after his death, begs Mme Caroline to save them: "Look! madame, they are over there on the table. Please give them to me so that we can tie them in a bundle and you can take them with you, take everything...Oh! I was calling for you, I was expecting you. My papers destroyed! My lifelong research and efforts reduced to nothing!"[68] But, as soon as his brother comes home and finds Sigismond dead, in a passionate outburst of grief, he turns on the papers: "And, in a fit of frantic despair, he gathered up the papers scattered over the bed and tore and crumpled them, as though to destroy all that senseless and resented work which had robbed him of his brother."[69]

Writing in Zola always provokes family quarrels: the writer's relatives always experience the writer's texts as an outrage, an act of aggression directed against them, threatening their happiness and security. The scene I have just described is a recurrent one. Thus, in *Le Ventre de Paris*, when Lisa goes up to inspect Florent's room, she finds something ultimately far more precious and damning than the somewhat juvenile collection of red rags discussed in the previous chapter; she discovers Florent's revolutionary writings in note form. And these notes, this outline, is compared to the scenario of a play. Her reaction is as swift and "irrational" as Sigismond's; she feels Florent's writing activities are a personal affront. If Sigismond's response is to destroy the texts—the author being out of harm's way—Lisa, as we have already seen, sets out to destroy the author, and succeeds.

Contrary to appearances, however, the family quarrel is not fraternal; both Busch and Lisa are maternal imagos. The "real" quarrel is between mother and son, but because writing for/in Zola is fraught with conflict

and guilt, it is only in *Le Docteur Pascal* that the real enemies meet face to face, unmasked. The war between Pascal and his mother, Félicité, brings out into the open an issue that far exceeds one text or one author: writing as matricide.[70] Pascal, Zola's artist persona and alias, has for thirty years devoted all his energies to accumulating voluminous dossiers on the Rougon-Macquart family, evidence which his mother, obsessed as she is with the family's glory, wants to destroy: "Ah! those wretched files! Every night she saw them in her nightmares, proclaiming in fiery letters the true stories, the physiological taints of the family, that other side of its glory which she would have liked to bury forever along with her long-dead ancestors" ("Ah! ces dossiers abominables, elle les voyait, la nuit, dans ses cauchemars, étaler en lettres de feu les histoires vraies, les tares physiologiques de la famille, tout cet envers de la gloire qu'elle aurait voulu à jamais enfouir, avec les ancêtres déjà morts!" [*R-M,* 5: 929]). The most damning of these "taints" is the original one — the insanity of tante Dide — which casts doubt on the sanity of the whole family: "What exasperates me, what must not happen, is for people to say that we are all mad" ("Ce qui m'exaspère, ce qu'il ne faut pas, c'est qu'on dise que nous sommes tous fous" [p. 930]).

No sooner has her son died than Félicité carries out her long-nour-ished project, burning the hateful papers, fighting the figurative letters of fire with the literal fire of the chimney. As the ashes lie smoldering in the fireplace, Clotilde — Félicité's granddaughter and Pascal's niece, ward, and finally mistress — rushes in and attempts to halt the sacrilegious destruction, but Félicité triumphantly points to the metonymic signs of her success — an empty container, parts that were a whole:

> With a sweeping gesture she pointed to the empty cupboard and the embers dying in the fireplace. "Now it's all over; our reputation is secure. Those dreadful papers will no longer incriminate us, and I will leave not a shred of evidence behind me: The Rougons are triumphant."[71]

Félicité's exaltation is premature, for, unlike Mme Caroline, Clotilde does manage to save a few charred fragments from the pyre, as well as the Genealogical Tree, miraculously spared despite or because of its pur-loined letter-like visibility. In the final chapter of the novel, Clotilde studies these precious relics of Pascal's lifework. Given Zola's passion for symmetry, we expect this final chapter to mirror the inaugural one, and we are not disappointed: the fertile cemetery is recalled by and opposed to the newborn infant suckling at Clotilde's breast because that infant is Pascal's posthumous offspring. But Zola's most remarkable symmetry is neither expected nor predictable: it pertains to the tombstone which stands at the center of the circle-cycle. The tombstone reappears in this crowning chapter but parceled out ("morcelé"); and here, dissemination

is a form of dissimulation. The stone in its very materiality recurs in the shape of the cornerstone Félicité is about to lay for the Asile Rougon, an old-age home and sort of anti-Tulettes, "a triumphant monument, intended to convey the family's renown into the distant future" ("le monument victorieux, destiné à porter la gloire de la famille aux âges futures" [*R-M*, 5: 1213]). This "first stone," as it is referred to, is no more the *first* stone than Silvère is the *first* victim; it is simply a laundered, purified version of the bloody tombstone which is the true cornerstone of the Rougon empire, the one tainted with the ritual victim's blood: "And, far away, at the lower end of the Aire Saint-Mittre, on the tombstone, a pool of blood congealed" ("Et, au loin, au fond de l'aire Saint-Mittre, sur la pierre tombale, une mare de sang se caillait" [*R-M*, 1: 315]). Félicité is a Lady Macbeth who succeeds in washing out the "damned spot."

As the tombstone's *substance* is duplicated by the cornerstone, its *surface* — the half-erased words engraved on its face — is duplicated by the charred fragments which Clotilde attempts to decipher: "When she had removed the fragments one by one, her previous suspicions were confirmed: not a single page of the manuscript, not a single meaningful note remained intact. There were just scraps left, blackened bits of scorched paper, disconnected and incoherent" ("Quand elle eut sorti les débris un à un, elle constata, ce dont elle était déjà à peu près certaine, que pas une page entière de manuscrit ne restait, pas une note complète ayant un sens. Il n'existait que des fragments, des bouts de papier à demi brûlés et noircis, sans lien, sans suite" [*R-M*, 5: 1215]).

This "logogriphe," to use Serres's expression, closes not one but two circles: *Le Docteur Pascal* and the *Rougon-Macquart.* Serres's concern is with the first circle; ours is with the second.[72] At the close of the cycle, as in the beginning, there is an elliptic message, a message scrambled, censored by time or fire, a message composed of words unlinked even by the most elementary syntax. Yet at the close, unlike in the beginning, the mangled message is not left in its gaping, fragmentary state, open to each reader's interpretation. Unlike Miette and Silvère, who refuse to probe the mystery, unlike Lisa, who is terrified by the scraps of paper she reads uncomprehendingly, unlike Eugène Rougon, who perpetuates the mystery by carefully burning his records, Clotilde does decode the message, does fiil in the blanks. Coming, as she does, at the end of the *Rougon-Macquart,* her act is exemplary; she represents the *first reader of the completed work,* and this passage provides a protocol for all future readers: "But as she examined them, these mangled sentences, these words half eaten by fire, which none other but she could have made out, excited her interest . . . .And each fragment came to life; the loathsome yet fraternal family was reborn from these scraps, these black ashes where only incoherent syllables still stood out."[73]

This passage is Zola's literary testament and, as such, merits the closest scrutiny. On one level, the passage attests to Zola's final realization that the twenty novels which comprise the *Rougon-Macquart* are fragments with no connecting link between them save the essential document which survives the fire intact, the key to the code, the Genealogical Tree. Once again we are confronted with the dialectic between continuity and discontinuity that characterizes so many nineteenth-century works, as Proust observes apropos of Wagner: "I thought how markedly, all the same, these works participate in that quality of being—albeit marvelously—always incomplete which is the peculiarity of all the great works of the nineteenth century."[74] Proust goes on to say that the authors of these great works—Balzac, Hugo, and Michelet—attempted to palliate this lack by imposing on their fragmented productions a retroactive unity, a unity of hindsight. The last in line of these demiurges, Zola very deliberately set out to avoid his predecessors' mistakes; he sought, in particular, to set himself off from Balzac—see the "Differences between Balzac and Me"—among other ways by incorporating unity into his project from the outset. How extraordinary then this testament: far from enhancing his work, Zola's backward glance reduces his achievement, denies his original intention, imposes, in short, a retroactive disunity. But at the same time as Zola recognizes the folly of his youthful ambition —an impossible totalization—he also sets his novels free from the constraints of the series, letting each one stand on its own. Zola's parting gesture signals the end of an era and is part of the movement towards the detotalized family sagas of the twentieth century, in particular Proust's own "genealogical" epic.

On another level, this passage, when superimposed on the like passage from *La Fortune*, reveals Zola's attitude toward the written word, which is throughout the *Rougon-Macquart* consistently opposed to the spoken word. Indeed, from first to last, for Zola the written word is associated with death and dismemberment. Writing is in its very materiality eminently perishable; the plaything of the elements, the toy of time, it is malleable, pulverizable, hardly the stuff that immortality is made of. The association of writing and death produces the hyperbolic illustration of the written word's fragility: the epitaph. The exemplary quality of the epitaph is hardly a novelty in literature; to cite an example familiar to Zola, the last chapter of *Les Misérables* is entitled "The Grass Covers and the Rain Effaces," and it features a moss-eaten tombstone bearing only "four lines, which have become gradually illegible beneath the rain and the dust, and which are, to-day, probably effaced."[75] The differences between Hugo's and Zola's use of this *topos* are illuminating: whereas Hugo's tombstone occurs in the final chapter, Zola's occurs in

the first; whereas Zola's tombstone bears a name, albeit half erased, Hugo's bears no name, only a poem.

The epitaph is then an examplary form of writing not only because of its extreme vulnerability to erasure, but also because for Zola it consists necessarily of that most privileged of written words, the proper name. According to Jacques Derrida's myth of the origins of writing, the three violent stages of the proper name are one and the same as those of writing in general; their destinies are identical. The following somewhat lengthy and difficult quotation gains full meaning when seen in the context of Derrida's frontal attack on Lévi-Strauss, who in *Tristes Tropiques* equates the concealment of proper names among the Nambikwara Indians of Brazil with an absence of writing; for Derrida, naming, even if the names are subsequently elided and even if the names are not transcribed in phonetic, linear script, is "always already" writing. Derrida replaces Lévi-Strauss's equation (no names = no writing) with his own (naming = violence = writing):

> There was in fact a first violence to be named. To name, to give names that it will on occasion be forbidden to pronounce, such is the originary violence of language which consists in inscribing within a difference, in classifying, in suspending the vocative absolute. To think the unique *within* the system, to inscribe it there, such is the gesture of the arche-writing: arche-violence, loss of the proper, of absolute proximity, of self-presence, in truth the loss of what has never taken place, of a self-presence which has never been given but only dreamed of and always already split, repeated, incapable of appearing to itself except in its own disappearance. Out of this arche-violence, forbidden and therefore confirmed by a second violence that is reparatory, protective, instituting the "moral," prescribing the concealment of writing and the effacement and obliteration of the so-called proper name which was already dividing the proper, a third violence can *possibly* emerge or not (an empirical possibility) within what is commonly called evil, war, indiscretion, rape; which consists of revealing by effraction the so-called proper name, the originary violence which has severed the proper from its property and its self-sameness [*propreté*].[76]

The violence against the surrogate victim, which I posited at the outset as the founding myth, is in no way incompatible with Derrida's "arche-violence"; on the contrary, Derrida's origin myth complements Girard's. Whether or not one believes that the absolute origin can be apprehended, the preoccupation with origins common to both thinkers evidences a shared epistemological framework. Both Girard and Derrida contribute to valorizing the tombstone as the sole *trace* of a pre-text no longer available, an origin receding into the unknowable. With Girard we dwell on *who* is buried *below* the stone; with Derrida we focus on *what*

is erased *on* the stone. But the victim (signified) and the epitaph (signifier) are inseparable; together they constitute a *sign* of the original violence. For Zola, writing participates in the system of the victim; the founding myth is also—perhaps, above all—a myth of the origins of (his) writing. The significance of what has been obliterated from the tombstone's face now becomes inescapable: it is Marie's family name, her "Nom-du-Père" in Lacanian terms; what remains is a sort of degree zero of the proper name, *Marie* being the most common of proper names in a Christian society.

The *Rougon-Macquart* alludes to the arche-violence of naming, then retraces the passage from the secondary violence of the proper name's obliteration to the tertiary one of its restitution. The space of twenty volumes will be taken up with the lifting of the interdict, the transgression of the taboo: for Zola, to write is to name the unnamables. In the passage alluded to earlier in *Son Excellence*, the interdict still holds. No sooner has Eugène been toppled from power than he burns his (incriminating) files; his secretary comments: "What a funeral, my dear fellow! How many dead you have to lay on the pyre!" ("Quel enterrement, mon pauvre ami! comme on a des morts à coucher dans la cendre!" [*R-M*, 2: 38]). But by the time we arrive at *Le Docteur Pascal*, the signs have been reversed, and transgression has become positively valorized: Pascal is the supreme author of epitaphs. What is the family tree but a series of epitaphs, a textual graveyard? The onomastic project culminates in a necronomy. The Genealogical Tree is made up of interrelated necrologies; the elision of the proper name has given way to its proliferation; each leaf-tombstone is complete, including (especially) Pascal's: "How valiantly he had inscribed the date of his own death!" ("Avec quelle bravoure il avait inscrit la date de sa mort!" [*R-M*, 5: 1216]).

The Genealogical Tree has too often been considered a cumbersome, even ridiculous appendage to the *Rougon-Macquart*, yet another unfortunate product of Zola's pseudoscientific method. But further examination of Zola's implicit theory (myth) of the origins of writing, as contained in the final pages of *Le Docteur Pascal*, cannot but lead us to reverse the order of the terms dossiers (metonyms for the novels) / tree. This relationship is presented here as essentially one of *supplementarity*, with the dossiers serving as discursive commentaries on the tree. It is surely no accident that while the dossiers are reduced to ashes, the tree survives intact, for it is truly the doctor's masterpiece: "The lifework of the master was there in that classified and documented family vegetation" ("Toute l'oeuvre du maître était là, dans cette végétation classée et documentée de la famille" [ibid.]).

Here, once again, we are guided by Derrida, who reminds us that "it is now known, thanks to unquestionable and abundant information, that

the birth of writing (in the colloquial sense) was nearly everywhere and most often linked to genealogical anxiety."[77] The key words in this passage are those set off by parentheses—"in the colloquial sense"—for if in its conventional acceptation, writing functions as a means of preserving genealogical records that would otherwise be lost, in its nonconventional, Derridean acceptation, writing—that is, "arche-writing"—informs the genealogical project from the first: "The genealogical relation and social classification are the stitched seam of arche-writing, condition of the (so-called oral) language, and of writing in the colloquial sense."[78]

We can read Zola *with* Derrida only up to a point, for though, implicitly, Zola's writings on writing constantly refer back to an "arche-writing" and an "arche-violence," Zola remains too much the prisoner of what Derrida exposes as the "phonocentrism" of Western thought to endorse, let alone articulate, the primacy of writing over speech, with all the consequences that such a position entails. In the end, the debate as to which came first, the dossiers or the tree, becomes academic, for finally both are juxtaposed to and superseded by Clotilde and her infant son. Already doubly negatively valorized as being destructive and destructible, writing is further devalorized in the perspective of the vitalistic philosophy Zola expounds in the final pages of *Le Docteur*. In the light of this vitalism, the child is Pascal's true masterpiece, his proudest legacy, by virtue of his potential as a powerful leader or even redeemer of mankind:

> The child had come, perhaps the redeemer. . . . What would he be once her selfless devotion had made him big and strong? A scholar who would teach the world some aspects of eternal truth, a captain who would bring glory to his land, or better yet, one of those shepherds of men who quell passions and make justice reign? She saw him as very handsome, very good, very powerful. It was every mother's dream, the conviction that she had given birth to the Messiah, and that hope, every mother's stubborn belief in the certainty of her child's triumph, was the very hope that produced life.[79]

The progression "scholar" → "captain" → "shepherd," echoed in the following sentence by the triad "handsome" → "good" → "powerful," bears ample witness to Zola's priorities. Better than the scholar—that is, the writer—influencing the world from afar through his writings, better even than the captain influencing the world through his acts, is the shepherd—that is, the orator—who through his speech brings peace to mankind. To the system of the victim—that is, writing—Zola prefers the system of the leader—that is, speech. This double postulation is represented in the following equivalence:

$$\frac{victim}{writing} \sim \frac{leader}{speech}$$

As we turn our attention to the system of speech in Zola, the shakiness inherent in his position will quickly become apparent, for even as Zola is vaunting the superiority of speech over writing, his descriptions of speech —transcriptions—are haunted by the written word.

Let us circle back to the leader's apotheosis. In my analysis of this hyperbolic moment, I purposely omitted any consideration of the actual form that the leader's power over the crowd takes, reserving the subject for later. The euphoria of the leader's omnipotence derives from the sensation of direct, unmediated contact between speaker and audience: "Etienne was tasting the heady wine of popularity. This was *power* that he was holding in his hands, *materialized* in the *three thousand breasts* whose hearts were beating at *his bidding*" (*G*, pp. 276-77; "Etienne goûtait l'ivresse de sa popularité. C'était son *pouvoir* qu'il tenait, comme *matérialisé*, dans ces *trois mille poitrines* dont il faisait d'*un mot* battre les coeurs" [*R-M*, 3: 1381; emphasis added]). Here, the French text is essential; the italics serve to underscore the particular form of power Etienne enjoys: the inverse proportion of the means (one word) and the end (three thousand hearts beating). No matter how widely read, no matter how influential a writer is, this heady sensation of power materialized, palpable and audible, is out of his reach, the privilege of the orator.

As if to point up the importance of oratory in *Germinal*, Etienne's speech is the culmination of a series of speeches by other orators, each possessing his own distinctive speaking style. Indeed, this technique of reduplication of the leader by other orators takes the form of a veritable rivalry between two types of speakers: on the one hand, the amateurs, represented by Maheu and his father Bonnemort; on the other, the professionals, represented by Rasseneur and Pluchart. The amateurs' sudden verbal outpourings contrast with their usual laconism (Maheu) or mutism (Bonnemort):

> But it was Maheu who did the cutting short. Now that he was well launched the words came of themselves. At times he was surprised at the sound of his own voice, as though it were a stranger speaking inside him. Things stored up in his heart, that he did not even know were there, now came tumbling forth in a great outpouring of emotion. (*G*, p. 213)

> And to everybody's amazement old Bonnemort could be seen standing on a log and holding forth in the midst of the uproar....Probably he was over-come by one of those garrulous fits which suddenly came and stirred up the past so violently that his memories welled up and poured out of his mouth for hours. (*G*, p. 278)[80]

This intermittent speech from the depths is diametrically opposed to the smooth, even flow of the professional orators, who are masters of the *logos*, instead of its slaves. First Rasseneur, then Pluchart:

His influence over the miners was due to his verbal facility, the good-natured way he could go on addressing them for hours without ever tiring. He did not venture on any gestures, but stood stolidly smiling, drowning them with words and hypnotizing them. (*G*, p. 240)

He spoke. His voice was hoarse and painful to listen to, but he was used to that, as he was always on the move and took his laryngitis with him as part of his performance. He strengthened his voice in a gradual crescendo, which produced effects of pathos. He stood with his arms open and punctuated his periods with a swing of his shoulders, giving his eloquence some of the character of the sermon, dropping his voice at the end of each sentence in a religious way which carried conviction by its very monotony. (*G*, p. 241)[81]

The rivalry between different styles of elocution, different voice timbers, is admirably foreshadowed by what might appear to be a mere touch of local color, a curious piece of folklore inserted in the Ducasse chapter; I am referring to the contest between two types of chaffinches:

The point of the contest was to decide which one would repeat his particular song the most times in an hour. . . . Off went the finches, the *chichouïeux* with a deeper note, and the more high-pitched *batisecouics*, timid at first and only venturing an occasional phrase, but working each other up and quickening their pace, and finally carried away by such furious rivalry that some even collapsed and died. (*G*, p. 156)[82]

Etienne's speaking style lies midway between that of the amateurs and that of the professionals. It is strikingly similar to Eugène Rougon's; their apotheoses are identical, synchronized with their oratory:

They applauded his triumph. His massive frame towered over the rostrum. His shoulders moved from side to side, keeping time with the rise and fall of his sentences. His speaking style was pedestrian, careless, and studded with issues of law; he would inflate commonplaces only to explode them with lightning bolts. He thundered, brandishing trivialities. His advantage as an orator consisted solely in his extraordinary long-windedness; he was tireless and could go on grandly for hours, rolling his periods, mindless of what they carried along in their path.

Gradually Etienne was warming up. He lacked Rasseneur's facile stream of words. Often he was at a loss, and had to use tortuous sentences from which he emerged with an effort emphasized by a forward lunge of his shoulders. But when he was pulled up in this way he found simple, energetic images which struck home to his audience, whilst his movements, those of a workman on the job, elbows now well back and now thrust forward to strike out with his fists, his jaw suddenly jutting out as though to bite, had an extraordinary effect upon his mates. As they all said, he was not very big but he made you listen. (*G*, p. 274)[83]

No two orators could differ more in physical appearance—Eugène is

big, Etienne, small—nor in speaking style—Eugène, the professional, speaks with great ease; Etienne, the autodidact, with great difficulty. But below these surface differences, the common feature stands out: both Eugène and Etienne capitalize on the "living" quality of speech. The cliché "la parole vive" (as in *viva voce*) lies at the heart of every discourse on language shown by Derrida as sharing in the myth of phonocentrism. Thus Plato follows preestablished traditions when he equates *logos* and *zôon:*

> In describing *logos* as a *zôon*, Plato follows certain rhetors and sophists who had before him opposed the corpselike rigidity of writing to live speech, which unfailingly adapts to the necessities of the current situation, the expectations and the demand of the interlocutors present, sensing the places where it must come forward, pretending to yield at the moment when it becomes both persuasive and compelling.[84]

The doubly determined lifelike quality of speech is clearly manifested in our two passages. The flexibility, the adaptability of speech contribute to Etienne's success in persuading the miners to strike. The possibilities that speech offers for supplementing one inadequate semiology (Etienne's lack of words) with an adequate one (his expressive gestures) are very markedly emphasized in the passage from *Germinal*. Etienne's rhetoric of persuasion relies heavily on body language.

In Eugène's case, it is the pneumatic aspect of speech that is stressed (though he too avails himself of the resources of body language), for if speech = life and life = breath, then speech = breath. The positive valorization in Zola of all expressions drawn from the paradigm of breath (*pneuma*) can hardly be exaggerated. In his earliest notes he sets a goal for himself from which he never swerved: "To maintain throughout my books a single and sustained inspiration which, arising on page one, would carry the reader to the end" ("Garder dans mes livres un souffle un et fort qui, s'élevant de la première page, emporte le lecteur jusqu'à la dernière" [*R-M*, 5: 1742]).

The consequences of this premium placed on the lifelike quality of speech is the formulation of an ideal writing which would represent the synthesis of the *animation* of speech with the *extension* of the written word. The union of the positive semes of both speech and writing is actualized in *Au bonheur des dames,* in the form of Octave Mouret's most brilliant innovation in advertising: "These balloons were a stroke of genius, red balloons with fine-grained rubber skins emblazoned with the store's name, given away as bonuses to each customer. They floated in the air attached to a string, *live advertisements* spread about in the streets" ("Un trait de génie que cette prime des ballons, distribuée à chaque acheteuse, des ballons rouges, à la fine peau de caoutchouc, portant en grosses lettres le

nom du magasin, et qui, tenus au bout d'un fil, voyageant en l'air, promenaient par les rues une *réclame vivante!*" [*R-M,* 3: 612-13; emphasis added.]).

Just as these "floating signifiers" are likened to speech by virtue of their living quality, speech as described in both *Son Excellence* and *Germinal* bears a curious resemblance to writing. Eugène's eloquence is informed by punctuation, by the rhythms and divisions of classical literature, as indicated by the word "periods"; Etienne's struggle to find the "mot juste," to get out his sentences, are a mimesis of what Flaubert described as "les affres du style" (the pangs of style), the agonizing effort to write beautiful sentences—that is, eminently linear, graphic units. (It is worth noting that Flaubert's struggle was waged on two fronts: the scriptural and the oral. In order to test his written sentences, to assure himself of their harmony, Flaubert submitted them to the trial of the so-called *gueuloir,* a neologism Flaubert coined to describe his readings.)

Sandoz (*L'Oeuvre*), Zola's anagrammatic persona, or Pascal, his alias, are both transparently autobiographical figures, but they reveal only the anecdotal side of writing, whereas the composite figure of Eugène, Etienne, and Octave provides a fairly complete commentary by Zola on his own writing. Zola's leaders are all variants on the writer, a writer profoundly dissatisfied with the inadequacies of (his own) writing and desirous of immediate, aggressive contact with an audience, but a writer aware, at some level, that there is no form of speech, even aided and abetted by physical supplements such as gestural language and stamina, which does not imply writing and its system. Just as the leader cannot be separated from the victim, speech cannot be detached from writing. Ultimately, the only distinction between the leader's and the victim's use of language is one of effectiveness. When the leader uses language it carries; indeed, whatever the sign system adopted by the leader, he establishes communication with and power over the crowd. A confirmation of this rule by the negative occurs in *Nana.* Her moment of apotheosis is a moment of silence; yet even her silence is golden:

> She didn't say a word; the authors had even cut the line or two they had given her, because they were superfluous. No, not a single word: it was more impressive that way, and she took the audience's breath away by simply showing herself.... Paris would always see her like that, shining high up in the midst of all that glittering crystal, like the Blessed Sacrament (*N,* pp. 459-60).[85]

When, on the other hand, the victim uses language, it miscarries. Etienne's lapidation coincides with a loss of verbal power; his speech has become impotent:

> He was too dazed to try to turn away, but faced up to them, trying to calm

them down with words. His old speeches, once so warmly applauded, now came back to his lips. He repeated phrases with which he had had them spellbound when he held them in the palm of his hand like a flock of sheep. But the old magic had gone, and the only answer was brickbats. (*G,* p. 423)[86]

The pharmakos is, of course, double and contradictory not only in its anthropological function, but also in its semantic composition: *pharmakos* is a primal word with antithetical meanings—poison and cure—and therein lies its "literariness." Etienne is not only pharmakos, but pharmakeus, a sorcerer whose speech is like a magic potion: now healing, now poisonous. The words remain the same, but depending on the state of the I/C relationship, they take on different, indeed opposite meanings and produce different effects. We can now add to our initial equation a new one which binds together the anthropological and the linguistic significance of the pharmakos, a double ambivalence which Zola exploits thoroughly and repeatedly:

$$(1)\ \frac{\text{victim}}{\text{writing}} \simeq \frac{\text{leader}}{\text{speech}} \qquad (2)\ \frac{\text{victim}}{\text{poison}} \simeq \frac{\text{leader}}{\text{remedy}}$$

By way of conclusion, we might attempt a comparison of Zola's founding myth and its Romantic counterparts or models. The differences —for those are what interest us—seem to pertain to the leader/victim's relationship to language and his attitude toward power.

The individual protagonist of a Romantic crowd-fiction is either a writer-victim (Chatterton) or a social-victim (Jean Valjean). Though Jean Valjean, the convict, may bear certain biographical similarities to Hugo, the proscript, unlike Hugo's, his relationship to the society that persecutes him is not mediated by language—that is, language as an instrument of power: Valjean is neither an author nor an orator. Similarly, Vigny maintains throughout his works a clear-cut distinction between his doomed poets (*Chatterton, Stello*) and his sacrificed soldiers (*Servitude et grandeur militaires*): his soldiers are not men of letters, and his poets *do* nothing. Zola, neither by design nor intention, but in response to inner needs and a changed cultural climate, achieves a synthesis of the two functions disassociated by the Romantics, syncretizing two actors: the writer-victim and the social-victim. His main protagonists are all men of words, though not of letters: Eugène Rougon, Octave Mouret, and Etienne Lantier all use language to establish and extend their influence over the crowd, that is, to further their ambitions.

This remark brings us to the second of Zola's innovations. In contradistinction to his Romantic forefathers, who confided the "dirty secret" of their will to power only to their journals (see Vigny's *Journal d'un poète* or Baudelaire's *Mon coeur mis à nu* and *Fusées*), Zola broadcasts his via his power-hungry protagonists. Furthermore, breaking with a

Romantic tradition, Zola makes it perfectly clear that the writer's apostolic mission is motivated not only (if at all) by altruistic feelings of brotherhood and compassion, but also/rather by egotistical desires for fame and fortune. The crowd's hostility to the man of genius is then shown as motivated not by ignorance or ingratitude (a common complaint among the French Romantics), but by a very strong desire for independence. Persecution is the proper response to the superman's will to power, and Zola's writer personae are contemporaries of Nietzsche's Superman and Carlyle's Heroes. Whereas the aristocratic Romantics fled to the ivory tower in droves, terrified by the rising tide of barbarism, Zola, the self-made man, the nouveau riche, refuses to stand and wait: "Unlike you, I cannot afford to go to sleep, lock myself up in an ivory tower, on the pretext that the crowd is stupid. *I need the crowd;* I approach it as best I can; *I try every means available to master it"* ("Il ne m'est pas permis comme à vous de m'endormir, de m'enfermer dans une tour d'ivoire, sous prétexte que la foule est sotte. *J'ai besoin de la foule,* je vais à elle comme je peux, *je tente tous les moyens pour la dompter").*[87]

Once the leader-victim's will to power is out in the open, the Christian model of persecution which informs both Hugo's and Vigny's previously cited works becomes either an object of parody (*La Conquête de Plassans*) or an empty cliché (*Travail*). In Zola's crowd-fictions, sacrifice is never a prelude to self-sacrifice; persecution of the victim by the crowd never results from or leads to the victim's selfless devotion to others. Persecution and sacrifice fulfill many functions in Zola's fictional universe: they are the wages of the sin of pride; they gratify masochistic fantasies; they serve political rather than ethical needs; they reenact a primitive ritual of catharsis—in short, they do everything but *improve* the individual victim. The Saccard of *L'Argent* is perhaps the best example of the unrepentant leader-victim. Even as he is in prison for having gone bankrupt and dragged hundreds of small investors down with him, he is already hatching his next grandiose scheme, to Mme Caroline's great astonishment and, finally, admiration: "Do you think I've given up my ideas?...For six months now I've been working here, staying up nights so that everything can be rebuilt....when I become the master again, you'll see, you'll see..." ("Est-ce que vous croyez que je lâche mes idées?...Depuis six mois, je travaille ici, je veille les nuits entières, pour tout reconstruire....quand je redeviendrai le maître, vous verrez, vous verrez..." [*R-M*, 5: 387]).

Considered in a diachronic perspective, over the years the leader-victim's fate is softened, going from the premature death of Silvère in *La Fortune des Rougon* to the advanced old age of the brothers Froment in *Travail* and *Vérité*. The final segment of the early novels—death or exile—gives way to conquest and apotheosis. The instinct for survival

wins out over the instinct for death; the victimization of the leader becomes a part of natural selection, which only the fittest survive.

The predominant role played by the individual protagonist in the I/C relationship has been sufficiently stressed throughout this first part of our study to lay to rest the notion that Zola's predilection for the crowd signifies the downgrading of the individual. What it does mean is the reduction of the individual to a single, all-encompassing drive: the will to power over the crowd. On the other hand, the predominance of the individual protagonist should not be taken to mean that the crowd is of secondary interest and importance, that it does not exist and function outside of the master/slave dialectic and the sacrificial ritual. Thus, in the following chapter we will consider the crowd-in-itself, the crowd per se.

Part II

Chapter 3

Polarization

Flying in the face of my own title, I have thus far spoken not of Zola's crowds, but of his crowd, proceeding as though Zola's much-vaunted variegated crowds—his marchers, his theater audiences, his shoppers, his soldiers, to mention just a few—were monolithic, without ever articulating the reasons behind this shift from the plural to the singular. We can no longer put off considering the question: Zola's crowds or Zola's crowd—are they mutually exclusive, or one and the same?

In the previous chapter we have seen one aspect of the crowds' underlying unity: an unvarying opposition to the individual protagonist. Let us examine here a somewhat different crowd constant, one immanent to the crowd: its unvarying temporal cycle, its curve. If we superimpose three celebrated crowd scenes—the races in *Nana,* the sales in *Au bonheur des dames,* and the exhibition opening in *L'Oeuvre*—we can distinguish a number of stages in the crowd's (or crowds') development which recur in Zola's crowd-fictions with amazing regularity. Not, I hasten to add, that all are necessarily manifested, but the actualization of any one of these stages presupposes the whole cycle. Each stage corresponds to a higher degree of crowd density; thus, the progression in time is projected into space.

1. Emptiness. The first stage is the crowd degree zero. The stage is set for the crowd's appearance; there is a sense of expectation as the vacant spaces—the "cases" (squares)—the crowd is to occupy are designated and the crowd begins to trickle in:

In the bright bursts of sunlight which alternated with the clouds the whole scene lit up, from the public enclosure, which was gradually filling with a

crowd of carriages, riders and pedestrians, to the still vacant course. (*N*, p. 345)

In walking around the departments, he had found them empty....Of course, it had barely struck eleven; he knew from experience that the crowd came only in the afternoon.

But his persistent fear of the famous public present at this solemn occasion made him take another look at the gradually thickening crowd....Some spaces remained empty.[1]

It is interesting to note in the second quotation that Octave Mouret is perfectly aware of the existence of a crowd curve; as the head of a department store he possesses a professional knowledge of the crowd. In contrast to Mouret, Claude Lantier, the figure in the third quotation, is a novice; through his eyes we discover rather than confirm a pattern.

 2. Swelling. The second stage consists in the swelling of the crowd, generally accompanied by a rise in the noise level:

Meanwhile the enclosure was filling up....now nothing could be heard but the hubbub of the swelling crowds, shouts, calls and the cracking of whips carrying loudly through the open air. (*N*, pp. 348-49)

The afternoon crush, the expected push had come at last....And there was no mistaking the noises which reached him from the outside, the rattle of cabs, the slamming of cab doors, the growing hubbub of the crowd.

And when he ended up again in the main gallery, the throng gathered there had increased rapidly. It began to be difficult to move about.[2]

 3. Saturation. At this stage the crowd has reached its maximum density, occupied every empty square. Zola's recurrent crowd metaphor to describe this stage is oceanic. One might say that this is the stage of the crowd's naturalization:

Meanwhile this downpour had suddenly filled the stands. Nana looked at them through her field-glasses. At that distance, she could only distinguish a compact, confused mass of people, piled up in row upon row. (*N*, p. 357)

It was no longer a simple matter to reach the staircase. A closely packed mass of heads surged through the galleries.

After wandering about at some distance, he ended up in the main gallery for the third time. The crush there was dreadful now. All the Parisian lions... men who belonged to smart clubs...women of all ranks...surged through in an endlessly rising tide.[3]

 4. Discharge. The fourth stage is perhaps the most complex, because it comprises both the moment of what Elias Canetti terms "discharge"—"this is the moment when all who belong to the crowd get rid of their

differences and feel equal"[4] — and the beginning of the crowd's disintegration and dispersal. This moment of supreme integration and incipient dissolution is generally signaled by a common song ("La Marseillaise" in *La Fortune des Rougon* and *Germinal*; "Ave Maria" in *Lourdes*) or cry ("Nana! Nana! Nana!" and "A Berlin! A Berlin! A Berlin!" in *Nana*) or other sound (the "fou rire" — uncontrollable laughter — that sweeps the exhibition halls in *L'Oeuvre*). The simultaneity of oneness, dissolution, and sound is most apparent in *Nana*: "It was the brutal climax of a colossal game, with a hundred thousand spectators possessed by a single passion....And the cry of the multitude, the cry of a wild beast reappearing in a frock-coat, grew more and more distinct" (*N*, p. 376; "C'était la brutalité dernière d'une colossale partie, cent mille spectateurs tournés à l'idée fixe....Et le cri de tout ce peuple, un cri de fauve reparu sous les redingotes, roulait de plus en plus distinct" [R-M, 2: 1403]).

The recurrent sentence structure (*C' + être + le/la*) in the passages quoted above and below, characteristic of "le style artiste,"[5] confirms the existence in Zola's crowd-fictions of a predictable curve of collective behavior:

> *It was that* hour of the day when the throng which had been whipped up by all the advertisements went berserk....The fever had been gradually rising since morning, very much like the sort of intoxication which emanated from the handling of all those fabrics....Now Mme Marty's face was flushed and nervous, like that of a child who has drunk a glass of pure wine.

> By five o'clock the atmosphere was sultry and stifling; *it was that* time of day when the throng, tired of milling about the halls, is seized with the dizzy panic of cattle let loose in a pen....And these thousands of people were wracked with the pains of this late afternoon fatigue which attacked their legs, tore at their faces, and ravaged their foreheads with migraines.[6]

The crowd's curve is patterned not merely on a pathological model (a fever), but mainly on a sexual one: the discharge is orgasmic in its intensity and physiological manifestations: the bestial cry (*Nana*), the flush (*Au bonheur des dames*), the fatigue (*L'Oeuvre*). In this monstrous coitus, the crowd is neither male nor female, but a combination of both — a combined-parent figure, as it were. The crowd's rapid movement and extreme noisiness, which place it somewhere in the same paradigm as Zola's trains and other machine-monsters, are further indications of its sexuality. Like the runaway train at the end of *La Bête humaine*, the crowd, that uncontrollable force of nature, is an impressive representation of desire.

5. Emptiness. The fifth and final stage is the coda, the symmetrical reprise of the initial emptiness: "Now the lines were growing shorter....

Having emptied out the stores with the thunderous roar of an open sluice gate, the clientele began to radiate forth, released, as it were, and carried back to the four corners of the city" ("Les queues diminuaient maintenant....Il y avait comme un élargissement continu, un rayonnement de la clientèle, remportée aux quatre points de la cité, vidant les magasins avec la clameur ronflante d'une écluse" [R-M, 3: 798-99]).

Zola's complete crowd curve can be drawn as shown in Figure 2. His insistence on the existence and the representation of a complete cycle serves as one of the distinctive features of his crowd scenes, for it could easily be demonstrated that in literature as a whole, and in the nineteenth-century French novel in particular, crowds are almost always presented only in their swelling and saturation stages. The emptiness which frames Zola's crowd scenes like ominous parentheses is theatrical, and it is surely no coincidence that the most insistently cyclical crowd scene in the entire Zola canon occurs in the first chapter of Nana, which describes Nana's debut on the Paris stage. Speaking somewhat mathematically, one might say that, using crowd density as a variable, the chapter can be broken down into a series of alternating emptiness/fullness segments (beginning and ending with emptiness), corresponding in mimetic terms to the various acts and intermissions. In effect, the first chapter produces in microcosm the cyclical structure of the entire novel, as evidenced by the juxtaposition of the first and last sentences of the novel: "At nine o'clock the auditorium of the Théâtre des Variétés was still virtually empty" (N, p. 19; "A neuf heures, la salle du théâtre des Variétés était encore vide" [R-M, 2: 1095]); "The room was empty. A great breath of despair came up from the boulevard and filled out the curtains" (N, p. 470; "La chambre était vide. Un grand souffle désespéré monta du boulevard et gonfla le rideau" [R-M, 2: 1485]).

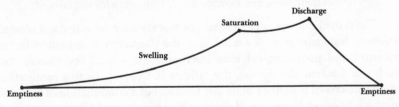

Figure 2

Not only does Zola's model allow for structural permutations, but it also provides an insight into the crowd's function in the economy of his mental and fictional universe. The writer's repeated exercise of his power to alternate excessive emptiness (absence of a crowd) with excessive fullness (presence of a crowd) recalls the child's game analyzed by Freud in Beyond the Pleasure Principle, the hiding and retrieving of a wooden

reel: "This, then, was the complete game—disappearance and return."[7]
The exceptional interest of the *Fort/Da* (gone/here) game, which links an
"instinct for mastery" to the acquisition of language, has not been lost on
Lacan (who terms this event "the primordial symbolization"[8]) and other
structuralists, who have made the Fort/Da a parable of structural linguis-
tics. Seen in the light of the isomorphism between the child's game and
the writer's activities, it would seem that Zola's most elaborate crowd
scenes, when reduced to their invariant cycle, are designed to gratify an
archaic instinct, to reenact an infantile experience. One difference
between the child and the writer is noteworthy: whereas the child attaches
the greatest pleasure to the return of the reel (which represents its
mother), Zola privileges the crowd's disappearance by adding a third act
to his play: Fort/Da/Fort. Ultimately, however, the author's greatest
pleasure is the verbal activity associated with the game: the alternating
absence/presence of the crowd generates language, and that is the writer's
specific concern.

In sum, whether considered from the point of view of the I/C
relationship or in terms of their temporal cycle, Zola's crowds can be
reduced to a synthetic abstraction, the singular CROWD. And yet to
leave matters at that would be not so much to impoverish Zola's texts as
to miss one of their key structuring devices. For the binary oppositions
which play such an important role not only in the I/C relationship but
also in the crowd cycle (empty/full), also obtain *within* the crowd. Zola's
crowd, as I shall seek to demonstrate throughout this chapter, is always
double, based on what Canetti describes as a "double crowd structure":

> The surest, and often the only, way by which a crowd can preserve itself
> lies in the existence of a second crowd to which it is related. Whether the two
> crowds confront each other as rivals in a game, or as a serious threat to each
> other, the sight or simply the powerful image of the second crowd, prevents
> the disintegration of the first. . . .
>
> In order to understand the origin of this structure we have to start from
> three basic antitheses. The first and most striking is that between men and
> women; the second that between the living and the dead; and the third that
> between friend and foe.[9]

1. The Sexual Axis: Male/Female

Had Zola never written another crowd-fiction, "Celle qui m'aime", a
short story included in the *Contes à Ninon,* would appear merely as the
most Baudelairean of Zola's works, a parable which owes much to the
prose poem "Le Vieux Saltimbanque" ("The Old Showman").[10] The
common features they share are

1. a "flâneur" type first-person narrator;

2. a similar setting: a fairground on the outskirts of Paris, rich in color, sights, and smells;

3. a symbolic encounter: in Baudelaire's prose poem, with the old showman, whose sorry fate is likened to that of the artist who has outlived his usefulness to society; in Zola's novella, with two complementary figures—the "ami du peuple" (the earliest incarnation of a typical character in Zola, the "faux ami," or false friend of the people, the revolutionary-provocateur), symbolizing the failure of a materialistic ideology to satisfy man's longing for an opiate, and "celle qui m'aime," representing in the form of a contrived fantasy the illusory quality of any dream.

But seen as the first in a long series of crowd-fictions, this short story takes on another dimension: with the wisdom of hindsight, we can read it, not as an awkward imitation, but rather as the matrix of Zola's original contributions to the genre. For the retrospective reader, many of the distinctive features of Zola's later crowds are already in place here. Foremost among them is the sexual segregation of the crowd.

In the course of his wanderings about the fairgrounds, the narrator is drawn into a tent by a magician who promises a glimpse of the lady of one's dreams ("celle qui vous aime"). As the narrator steps inside, he describes the scene:

> I let the curtain drop and found myself inside the temple. It was sort of a long, narrow room lined with canvas, with no seats, and lit by a single lamp. Several people—curious girls and boisterous boys—were already gathered there. Everything, it must be added, took place with maximum decorum: a rope stretched across the middle of the room separated the men from the women.
>
> Truth to tell, the Mirror of Love was nothing but two sheets of plate glass, one in each compartment, small, round windowpanes looking into the back of the booth.[11]

As such, the rope will never reappear in Zola's fiction; but its trace, its invisible presence, will continue to delimit two separate, but not identical (or equal) worlds in all the crowd-fictions to come. Just as the mirror of love is not a real mirror, the mirrorlike symmetry of the tent is an optical illusion. Extending the segregation throughout the description of the scene (some two pages in length), the narrator contrasts the male and the female reactions to their respective visions:

> Thus the interested spectators filed past the window....O vision of the beloved! what harsh truths you drew forth from those wide-open eyes. They were the true Mirrors of Love, mirrors where feminine grace was reflected in eyes gleaming with a lust so lewd it bordered on stupidity.
>
> At the other window the girls amused themselves in a more seemly fashion.

On their faces I detected only a great deal of curiosity, but not the slightest sordid desire, not the slightest wicked thought.[12]

Thus, from the first, the sexual axis runs parallel with an axiological one: male : female : : impure : pure. The combination of a spatial separation and an axiological opposition will recur throughout Zola's fiction, though the rope will be replaced by other, less tangible barriers, and the stereotyped Romantic opposition of impure/pure will be reformulated in other, less obvious terms. Hyperbolized, the two-crowd structure will burst the boundaries of a single novel, producing novels where the crowd is coextensive with a single sex: e.g., *Au bonheur des dames* (female crowd), *La Débâcle* (a *double* male crowd, as we shall see in the next section). These hyperbolizations are the exceptions that prove the rule; and were our primary concern the changing contents of the male/female opposition, we should certainly have to examine them closely. But since we are focusing here on the manner in which the male/female opposition informs individual novels, we will concentrate our attention on that novel where the sexes confront each other directly: *Nana*.

If we compare the opening and closing scenes of *Nana*—scenes which are, as always in Zola, rigorously symmetrical—the form and function of the double crowd structure stand out. The opening scene consists in part of a description of the theater audience. This "audience" or "spectator crowd"—to adopt the convenient jargon of sociology—bears the unmistakable imprint of the segregation noted in "Celle qui m'aime"; though the rope has vanished, its mark is everywhere in evidence, for even as they are standing or sitting side by side, the men and women in fact form two distinct crowds:

> Downstairs, in the big marble-paved vestibule where the ticket-barrier was installed, the audience was beginning to arrive. . . . The rumbling of carriages stopped short, doors slammed, and people entered in little groups, waiting at the barrier before climbing the double staircase behind, where the women, their hips swaying, lingered for a moment. In the crude gaslight, on the pale bare walls skimpily decorated in the Empire style to form a peristyle like a cardboard temple, tall yellow posters were boldly displayed with Nana's name in thick black letters.
>
> Some gentlemen were reading them, as if accosted on the way; others were standing about chatting together, blocking the doors. (*N*, pp. 20-21)[13]

This crowd is a microcosm of the sexually polarized society represented in *Nana*. At first the crowd is undifferentiated, unisexual: the "audience," "people." Then, as if split by the "double staircase," the single crowd is divided into two separate groups, which are spatially distinct—the women above and the men below—and connotatively

opposed as prostitute vs. client. Bordenave's insistent refrain with reference to his theater—"You mean my brothel" (*N*, p. 21; "Dites mon bordel" [*R-M*, 2: 1097])—should be taken at face value. Having crossed the threshold of the theater, the women adopt a provocative pose ("their hips swaying"), while the men hover at the entrance "as if accosted on the way." Zola's use of the French word *accrochés* for "accosted" confirms this reading: when asked by Dr. Toulouse for his free association with the word *fille* ("prostitute"), Zola responded "une raccrocheuse" ("streetwalker"), specifying further that it is a "visual image."[14]

This initial opposition is reiterated in various terms throughout the rest of the chapter. Thus, in the following passage, male is to female as loud is to soft: "And there was a din of voices, in the midst of which Nana's name sounded with all the lilting vivacity of its two syllables. The men standing in front of the playbills spelt it out aloud;...while the women, at once uneasy and smiling, repeated it softly with an air of surprise" (*N*, p. 24).[15]

Elsewhere the opposition is reformulated in terms borrowed from the vestmental code:

> There were signals, rustlings of fabrics, an endless procession of skirts and coiffures, broken now and then by the black of a dress-coat or a frock-coat. All the same, the rows of seats were gradually filling up, while here and there a light-coloured dress stood out from its surroundings, or a head with a delicate profile bent forward under its chignon, in which there flashed the lightning of a jewel. In one of the boxes a bare shoulder gleamed like snowy silk. Other women sat languidly fanning themselves, following with their gaze the movements of the crowd, while young gentlemen, standing in the stalls, their waistcoats open, gardenias in their button-holes, pointed their opera-glasses with gloved fingertips. (*N*, p. 27)[16]

One set of oppositions seems to lead to another, since this representation of the male vs. female crowd entirely by metonyms (parts of bodies, elements of dress) is not only reinforced by a light (female) vs. dark (male) contrast, but also relayed by an expansion of the cliché active/passive paradigm: male activity (= verticality + mobility) vs. female passivity (= horizontality + immobility). This series of escalating oppositions culminates in the masculine crowd's use of opera glasses to view the feminine crowd, the optical instrument serving to dramatize the distance which separates them.

When Nana finally appears on stage and begins to sing, the male response to her extraordinary sex appeal is emphasized, while the female is omitted, but the absence of a specific female response only confirms the difference: it is not necessary for both terms of an opposition to be manifested at all times, once the basic terms have been set up. In fact, the direction in which the men now point their opera glasses reveals the new,

otherwise hidden opposite pole; at this moment Nana embodies all the women in the audience: "Little by little Nana had taken possession of the audience, and now every man was under her spell" (*N*, p. 45; "Peu à peu, Nana avait pris possession du public, et maintenant chaque homme la subissait" [*R-M*, 2: 1119]).

All that is implicit in the first chapter is made quite explicit in the final one. The spatial distribution is the same: the crowd on the boulevards marching by, shouting "A Berlin," Nana's male friends gathered downstairs, while the women—friends and (former) rivals—are upstairs in Nana's mortuary chamber. The geometry is not a gratuitous, purely ornamental effect of symmetry, but rather the visible, visual expression of the profound male/female split that runs throughout the work. Zola has gone far beyond the stereotyped male impurity vs. female purity opposition of "Celle qui m'aime"; what he promotes here is perhaps the most significant variant of our basic paradigm (male/female), a variant which might be formulated as male selfishness vs. female compassion. Whereas, throughout the novel, the men have sacrificed their fortunes and reputations to Nana while the women alternated between envy and competition, in the end it is the women who risk their lives and beauty for her (she dies of smallpox) while the men save their skins. Ultimately then, the male/female opposition comes down to a male bonding / female bonding opposition.[17]

Once the antitheses and distance between the male and female crowds have been brought out where they are most prominent, hence most perceptible, the extent to which this agonistic structure pervades the novel as a whole can be more easily apprehended. Most critics who have dealt with Nana have portrayed her primarily as a "mangeuse d'hommes" ("man-eater"), emphasizing Nana's relations with men to the exclusion of her relations with women. Nana's lesbianism has not, of course, gone completely unnoticed, but it has been, I would suggest, underestimated, misdiagnosed as little more than a symptom of decadence, a *topos* of decadent literature. To fail to measure the depth not only of Nana's contempt for men but also of her love for women is to overlook the open war between men and women waged from page 1 onward. The battle of the sexes is a difficult cliché to renew, but Zola rises to the challenge.

To the extent that Nana incarnates a familiar *fin de siècle* female literary stereotype, one which Mario Praz has termed the "Fatal Woman," her contempt for her male victims is generically determined, her impassivity in the face of the disasters she causes, predictable. But Zola carries this conventional representation to its logical conclusion: Nana's scorn for men is matched, counterbalanced, by her sense of "comradeship" with other women. Elements of this compensatory theme of female bonding are disseminated throughout the literature of the courtesan,[18]

but in *Nana* they all converge, producing a vision of an antisociety composed exclusively of women.

The contrast of the contempt for men/need for women is the structuring device of chapter II. Here, while Nana's male admirers invade her apartment, cooling their heels for hours in the hope of seeing her, she seeks refuge in the kitchen, that locus of female bonding par excellence: "She regretfully abandoned the kitchen, that snug refuge where you could chat and relax amid the pleasant fumes of the coffee-pot while it was warming on the embers" (*N*, p. 65; "Elle quitta la cuisine à regret, ce refuge tiède où l'on pouvait causer et s'abandonner dans l'odeur du café, chauffant sur un reste de braise" [*R-M*, 2: 1136]). With Nana in the kitchen are her three surrogate mother figures: her aunt Mme Lerat— "Wasn't she a second mother to her since the first had gone to join Papa and Grandmama?" (p. 55; "Est-ce qu'elle n'était pas sa seconde mère, puisque la vraie avait rejoint le papa et la grand-maman?" [p. 1127]); her companion Mme Maloir, Mme Lerat's double and rival; and Zoé, her maid and "manager." The only men admitted into the inner sanctum, the hearth, are two minimal males, two almost women—Francis, the hairdresser, and Labordette, the "eunuch": "He never asked for any favours. He was just a friend doing little services for the women he knew" (p. 73; "Jamais il ne demandait rien, lui. Il n'était que l'ami des femmes, dont il bibelotait les petites affaires" [p. 1143]).

This all-female society gathered around a coffeepot will be expanded into the larger all-female society gathered to eat at Chez Laure, the lesbian restaurant which Nana visits with Satin. This restaurant is remarkable for its almost exclusively female clientèle; it is a sort of women's club where men are tolerated on sufferance, relegated to the role of (humble) spectators: "There were about a hundred women there....As for the men, there were very few of them—between ten and fifteen—and apart from four jolly fellows who had come to see the sight, and were cracking jokes, very much at ease, they were behaving very humbly in the midst of an overwhelming flood of petticoats" (*N*, pp. 257-58; "Il y avait là une centaine de clientes....Quant aux hommes, ils étaient peu nombreux, dix ou quinze au plus, l'attitude humble sous le flot envahissant des jupes, sauf quatre gaillards qui blaguaient, très à l'aise, venus pour voir ça" [*R-M*, 2: 1300-1301]). This restaurant is an extension of the theater world: the real men are overshadowed by the make-believe men, the (wo)men who act and dress like men:

> For a moment her attention was drawn by a young man with short curly hair and an insolent face, who was keeping a whole tableful of enormous women breathlessly attentive to his slightest caprice. But when the young man began to laugh, his chest swelled out.
> 'God, it's a woman!' she blurted out. (*N*, p. 258)[19]

Transvestism in *Nana* is not unilateral: if women act and dress like men, the corollary is also true. The high point in Nana's idyll with Georges Hugon comes when she dresses him in one of her nightgowns, his own clothing having been soaked in the rain:

'He'll never get dry,' said Nana, seeing Georges beginning to shiver. 'He's going to catch cold.'

And there were no men's trousers in the house! She was on the point of calling the gardener back, when an idea occurred to her. Zoé, who was unpacking the trunks in the dressing-room, had brought Madame a change of linen, consisting of a chemise, some petticoats and a dressing-gown.

'But that's perfect!' cried the young woman. Zizi can put all that on. You don't mind wearing my things, do you, Zizi?...When your clothes are dry, you can put them on again and go straight back home, so as not to have a scolding from you mama...Hurry up. I'm going to change too, in the dressing-room.'

Ten minutes later, when she reappeared in a tea-gown, she clasped her hands together in ecstasy.

'Oh, the darling! Doesn't he look sweet dressed like a woman!' (*N*, p. 182)[20]

What the English translation does not render at all is Nana's *shame* at enacting (acting out) a fantasy scenario: where the translator writes, "You don't *mind* wearing my things," the original text reads, "Tu n'es pas *dégoûté* de moi"—that is, "do I *disgust* you?" Disgust is a strong word in Nana's mouth, for even though she remains "innocent" and intact throughout the most sordid episodes, she does not, so to speak, blush easily. One might well question her sudden moral scruples: my hypothesis is that this little interlude with Georges is presented as shameful because it is a rehearsal for the Sapphic love scenes with Satin. Once Georges has agreed only too willingly to participate, Nana directs the scene as if following a preexistent script. First she dresses Georges up in women's clothes, and not just any woman's, but her own. The narcissism inherent in homosexuality determines her choice of Georges as a partner, for they are look-alikes; like Nana he has "tawny hair" (*N*, p. 182; "cheveux fauves" [*R-M*, 2: 1236]), and as Nana discovers to her delight, "he's as slim as I am" ("il est aussi mince que moi" [ibid.]). Dressed up in Nana's clothes, Georges becomes her male double. This specular relationship is apparent on the level of the signifier; both have nicknames consisting in the repetition of a single syllable, and furthermore, each one of these syllables contains a prominent letter in Zola's own name: N*a*na/*Z*izi, suggesting that for Zola his very surname bodied forth his bisexuality. And, indeed, if *a* is the feminine suffix par excellence, *zizi* signifies penis in French argot. Once Georges is costumed, Nana proceeds to address him as a woman for reasons which are certainly worth noting: "Nana kept calling Georges 'my sweet', a form of address which struck her both as affectionate

and familiar" (p. 183; "Nana appelait Georges: 'Ma chère'; ça lui semblait plus familier et plus tendre" [p. 1237]). Finally, overcoming "her embarrassment and her scruples" (p. 185; "sa gêne et ses révoltes" [p. 1239]), she gives in to Georges's advances.

The line of interpretation built into the scene deviates from my hypothesis by emphasizing the incestuous aspect of the Nana/Zizi affair. Nana's shame and reluctance result from a violation of the incest taboo: "'No, leave me alone. I don't want to....It would be very wrong at your age....Listen, I'll just be your mama'" (p. 185; "Non, laisse-moi, je ne veux pas... Ce serait très vilain à ton âge... Ecoute, je resterai ta maman" [R-M, 2: 1239]). But this deviation is a detour, a "snare," for the incest motif produces the following fantasy:

> And at night, when she went upstairs dazed by her day in the open air, and intoxicated by the scent of the leaves, to join her Zizi behind the curtain, she felt like a schoolgirl having a holiday escapade, a love-affair with a young cousin to whom she was going to be married, trembling at the slightest noise, terrified lest her parents should hear her, and savouring the delicious novelty and the voluptuous terror of a first affair. (N, p. 191)[21]

We have only to let ourselves be guided by the distinctly (and surprisingly) Proustian ring of this passage[22] to discover that the relatively minor transgression represented by an affair between cousins intended for marriage conceals the major transgression represented by homosexuality. The highly implausible attribution of this fantasy to Nana should alert our attention: given what we, as readers of L'Assommoir, know of Nana's socioeconomic background, this fantasy's presence at this juncture of the text can only be explained by its latent content, because its manifest content signals a lapse in Zola's realistic portrayal of Nana, "the golden fly" ("la mouche d'or"). This fantasy is an eminently bourgeois fantasy, one unlikely to occur to an unread slum child whose "boarding school" ("pension") was a sweatshop and whose parents were too busy drinking to eavesdrop on her sexual initiation. The use of a chiasmus—"les tâtonnements délicieux et les voluptueuses épouvantes"—, a comparatively rare figure in Zola's rhetoric, further underscores the literariness of this scene.

It is, in fact, the word pensionnaire (translated as "schoolgirl" but actually signifying "boarding-school girl") that gives us access to the latent content of this passage, for in Zola's idiolect, "pensionnaire" is another way of saying "lesbian." In an early newspaper article entitled "Au couvent" ("In the Convent"), Zola launches an attack (to be taken up again in future novels, in particular La Curée) on that bourgeois institution, the convent education. According to Zola (here, too, following in Balzac's footsteps), boarding schools are hotbeds of vice, breeding grounds for homosexuality. The narrator of this article compares two young girls

—Lucie, who was educated at home, and Jeanne, who was educated in a convent. This is how he imagines Jeanne's life in the convent:

> I can still see her—and it is this image that should strike fear in the hearts of all mothers—I could see her sneaking off into a corner with an older student; she would call her "my little mama," and let her put her arm around her waist and kiss her on the lips; and then both of them would go off behind the lilac bushes, like two lovers giddy with the warm scents of springtime.[23]

Just as in *Nana*, there is an initiator and a novice, the initiator being cast in a maternal role. There is nothing fixed about this role, however, for if in the scene under study, Nana plays the role of initiator, in the later scenes with Satin, the roles are reversed.

Our suspicions once aroused by the incongruity of this fantasy, other details draw our attention, in particular the choice of a "young cousin" ("petit cousin") as a sexual partner. If one were to write a structural anthropology of the nineteenth-century French family as represented in the novel, the "petit cousin" would deserve a chapter to himself. It seems quite clear, based on the evidence, that in the society at large, this family member was viewed with distinct misgivings: at best, he was a dangerous heterosexual (a seducer), at worst, a contemptible homosexual (the passive partner). These connotations of the word *cousin* are contained in two invaluable repertoires of the clichés and stereotypes which inform the nineteenth-century mentality—first, Flaubert's *Dictionnaire des idées reçues* (≃ Commonplace Book), and second, the *Larousse du 19ᵉ siècle:*

> COUSIN. —Advise husbands to beware of the "young cousin."
>
> Slang. A man guilty of shameful sexual submission to other men.[24]

Given the restrictions imposed upon young women by nineteenth-century mores, the petit cousin was clearly a privileged family member —the most easily available sexual partner. (The narrator of *A la recherche* is initiated by a mysterious "petite cousine" on tante Léonie's sofa, indicating that the degree of kinship matters more than the sex of the cousin!) Thus, by extension, the petit cousin was also the most obvious "cover" for a lover. When, in *Une Page d'amour,* the maid Rosalie is visited by her fiancé, young Jeanne Grandjean asks: "Mother, is he Rosalie's brother?" ("Maman, c'est le frère de Rosalie?"). Her mother's answer is ready, spontaneous: "No, he's her cousin" ("Non, c'est son cousin" [*R-M*, 2: 862]). *Eugénie Grandet* is only the best known of a series of novels depicting love affairs between cousins. Indeed, Nana's apparently innocent fantasy about a cousin leads us to a peculiar disparity between information provided by *Nana* and by the Genealogical Tree with reference to the father of Nana's child: whereas in the novel, Louiset's father is unknown, evasively described as "a gentleman" (*N*, p. 55), the

family tree specifies that Nana "has a child by a cousin." The unfortunate consequence of Nana's family romance—her sickly offspring—is typical of all such relationships featured in Zola's novels: e.g., Thérèse and Camille in *Thérèse Raquin,* or Pauline and Lazare in *La Joie de vivre.* These affairs are perhaps all ill-fated because they presuppose the equation of the female cousin with a male; they are thinly disguised accounts of adolescent male homosexual relationships: "When he [Camille] played with her and held her in his arms she might just as well have been a boy" (*TR,* p. 41); "Lazare, from the very first, had accepted her as a boy, a younger brother."[25]

When situated in the context of Zola's idiolect and the "mythologies" of the nineteenth century, both "pensionnaire" and "petit cousin" bring us back to the theme of homosexuality. The revelation of the strata of associations deposited below the surface linear simplicity of Nana's fantasy is meant to show the pervasiveness of the homosexual theme in the novel, demonstrating how it is present even when and where it appears absent. Transvestism is only the tip of the iceberg; indeed, the very explicitness of the scene with Georges diminishes its effectiveness. Furthermore, transvestism is a commonplace of decadent literature.[26] Zola himself depicts similar scenes elsewhere, as in *La Curée,* where Maxime and Renée finally consummate their incestuous relationship when Renée is disguised as a man, or in *Germinal,* where Etienne's desire for Catherine is aroused by her boyish getup: "These boy's clothes, this jacket and breeches on a girl's body, excited and troubled him" (*G,* p. 59; "Ces vêtements de garçon, cette veste et cette culotte sur cette chair de fille, l'excitaient et le gênaient" [*R-M,* 3: 1173]). And, as Mitterand has argued, Etienne's desire for Catherine is incestuous: "Etienne shares Catherine's room as though he were another brother. Hence the desire that arises between the two young people can only be an incestuous desire. Catherine cannot be both sister and mistress. . . . For the shadow of incest and its prohibition to disappear, Maheu must die. It is he who prevents Etienne from touching Catherine, and not Chaval."[27] What distinguishes the transvestism scene in *Nana* from those in *La Curée* and *Germinal* is of course the *sex* of the transvestite. Instead of a female → male transformation, we have a male → female one; the direction of the vector points up the importance of lesbianism in *Nana.*

In the light of this interpretation of the transvestism scene with Georges, Nana's actual initiation by Satin is, so to speak, an anticlimax. What becomes significant is not the final consummation of this passion, but its constant retardation, deferring. Indeed, some sixty pages elapse between Nana's first visit to Chez Laure, where Satin drops her for Mme Robert (the perfect oxymoronic name for a hermaphrodite), and their final union, after which Satin again drops Nana for Mme Robert. But it is

not Mme Robert (feminine rival) who prevents Nana from making love with Satin, but men; and not just any men, but the police, those enforcers of male law, the law of the father. The confrontation between the prostitutes and the police is a hyperbolization of the war between the sexes; the interruption of Nana and Satin's lovemaking by a police raid on the hotel where they are spending the night (both having been evicted by men from their respective apartments) dramatizes the inseparability of the social and sexual axes, of the class struggle and what Ralph Ellison has so aptly called the "ass struggle."[28] The police enforce bourgeois law and order, an order consisting of two forms of oppression: that of women by men and that of the poor by the rich. The street prostitute (as opposed to the courtesan that Nana becomes), being both female and poor, is the prime victim of this sociosexual oppression, as Satin explains to Nana:

> According to her, the police arrested as many women as possible, in the hope of earning bonuses; they grabbed everybody and silenced you with a slap if you shouted, for they were sure of being defended and rewarded, even when they had taken a respectable girl among the rest. In the summer they would carry out raids on the boulevards in parties of twelve or fifteen, surrounding a long stretch of pavement and picking up as many as thirty women in an evening.... Nana listened to these stories in growing terror. She had always been afraid of the Law, that unknown power, that instrument of male vengeance which could wipe her out without anybody in the world lifting a finger to defend her. (*N*, p. 274)[29]

Rising up from the gutter, Nana's triumph will consist in reversing the reigning power structure by oppressing *rich men.* Satin, a "sister" and childhood friend, is Nana's natural ally in this all-out war against the rich, the powerful, and the male. The aggressive nature of Nana's lesbianism appears in chapter X, where, in the course of an elegant dinner given in Nana's town house, Nana and Satin humiliate the male guests by forcing them first to grovel in the dung heap whence they came and second to approve their open display of affection for each other and their contempt for men:

> While the roast was being served the two women plunged into an orgy of reminiscences. They used to have frequent fits of chattering of this kind when a sudden urge to stir up the mud of their childhood would take hold of them; and these fits always occurred when men were present, as if they were giving way to a burning desire to smear them with the dung on which they had grown to womanhood. The gentlemen turned pale visibly and exchanged embarassed looks. (*N*, p. 333)[30]

The discomfort displayed by the men when treated to a brief plot summary of *L'Assommoir* is contrasted with their relatively good-humored acceptance of Nana and Satin's show of affection: "There were no more

protests. In the midst of these fine gentlemen with their great names and their ancient traditions of respectability, the two women sat face to face, exchanging tender glances, triumphant and supreme in their tranquil abuse of their sex, and their open contempt for the male. And the gentlemen applauded them" (p. 335).[31]

The repetition in the French text of these two passages of the word *imposer* ("imposer le fumier"; "s'imposaient et régnaient") to describe the female/male relationship serves to underscore the identity of the two episodes; the gentlemen's constant tension (relieved either by pallor or applause) attests to the parallelism of the evocation of the lower classes' misery and the flaunting of female homosexuality. But of these two *obscenities*, the second is the more important. Although, in the course of the evening, Nana completely contradicts her earlier sentimentalization of the people—"A nice lot *they* were, and no mistake! She knew them and she could talk about them" (*N*, p. 337; "Une jolie ordure, le peuple! Elle le connaissait, elle pouvait en parler" [*R-M*, 2: 1369])—she remains true to her lesbianism, sending home all the men, including Muffat, who is footing the bill, to be alone with Satin. Once again the vertical axis translates the separation of the sexes and the (spatial) superiority of women. In order to fully savor the humiliation inflicted on Muffat, Nana and Satin watch from the window as he slinks off into the night: "And the two women rocked with helpless laughter as they saw Muffat's rounded back and watery shadow disappearing along the wet pavement, across the icy, empty plains of the new Paris" (p. 342; "Et elles eurent un fou rire, en voyant le dos rond de Muffat, qui s'en allait le long du trottoir mouillé, avec le reflet éploré de son ombre, au travers de cette plaine glaciale et vide du nouveau Paris" [p. 1374]). To do justice to the complexity of Zola's vision, it should be noted that this successful humiliation is offset by two other sights Nana and Satin see while at the window: first, two policemen walking the beat, an insistent reminder of the vigilance and supremacy of male law; second, "la reine Pomaré," once the toast of Paris, now a ragpicker, a none-too-subtle reminder of the fleetingness of Nana's triumph.

Fleetingness or emptiness? The acquiescence and tolerance displayed by the men gathered around Nana's dinner table should not be taken for mere signs of male weakness. The lack of masculine protest means something quite different: it indicates that though a titillating and extreme form of female bonding, lesbianism is not in any real sense disruptive or a danger to the patriarchal-paternalistic system. Like "the golden fly" carrying its poison up from the dung heap, the threat in *Nana* always comes from below, corroding the vertical axis which supports, or *is* social hierarchy. Women of the same class kissing in public may embarrass their male spectators, but whatever the blows endured by the

male ego, male hegemony remains intact. Female bonding becomes a danger for the male social order only when it crosses class lines, calling into question the differences that separate rich women and poor women, for when this phenomenon occurs, it is an epiphenomenon of a larger event: a calling into question of all structuring differences. One of the major themes in *Nana* is the notion that once the veneer of civilization/ repression has been stripped away, there is no innate qualitative difference between the sexuality of the upper and lower classes; indeed, the excessive repression of the upper classes breeds excessive perversion:

> From the top of the social ladder to the bottom, everybody was at it! Well, there must be some nice things going on in Paris between nine o'clock at night and three in the morning! And with that [Nana] would laugh and say that if you could have looked into every bedroom in the city, you would have seen some funny sights—the ordinary folk going at it hammer and tongs, and quite a few nobs, here and there, wallowing in the filth even deeper than the rest. (*N*, p. 273)[32]

The subverting of class differences by sexual identity clearly applies to both men and women: the crowd of orgiasts is undifferentiated. For cultural reasons, however, the notion that "honest women" and courtesans are really sisters underneath it all is a far more explosive one than the concomitant identification of upper- and lower-class men, perhaps because it touches on a common (nineteenth-century?) male fantasy: any female sexual activity not connected to procreation—that is, the perpetuation and expansion of the bourgeois family—is somehow "louche," not to say lewd. Bourgeois morality in the latter half of the nineteenth century, even in non-Victorian France, was founded on the opposition between home and house, so to speak: thus, the antithesis between Mme Arnoux (Mother) and Rosanette (Whore) structures the mental universe of Frédéric Moreau, that bourgeois everyman in *L'Education sentimentale*. But try as he might to cling to the structuring differences (that is, to deny the mother's sexuality), Frédéric is forced to recognize that the two worlds are not hermetically sealed off from each other. In a sense, the objects which Arnoux puts into circulation are metonyms for the men who circulate between compartmentalized female circles. The interpenetration of home and brothel which is only incipient in *L'Education* becomes widespread in *Nana;* thus, whereas the brothel is alluded to nostalgically as the paradoxical locus of a lost innocence on the last page of *L'Education,* in *Nana* it signifies only rampant corruption and commercialization. The omnipresence of the brothel is confirmed by the presence in the Muffats' otherwise austere salon of a piece of what might be described as "early bordello" furniture, a red silk easy chair:

> However, opposite the armchair in which the Count's mother had died—a

> square armchair with a stiff frame and inhospitable upholstery which stood on the other side of the fireplace — the Comtesse Sabine was seated in a deep easy-chair, whose red silk padding was as soft as eiderdown. It was the only piece of modern furniture there, a touch of whimsy introduced amid the prevailing severity, and clashing with it. (*N*, pp. 74-75)[33]

This chair, "this voluptuous piece of furniture" (p. 84; "ce meuble de voluptueuse paresse" [p. 1153]), stands for the countess's repressed sexuality. The "sign" next to her mouth is the sign of Sabine's identity with Nana; indeed, they are doubles: "In the glow of the fire the black hairs on the mole at the corner of her lips looked almost fair. It was Nana's mole, down to the colour of the hairs" (p. 96; "Dans la lueur du foyer, les poils noirs du signe qu'elle avait au coin des lèvres blondissaient. Absolument le signe de Nana" [p. 1163]). This observation made by Fauchery, who will become Sabine's lover, is reiterated by other characters, in particular Nana and Count Muffat. As soon as Nana sees Sabine, she recognizes Sabine's true female nature:

> '...she may be a countess, but she's no better than she should be....Yes, she's no better than she should be....I've got an eye for that sort of thing, you know! And now I know your Countess as well as if she were my own child....I'm willing to bet she sleeps with that snake Fauchery....Yes, I tell you she's his mistress! A woman can always tell that sort of thing about another woman.' (Pp. 200-201)[34]

The vindictive pleasure Nana derives from this feminine intuition/complicity is contrasted with Muffat's horrified and reluctant recognition of the identity of wife and mistress. As the ultimate representative of both the *repressed* (by his mother and her Catholic dogma) and the *repressive* (he is the emperor's chamberlain), Muffat is the character in the novel most threatened by the breakdown of structuring differences. The discovery that his wife has a lover gives rise to two independent, obsessive trains of thought. First, if Sabine, like the count, is having an affair, then count = countess as *desiring subjects:* "While he was taking off his clothes in a whore's apartment, his wife was undressing in a lover's room; nothing could be simpler or more logical" (*N*, p. 230; "Tandis qu'il se mettait en manches de chemise chez une catin, sa femme se déshabillait dans la chambre d'un amant; rien de plus simple ni de plus logique" [*R-M*, 2: 1277]). Second, if Sabine, like Nana, is attractive to other men, then Sabine = Nana as *objects of desire:* "Warm images pursued him. A naked Nana suddenly evoked a naked Sabine. At this vision, which brought them together in a shameless relationship, under the influence of the same desire, he stumbled into the roadway" (pp. 230-31; "Des images chaudes le poursuivaient. Nana nue, brusquement, évoqua Sabine nue. A cette vision qui les rapprochait dans une parenté d'impudeur, sous un même souffle de désir, il trébucha" [p. 1278]).

My initial emphasis on the segregation of the crowd in *Nana* now stands in need of qualification. The main line of the novel, as I have been reading it, is the definition of sexual roles, which transcend role-playing. Now in the bordello-theater world represented in *Nana,* where playacting is the rule and the real prince is indistinguishable from the false king, this endeavor is bound to fail. Georges Hugon embodies this dilemma; first described as a "girl dressed up as a boy" (*N,* p. 84; "fille déguisée en garçon" *R-M,* 2: 1152]), we later see him as a boy dressed up as a girl. His "real" sex, his gender, recede into the unknowable. Inevitably Nana's own polymorphous sexuality leads her down the path of transvestism; there is no barrier between the stage and the street, as the world of *Nana* verges on that of Jean Genet's *The Balcony:* "Nana deceived Satin as she deceived the Count, abandoning herself to monstrous caprices, and picking up girls on street corners. . . . Then again, disguised as a man, she would go to infamous houses and watch scenes of debauchery to relieve her boredom" (p. 433; "Nana trompait Satin comme elle trompait le comte, s'enrageant dans des toquades monstrueuses, ramassant des filles au coin des bornes. . . . Puis, sous un déguisement d'homme, c'étaient des parties dans des maisons infâmes, des spectacles de débauche dont elle amusait son ennui" [p. 1453]).

It is surely no coincidence that in a novel animated by an anguished and complex inquiry into sexual difference, the castration complex is a central preoccupation. As Borie had already noted, Nana's genitals are described in terms which instantly call to mind Freud's analysis of the myth of Medusa's head, but it is Freud's essay on fetishism that seems most relevant here, for in it Freud indicates that the little boy's horrified discovery of what he assumes to be female castration provokes vehement denial. Fetishism, the erotization of a substitute for the mother's missing phallus, is only the most extreme form this denial or protest takes; the clinging to a fantasy of the "phallic mother" is another. Now Nana's examination of her own body in the mirror seems to imply the persistence of just such a fantasy (on the part of the male author, who was once a little boy): how else are we to account for the amusement and surprise her self-examination evokes? "Then she studied *other parts of her body,* amused by what she was doing, and filled once more with the depraved curiosity she had felt as a child. The sight of herself always surprised her, and she looked as astonished and fascinated as a young girl who has just discovered her puberty" (*N,* p. 222; "Puis, elle étudia *d'autres parties de son corps,* amusée, reprise de ses curiosités vicieuses d'enfant. Ça la surprenait toujours de se voir; elle avait l'air étonné et séduit d'une jeune fille qui découvre sa puberté" [*R-M,* 2: 1270; emphasis added]).

Certain stylistic peculiarities of this passage reinforce our sense that what is being recounted here is a repetition of the child's crucial discovery

of anatomical difference, with the concomitant refusal of castration and search for the mother's hidden phallus. Zola's use of the vague, euphemistic expression "other parts of her body" is in marked contrast with the anatomy-lesson-like precision of the context, where, in the manner of the blazon, each member of the body is carefully enumerated. This euphemism is all the more remarkable because later on in the same scene, when we shift from Nana as spectator of herself to Muffat as spectator or voyeur of this specular love scene, Nana's genitals are referred to explicitly. Similarly, the choice of "puberty" as a synechdoche for budding breasts and pubic hair is euphemistic. The technique of euphemism is particularly appropriate in texts dealing with taboo subjects, for as the author of an article on lesbianism in Balzac's *La Fille aux yeux d'or* remarks: "Behind the conscious repression inherent in euphemism there is another repression."[35] The euphemization, or conscious repression, bears on Nana's genital organs, but the other, unconscious repression bears on the penis/phallus, curiously absent from this novel, which Zola describes in his notes as "the poem of male desire" (*R-M,* 2: 1665), as well as from all the others, with the possible exception of *Germinal,* where it features prominently, so to speak, in the scene of Maigrat's castration. But even there, it is referred to euphemistically as "his dead virility" (*G,* p. 351; "sa virilité morte" [*R-M,* 3: 1453]).[36]

The proliferation of androgynous protagonists in nineteenth-century French novels bespeaks a generalized breakdown in valid criteria for sexual classification, reflecting no doubt a questioning of traditional male/female roles in contemporary society. The conundrum posed by Emma Bovary — is she a woman infused with a male spirit (Baudelaire)? is she a man disguised as a woman (Sartre)? — is also posed by Balzac's Lucien de Rubempré, Stendhal's Lamiel, and Gautier's Mademoiselle de Maupin, to name a few. Intuitively the novelists had arrived at the fundamental principle of sexual differentiation which Freud would later articulate and theorize: castration. What Barthes says with reference to the characters in Balzac's *Sarrasine* can easily be extended to all the characters we have just mentioned: "Thus the symbolic field is not that of the biological sexes; it is that of castration: of *castrating/castrated, active/passive.* It is in this field, and not in that of the biological sexes, that the characters in the story are pertinently distributed."[37]

There is, however, a tremendous gap between the conclusions *implicit* in Zola's text and the ones he makes *explicit.* If there is any progression from chapter I to chapter XIV, it consists in replacing purely physical distinctions between male and female with spiritual ones: in chapter XIV, the difference between the sexes is ethical, not biological. Women are morally superior to men, for female bonding transcends petty rivalries in moments of greatest need. Thus Rose Mignon, Nana's archrival, rushes

to tend her, just as earlier on Nana, forgiving Satin for her infidelities, hurries off to visit her in the hospital, saying: "'I'm going to the hospital...Nobody's ever loved me as much as her. Oh, they're right when they say that men are heartless" (*N*, p. 452; "Je vais à l'hôpital... Personne ne m'a aimée comme elle. Ah! on a bien raison d'accuser les hommes de manquer de coeur!" [*R-M*, 2: 1470]). In fact, the union of all the warring female doubles around Nana's putrefying corpse suggests that Nana is a pharmakos, albeit an anomalous one. Anomalous for several reasons: for one, smallpox is a rather unorthodox cause of death for a ritual victim; for another, the reconciliation of former enemies around her dead body is only partial. Downstairs, Muffat stands conspicuously apart from Nana's other former lovers, and, what is even more telling, the women gather upstairs—that is, in a separate place from the men. Even the cadaver of the pharmakos cannot bring together the rival sexes.

The function of the double crowd structure in *Nana* is now clear; it magnifies, renders immediately perceptible, the central issue of the novel, which is not male desire, but sexual difference. Yet the clear-cut binary opposition between the male and the female members of the crowd does more than provide an enlargement of the conflict between animus and anima within Nana; it also serves as a reassuring foil for Nana's androgyny. The ultimate redistribution of male and female characters on either side of a secure boundary bespeaks a firm rejection of the threat posed by Nana's properly mythic bisexuality. Whether or not this solution is final, whether or not Nana's death ushers in a new order, will be seen in the following pages.

2. The Polemological Axis: Friend/Foe

The double crowd structure which opposes two warring, all-male crowds both presupposes male/female segregation and determines the separation of the living from the dead. Before turning our attention to *La Débâcle*, let us examine each of these propositions.

It would be a serious relapse into the mimetic or "referential" fallacy to take the absence of women from the front lines of the novel for granted, on the grounds that in actual historical fact there were no women on the front lines of the Franco-Prussian War. The assignation of secondary, supportive roles to the female characters in *La Débâcle* corresponds not so much to a verifiable outer reality, but rather and more significantly to an inner reality. That Zola felt quite free to upgrade or downgrade the importance of women in the novel, that his ultimate disposition derives from the structural logic of the text, is attested to by his preliminary

dossiers. Mitterand notes: "At first he does not want to 'give a woman an important role': 'the romantic interest of the novel will suffer accordingly'"; however, "gradually Zola seems to abandon his original intention to write a novel devoid of important female characters: 'I would like to have other women.'"[38]

The exclusion of women from the battle is already foreshadowed in *Nana*, where, in the final chapter, the women gathered in Nana's mortuary chamber watch from the window as the crowd surges by shouting: "To Berlin! To Berlin! To Berlin!" It is abundantly clear that the war will be fought by men, with women relegated to the role of spectators. Though written twelve years apart, *La Débâcle* picks up where *Nana* leaves off. There is, however, a seeming break in the continuity between the representation of women in *Germinal* and *La Débâcle* that must be accounted for. In *Germinal*, the miners' wives participate fully in the strike, alongside and, more often than not, ahead of their husbands. Nowhere does Zola exhibit more openly his espousal of the myth that women are innately more violent than men, though the celebrated fight between the laundresses in *L'Assommoir* (as well as Lisa's pugilistic talents in *Le Ventre de Paris*) leaves little doubt as to women's capacity to inflict punishment when aroused. Throughout the events of the strike, the miners' wives are cast as instigators of violence: "It was the screaming women who were egging the men on" (*G*, p. 308; "C'étaient les femmes qui poussaient, glapissantes, excitant les hommes" [*R-M*, 3: 1411]); "the men had now followed the women's example" (p. 410; "les hommes s'y mettaient, à l'exemple des femmes" [p. 1508]). As perceived by Etienne, this female fury is a terrifying sight: "It was above all the women who frightened him: la Levaque, Mouquette, and the rest, who were possessed with murderous fury and fighting tooth and nail, yelping like a pack of bitches and egged on by Ma Brûlé, whose skinny form towered above them" (p. 341; "Et les femmes surtout l'effrayaient, la Levaque, la Mouquette et les autres, agitées d'une fureur meurtrière, les dents et les ongles dehors, aboyantes comme des chiennes, sous les excitations de la Brûlé, qui les dominait de sa taille maigre" [p. 1443]). The final paroxysm of this subhuman, specifically female brand of violence is, of course, the castration of Maigrat.

The myth of female violence has, as I have already had occasion to mention, a long literary history, stretching back at least as far as Euripides' *The Bacchae*, but in nineteenth-century France it was reactivated by the decisive part played by women first during the French Revolution, and second, closer in time to the period when Zola was writing, during the Commune of 1871. The "pétroleuses" of that period fired up, so to speak, the imagination of many contemporary authors.[39] The question then becomes, If Zola gave credence to the myth that women are more prone

to violence than men, why is there not a single instance of a woman's actually firing a gun in *La Débâcle?* I think this apparent contradiction can be resolved by adopting the simple and useful distinction put forth by Lionel Tiger in *Men in Groups.* This distinction is the one between "violence" and "aggression": "'Aggression' is a social-organizational term referring to a process, while 'violence' describes an event which is only one possible outcome of the aggressive process." Tiger goes on to say that "males are prone to bond, male bonds are prone to aggress, therefore aggression is a predictable feature of human groups of males."[40] Zola's so-called anthropology, as set forth in *La Débâcle,* concurs with Tiger's—not surprisingly, as both are essentially Darwinians—in that it too posits a prehistoric male bond based on common dangers faced by males:

> Was this not the brotherhood of the earliest days of the world, friendship before there was any culture or class, the friendship of two men united and become as one in their common need of help in the face of the threat of hostile nature? (*D*, p. 136)

> The brotherly love that had grown up between this peasant and himself went down into the depths of his being, the very root of life itself. Perhaps it went back to the earliest days of the world. (P. 272)[41]

In discussing *Nana,* we saw that Zola also envisions a female bonding process at work in society, but unlike its male counterpart, it has no prehistoric origins, which is to say, is not determined by heredity, a very serious lack in Zola's system of values. The crucial distinction between a primeval male bond and a latter-day female bond overlaps the aggression/violence distinction, but it does not cover it. If in *La Débâcle,* male aggression, in the form of military combat is contrasted with female violence, in the form of Silvine's murder of Goliath (the German spy who raped her and fathered her child), the one being in the interest of national security, the other personally—read sexually—motivated, there is also a contrast between international conflict and civil war, the first being socially acceptable aggression, the second, reprehensible violence (see Table 4).

If in one direction the friend/foe opposition subsumes the male/female, in another it has direct bearing on the third of our posited double crowds, the living/dead, for, as Canetti remarks, in war, "each side wants to constitute the larger crowd of living fighters and it wants the opposing side to constitute the larger heap of the dead."[42] These are the very terms in which Weiss, the only French character who from the outset foresees the inevitable defeat, expresses his hope and consolation: "I still don't think we shall get out of this, and I want some Prussians not to get out of it either, *heaps* of Prussians, enough to cover all that land over there!" (*D*, pp. 172-73; "je crois encore que nous allons y rester, et je voudrais qu'il y

Table 4

Aggression (acceptable)	Violence (unacceptable)
Franco-Prussian War (male vs. male)	Silvine's murder of Goliath (female vs. male)
	Commune (male vs. male)

restât aussi des Prussiens, des *tas* de Prussiens, tenez! de quoi couvrir la terre, là-bas!" [*R-M*, 5: 559; emphasis added]). Thus each member of an army is doubly determined: "Every participant in the war belongs simultaneously to two crowds. From the point of view of his own people he belongs to the crowd of the living fighters; from that of the enemy to the potential and desired crowd of the dead."[43]

The crucial discriminant introduced here by Canetti is that of point of view, for in no other novel does Zola make such a deliberate and elaborate use of modulations of points of view; in no other novel is the proliferation of spectators less gratuitous, more congruent with the subject. This technique has direct bearing on one of the major problems confronting Zola: how to actualize the friend/foe opposition? how to distinguish the two armies? in short, how to institute (radical) difference? Point of view is everything here, for clearly the Prussians will look different to a French observer than to a fellow Prussian, and of course, vice versa. The problem is further complicated by the near absence of Prussian observers: King William is hardly a representative observer, as we shall see. Zola's *tour de force* consists in giving a "fair," or balanced, picture of the two armies through a series of subterfuges, or ruses.

In the absence of Prussian observers, Weiss, the patriotic but realistic Frenchman, functions in the opening chapter as a sort of pseudo-Prussian, in that he provides an exposition of the strengths and weaknesses of the opposing armies which is devastating in its implications for the French. Confusing the messenger with the message, the French officers attack Weiss, but his vision proves prophetic. The basic paradigm as Weiss sees it is simply PRUSSIANS (well prepared) vs. FRENCH (poorly prepared).

This impartial formulation of the situation will soon give way to more emotional and one-sided descriptions of the Prussians. One of the great sources of suspense throughout the first part of the novel is the invisibility of the enemy, which gains in power from this very mystery. The first description of the Prussians by first-hand witnesses occurs in chapter III, and it is brief: "I was on a little rise lying behind a bush and I

saw them coming out straight ahead of me and to right and left, real anthills and streams of black ants, so that when there weren't any more left there were still more to come" (*D*, p. 69; "J'étais, moi, sur un petit coteau, couché derrière un buisson, et j'en voyais déboucher en face, à droite, à gauche, oh! de vraies fourmilères, des files de fourmis noires, si bien que, quand il n'y en avait plus, il y en avait encore" [*R-M*, 5: 450]).

This account by a soldier who fought at Froeschwiller sets the tone for the longest description of the invading Prussians, delayed until chapter VII of part I. It is Silvine's terrified narration of the arrival of the Prussians in Raucourt:

'I had gone upstairs to a window looking on to the road and the open country. I couldn't see a soul, not one red-trouser, and then I heard loud, heavy steps, and a voice shouted something and all the rifle-butts hit the ground together. There, at the end of the street, were a lot of *little, dark, dirty-looking men with big ugly heads* surmounted by helmets like the ones our firemen wear... I was told they were Bavarians. Then as I looked up I saw, oh, thousands and thousands of them coming along all the roads, over the fields, through the woods, in close packed ranks, endlessly. *A black invasion, like black grasshoppers,* on and on, so that in no time you couldn't see the ground for them.' (*D*, p. 150)[44]

What we have here is a classic description of the enemy as nonhuman, animalistic. The anaphoric repetition of the adjective *black*, which is opposed in chromatic code to the red of the French soldiers' uniforms ("red-trouser"), culminates in the entomological analogy: Bavarians $\simeq$ grasshoppers. Tiger, borrowing the term from Eric Erikson, describes this process as one of "pseudo-speciation," and explains the benefits derived from this symbolic transformation: "This is a process of clearly defining an enemy or prey as different from members of the in-group, attributing especially disagreeable characteristics to the out-group, and finally coming to an implicit decision that the members of the out-group are not really human and may be killed without any of the inhibitions... against killing one's own kind."[45] However, Zola's concomitant use of hyperbole—"thousands and thousands"—suggests that this animalization is also a form of hyperbole; Silvine's point of view is revealed as unreliable because distorted by fear and ignorance. If we simply pursue the adjective *black* and/or the entomological analogy as they recur throughout the novel, we discover that the soldier's and Silvine's vision does not predominate.

First, a simple shift in perspective and mediating consciousness results in a French = Prussian equation. Blackness and animalism are qualities not specific to one nationality; they can attach themselves to

either army. Thus, when King William surveys the battlefield on the morning of Sedan, he sees the French troops as "lines of insects" (*D*, p. 196) or as "moving black dots" (p. 197). By the end of the passage, all the soldiers massing below are reduced to a common denominator—"these few black dots" (p. 198)—as hyperbole gives way to litotes.

Second, the initially negative valorization of the entomological analogy becomes positive, as the invading ant is replaced by the ant image familiar to the readers of La Fontaine's *Fables*, the hard-working ant. Watching the stretcher-bearers struggling with their heavy loads, Maurice is reminded of the ant which carries burdens many times its own weight. In the course of this passage the simile becomes metaphor:

> As Maurice was watching one of them on his right, a puny, delicate-looking young man who was carrying a heavily-built sergeant on his back and struggling along on his tired legs like a worker ant transporting a grain of wheat too heavy for it, he saw them pitch over and vanish in a shell-burst. When the smoke had blown away the sergeant reappeared, lying on his back but with no fresh wound, while the bearer lay with his belly ripped open. And another busy ant ran up, and after turning over and examining his dead comrade he picked up the wounded man again and carried him away on his back. (*D*, p. 254).[46]

Over and over again the initial French/Prussian opposition is subverted; when seen at close range the enemy becomes, if not a friend, at least human. The transformation of an animalistic, hated enemy into a suffering fellow man—a complete undoing of the process of pseudo-speciation—is illustrated by one of the episodic German characters, whose very name is his narrative program: Gutman. We first see him during the central scene in the book, Weiss's execution at the hands of the enemy in full view of his wife, Henriette. Gutman is the soldier who steps forward to restrain Henriette, who tries desperately to intervene. In this first appearance, Gutman is described in the expected negative animal code: "A soldier stepped forward, a thickset Bavarian with a huge head bristling with red beard and hair, in the midst of which all that could be seen was a wide potato nose and big blue eyes. He had blood on him and looked horrible, like one of those cave-dwelling bears, hairy wild beasts red with the prey whose bones they have been cracking" (*D*, p. 250).[47]

This bloodthirsty beast, this ogre straight out of a children's fairy tale, turns up again much later in the novel in a pitiable state, half his tongue shot off; and Henriette, despite her initial repulsion on encountering her nemesis on the ward of the infirmary where she is a nurse, ends up caring for him up to his death. In yet another instance of the passage from a negative to a positive valorization of an animal image, the term

bear takes on an affectionate connotation when Jean asks Henriette: "'And your bear, this Gutman of yours?'" (*D*, p. 407; "Et votre ours, votre Gutman?" [*R-M*, 5: 805]).

The hospital and the cemetery to which it all too often leads are the great levelers, reducing former ancestral enemies, with their seemingly irreconcilable differences, to comrades bound together by a similar fate: "The enemies who had flown at each other's throats were now lying side by side in the good companionship of their common suffering" (*D*, p. 405); "in the little cemetery of Remilly two trenches had been dug, and they all slept side by side, the Germans on the left and the French on the right, reconciled in the earth" (p. 406).[48]

The differences between the French and the Germans are undercut not only by the imagery and the progression of events, but by the very structure of the novel. Let us recall the tripartite structure of *La Débâcle:* part I recounts the events of the period extending from August 6 to the eve of the battle of Sedan (September 1); part II is coextensive with the battle itself; part III covers the period from September 1870 to May 1871. The extraordinary hypertrophy or, to use one of my own terms, hyperbolization of the day of the battle is certainly the novel's most striking structural feature. It is an extreme example of what Gérard Genette calls the "pause," and results from the maximization of the disproportion between "narrative time" ("temps du récit", abbreviated *TR*) and "historical time" ("temps d'histoire," or *TH*): $TR \propto > TH$.[49] This deliberately imbalanced structure, with its intensive focus on the battle of Sedan, contributes greatly to the transcendance of the original opposition, for the Battle as a literary *topos* is the single event where extreme difference produces extreme indifference. According to Gilles Deleuze, one of the leading contemporary French thinkers, who has made the concept of difference central to his philosophical inquiry, the Battle is the privileged literary event—that is, the Event par excellence—because like meaning, it is beyond oppositions:

> If a battle is not just one example of an event among others, but the Event in its very essence, probably it is because it is actualized in many ways at the same time, and each participant can apprehend it at a level of actualization which varies according to his own fluctuating present; this is the case for now classical comparisons between the manner in which Stendhal, Hugo, and Tolstoï "see" the battle and make their heroes see it. But it is above all because the battle *hovers* over its own field, neutral in relation to its temporal actualizations, neutral and impassive in relation to the vanquished and the victors, the cowards and the brave, all the more dreadful for that reason, never present, always still to come and already past. Thus it is apprehensible

only by the will it inspires in the anonymous participant: a will one might well term "of indifference" in a mortally wounded soldier who is no longer either brave or cowardly, can no longer be one of the victors or the vanquished, who is so far removed, in that place where the Event is taking place, sharing in this manner in its dreadful impassibility. "Where" is the battle?[50]

The impossible location of the battle haunts Maurice just as it troubles the heroes of Hugo, Stendhal, Tolstoï, and, one might add—always in the nineteenth century—Stephen Crane. In the midst of the battle of Sedan, Maurice asks himself: "They still could see nothing and knew nothing. It was impossible to have the slightest conception of the battle as a whole—was it even a real big battle?" (D, p. 210; "On ne voyait toujours rien, on ne savait rien. Impossible d'avoir la moindre idée de la bataille, était-ce même une vraie, une grande bataille?" [R-M, 5: 597]).

Nonetheless, in Zola the all-embracing, neutral/izing view is not that of the anonymous, fatally wounded soldier, but rather that of the invulnerable King William. Though certainly the preeminent enemy and victor, as he watches the battle unfold below him, the king's vision approaches that of a neutral, not to say godlike observer; from his exclusive, elevated vantage point, he is in a position to extract from thousands of individual conflicts, each singularized in time and space, a totalizing overview. This transcendent apprehension of the Battle arises from the king's identification with "impassive nature." The theme of the impassibility of nature, dramatized at several points throughout the "longest day" by the recurrent figure of the peasant tilling the soil, is nothing but the impassibility of the Battle itself, projected onto nature: "He [Maurice] was very surprised to see down in a lonely valley, isolated by steep slopes, a peasant unhurriedly ploughing, guiding his plough behind a big white horse. Why lose a day's work? The corn wouldn't stop growing or people living just because there was fighting going on" (D, p. 210).[51]

At the risk of belaboring the obvious, we must be careful to distinguish the concepts of indifference and impassibility from those of self-interest and egotism—incarnated in La Débâcle by the miserly, war-profiteering peasant Fouchard—for, as this extended quotation from the passage describing what the king sees should make clear, what is involved here is the impassibility of language and the art it produces:

The atrocious, bloody battle itself, seen from such a height in the setting sun, was like a delicate painting: dead horsemen and disembowelled horses flecked the plateau of Floing with gay splashes of colour; further to the right, towards Givonne, the final scramble of the retreat made an interesting picture with

the whirling of black dots running about and falling over themselves; and again in the Iges peninsula to the left a Bavarian battery with its guns the size of matches looked like a piece of nicely adjusted mechanism, for the eye could follow its regular, clockwork movements. It was unhoped-for, over-whelming victory, and the King had no remorse, faced as he was by these tiny corpses, these thousands of men less than dust on the roads, the great vale in which the fires of Bazeilles, the slaughter of Illy, the anguish of Sedan, could not prevent unfeeling nature from being beautiful at this serene end of a perfect day. (*D*, p. 295)[52]

The fierce opposition between the French and the Germans, in terms of the novel *qua* novel, has but one function: to "result in a beautiful book," to quote Mallarmé's celebrated dictum.[53] Just as binary oppositions between phonemes makes meaningful language possible, binary opposi-tions between what Deleuze terms "series" (e.g., the French / the Germans) produce fiction. Seen from the king's point of view, "the battle *hovers* over its own field"—that is, the Battle transcends such antitheses as victorious/vanquished, living/dead, and human/animal, to become a "delicate painting," where each negative detail is transformed into a positive one: e.g., "dead horsemen and disembowelled horses" → "gay splashes of colour"; "guns" → "matches." In the final analysis, the king is nothing but the author's regal (Prussian) persona. The discrepancy between the horror of the *real events* being evoked and the neutrality of the *ideal Event* inscribed both points to and confirms the Battle's meta-mimetic status.

This "formalist" truth was not only unavailable, but more, unac-ceptable to both Zola and his contemporaries. The Franco-Prussian War and its humiliations were still too fresh in many Frenchmen's minds for them to view *La Débâcle* as nonreferential. A ballet based on the events of the Holocaust might today provoke an analogous indignation. Hence the debate which raged over Zola's unflattering portrayal of the French army, compounded by his incomplete rendering of the German. However distorted his interpretation, however erroneous his conclusions, even a critic such as Eugène-Melchior de Vogüe correctly identifies an important feature of the novel, the imbalance between the two "series," the French and the German:

> This big book is one-sided because in the dreadful duel which he recounts, the author shows us only one of the two opposing forces. Let us grant him for a moment the correctness of his conception of France under the Second Empire, and admit that all its energies were exhausted. All the same, we feel entitled to an explanation of the nature of the adversary's superiority. The victim was not strangled by an anonymous hand, yet that is the impression

with which the novel leaves the reader; there is a gaping hole in the very place where we expect Germany to be. I ask to be shown Germany.[54]

Zola readily acknowledged that this imbalance did exist, but attributed it to the epic genre of the novel:

> M. de Voguë wonders where Germany is in my book. Why it lurks about us like fate itself. I thought it more forceful to show Germany on the horizon, keeping it off stage. One divines its presence, or rather, one perceives it. Its closely felt presence is the factor which determines the strategic movements of our armies. . . . It is a literary device, an idea derived from my conception of the epic which I adhered to throughout the novel.[55]

What escaped both author and critic was the *necessity* of this imbalance, the *law* that governs the relationship between series: "The law governing two simultaneous series is that they are never equal."[56] What the author, unlike the critic, did understand, however, is that while the French are "phenomenologically" dominant, they are "ontologically" inferior; the Germans' superiority consists precisely in the fact that it is they who call the shots.

Now what becomes crucial in this perspective is the mechanism which insures communication between the two series, what Deleuze variously calls the "paradoxical instance" or the "differentiator."[57] This "differentiator" or "discriminant" is indeed paradoxical because it both links up the two divergent series and accounts for their disparity; it is both excessively present and excessively absent:

> This element belongs to neither series or, rather, belongs to both at once, and circulates continually between them. Thus one of its properties is a constant displacement in relation to itself; it is always "absent from its proper place," its proper identity, its proper resemblance, its proper balance. It appears in one series as excess, but on condition that it appear at the same time in the other as lack. But if it is in excess in the one, it is in the form of an empty square; and if it is lacking in the other, it is as supernumerary pawn or "occupant without a square." It is both word and object: esoteric word, exoteric object.[58]

It has been suggested that Deleuze's "paradoxical instance" could be enlisted in the elaboration of a theory of fictional characters: "Because of the connection maintained with meaning and nonmeaning, fantasy and representation, this agency must be considered the kingpin of a potential theory of the *character*"[59] In fact, the description of the differentiator reads like a description of one of the most troublesome characters in *La Débâcle;* I am referring to the Emperor Napoleon III. Having left a vacuum at the head of the Empire ("an empty square"), he becomes a

spectacularly displaced person ("occupant without a square"), shunted about with his retinue. His absence/presence constitutes the convergence factor between the two armies; without him there can be no battle, no victory, no defeat:

> Then in the midst of this tragic struggle he suddenly had a clear vision of the Emperor deprived of his imperial authority which he had entrusted to the Empress-Regent, stripped of his position as commander-in-chief with which he had just invested Marshal Bazaine, no longer anything at all, a shadow emperor, vague and indefinite, a nondescript useless object and a nuisance that nobody knew what to do with, spurned by Paris and with no function left in the army, since he had undertaken not to even give an order. (*D*, pp. 63-64)[60]

The recurrent image which best translates the Emperor's paradoxical status is that of the "shadow"; even when and where present, the Emperor appears as a mere shadow of himself. This image leads to the image of the Emperor as actor, one of the most controversial aspects of the novel in the eyes of Zola's contemporaries. The combination of the excessive pallor of a ghost with the excessive color of the made-up actor is the physical equivalent of the Emperor's literary function as paradoxical discriminant, as oxymoron incarnate:

> It was indeed Napoleon III, who looked taller now that he was on horseback, and his moustache was so waxed and his cheeks so rouged that he at once thought he looked much younger, and made up like an actor. Surely he must have had himself made up so as not to go round displaying to the army the horror of his colourless face all twisted with pain, his fleshless nose and muddy eyes. Having been warned at five in the morning that there was fighting at Bazeilles, he had come like a silent, gloomy ghost with its flesh all brightened up with vermilion. (*D*, pp. 192-93)[61]

Napoleon III is the differentiator by virtue not only of his paradoxical situation and appearance, but also of his excessive mobility; spurred on by the Empress's orders—"March on! March on!" (*D*, p. 193) —he is constantly on the move, in circulation, so to speak. This extreme mobility guarantees the unity of the otherwise chaotic events which make up *La Débâcle;* Emile Faguet, yet another contemporary critic, comments shrewdly: "At carefully timed intervals the Emperor's appearance punctuates, as it were, the periods of this vast, rambling story, the episodes of this chaotic epic, reminding us of the central, indeed the essential idea of the poem: a crumbling Empire."[62] The Emperor's relentless movement up, down, and behind the battle lines culminates in his fleeing into exile, forever condemned to displacement and leaving behind him an empty

throne. With the disappearance of the convergence factor, the second part of the novel ends.

Many critics have strongly suggested that Zola would have done well to have ended his novel there; or, at least, to have concluded part III short of the two final chapters on the Commune. Attacked both on ideological and aesthetic grounds—as either inadequate or superfluous —these chapters constitute a sort of *pons asinorum* for Zola scholars. If my reading of *La Débâcle* as a crisis of distinctions of epic proportions has any *telos*, it is the reintegration of the final chapters, a "revisionist" affirmation of the coherence of Zola's war novel. It is surely no coincidence that at this juncture my reading intersects with Michel Serres's: the articulation of the inter- and intra-specific conflicts is, to take up Serres's running metaphor, a hermeneutic crossroad, our inevitable rendezvous. Serres's argumentation is syllogistic: if the enemies are brothers (and they are, for, as Serres reminds us, the family tree has branches on both sides of the Rhine), and if in Zola all brothers are by definition enemies, then it follows that brothers must fight brothers. Or: "The enemies were brothers. The brothers are enemies"; "The struggle is always intrafamilial, pitting a Same-Other against an Other-Same"; "The Same is Other, the Other is Same."[63] Structurally the repetition of the international conflict by an intranational one is as predictable as it is fitting.

In my concluding remarks on the double crowd structure in *Nana*, I observed that there exists a microcosm-macrocosm relationship between the crowd(s) and the main protagonists. If we seek to verify the accuracy of this observation by applying it to *La Débâcle*, the necessity for the final Commune chapters becomes inescapable: it is the macroconflict which reduplicates the central microconflict of the novel, the one opposing Jean to Maurice. That Zola chose as his nuclear male-male couple two Frenchmen, rather than a Frenchman and a German, is of the essence, for the one binary opposition where the difference remains insurmountable is the archetypal fraternal conflict on which the Rougon-Macquart series is founded.

The opposition initially posited between Jean and Maurice is distributed along several axes, in keeping with what Julia Kristeva calls the "idéologèmes" common to Michelet, Barrès, Péguy, and other practitioners of a dominant bourgeois discourse on the Commune.[64] These axes are outlined in Table 5.

As Serres has noted, the rhetorical figure that best describes the relationship of Jean and Maurice is not antithesis (a vs. b), but rather chiasmus (ab vs. ba). Each of the protagonists combines semantic components which seem a priori incompatible; thus: Jean = peasant + corpo-

Table 5

	Protagonists	
Axes	Maurice	Jean
Class	petit bourgeois *déclassé*	peasant
Education	literate	illiterate
Temperament	unstable	stable
Rank	private	corporal
Political allegiance	Empire	France

ral. But, what is more, each paradoxical combination is opposed to its symmetrical opposite: Jean (peasant + corporal) vs. Maurice (private + bourgeois). Serres goes on to remark that this initial chiasmus generates through a series of dialectical reversals the main events of this masculine friendship. Not the least striking of these reversals involves a paradigm already familiar to us, the dyadic protection scenario, or: Maurice (weak + bourgeois) protects Jean (peasant + strong).[65] But this paradigm does not, indeed cannot alone account for the unfolding of the plot; projected onto the syntagmatic axis, it enters into combination with another equally important paradigm, the separation/reunion segment. It is by alternating protection and separation/reunion segments that Zola builds his larger narrative sequences. Thus we can schematize the micromale-male relationship as follows:

1. Protection: Jean → Maurice (*D,* pp. 136-37; *R-M,* 5: 521).
2. Separation/Reunion: Jean // ∪ Maurice (pp. 158-67; 5: 544-54).
3. Protection: Maurice → Jean (pp. 272-73; 5: 663).
4. Separation/Reunion: Maurice // ∪ Jean (pp. 356-60; 5: 751-55).
5. Protection: Maurice → Jean (pp. 389-91; 5: 786-88).
6. Separation: Maurice // Jean

This separation is exceptional in several ways. First, unlike the two previous ones, it is not accidental (due to the chaos of battle and defeat), but planned. Maurice leaves for Paris, entrusting Jean, who is convalescing from his wounds, to Henriette. Second, because of the formal nature of this leave-taking, the significance of the repetition and variation of the protection segment is articulated: protection gives rise to gratitude, institutes a debt, as one good turn deserves another. The imbalance in Maurice's favor, made explicit in this "accounting" scene, is crucial in setting up the irony of the two concluding segments:

Jean stopped him with a gesture.

'You don't owe me anything, we're quits. I'm the one the Prussians would have picked up out of there if you hadn't carried me on your back. And only yesterday again you got me out of their clutches. You've paid twice over and it should be my turn to give my life for you. (*D*, p. 396)[66]

7. Reunion/Separation

This segment is like 2 and 4, also anomalous. Unlike the other reunions, which result from quests, this one is purely accidental; furthermore, it is very brief. Jean and Maurice find themselves in opposing camps—pursuing the initial paradox, Jean is a Versaillais, Maurice, a Communard—and the joy of their reunion gives way almost immediately to the distress of their separation. In this segment, both reunion and separation are, as it were, mutual.

8. Reunion: Jean ∪ Maurice

All the preceding narrative segments serve to overdetermine this *dysphoric reunion*, negatively valorized further by the ultimate reversal of the protection relationship: assassination, as Jean unwittingly bayonets Maurice. In addition, this scene also refers to an intertext, the celebrated 1848 barricade scene in Flaubert's *L'Education sentimentale*, where Sénécal bayonets Dussardier. Recalling his remarks in segment 6, Jean exclaims: "'We were quits, and it was my turn to give my life, and then I go and kill you'" (*D*, p. 487; "Nous étions quittes, c'était à mon tour de donner ma vie, et je te massacre" [*R-M*, 5: 890]).

9. Protection: Jean → Maurice

One excessive deed leads to another. Having seriously wounded Maurice, Jean proceeds to carry out a heroic rescue attempt, carrying Maurice back to his room in the midst of a burning Paris crawling with Versaillais soldiers hunting down the Communards: "And he had done this unspeakable thing, and yet he had saved Maurice once again, for he had brought him back here through so many dangers" (*D*, p. 495; "Et il avait fait cette chose abominable, et il venait pourtant de sauver encore Maurice, puisque c'était lui qui l'avait rapporté là, au travers de tant de dangers" [*R-M*, 5: 898]). But this hyperbolic protection scene presents a unique variant: the death of the protégé, which closes the series.

The male protector-protégé relationship poses with even greater urgency the problem already explored in *Nana:* that of sexual difference. There is no question but that in *La Débâcle*, Zola went as far as he could in depicting a male homosexual relationship, which, as we shall see, is well short of the explicitness of the female homosexual relationship in *Nana*.

For Jean, Maurice occupies the place left vacant in his affections by the death of his wife (see *La Terre*):

Since the violent death of his wife in a dreadful tragedy, he thought he had
no heart, he had sworn never again to look at those creatures on whose
account a man suffers so much, even when they are not being evil. And so
friendship became a sort of broadening out for both of them: they might not
kiss, but they touched each other's very souls, the one was part of the other,
however different they might be. (*D*, p. 137)[67]

As for Maurice, despite a passing cliché reference to women in his
dissipated student days in Paris—"money thrown away on gambling,
women and the follies of all-devouring Paris" (p. 27; "l'argent qu'il avait
jeté au jeu, aux femmes, aux sottises de Paris dévorateur" [p. 405])—it is
abundantly clear that there is not and never has been a single, important
female love-object in his life.

The male bond in *La Débâcle* bears a curious and significant resemblance to the female bond in *Nana:* homosexual love, whether consummated or not, in keeping with Platonic tradition is conceived of as a
higher form of love, where devotion looms larger than selfishness, where
a primitive unity is restored: "They hugged each other in a passionate
embrace, made brothers by all they had gone through together, and the
kiss they exchanged seemed the gentlest yet the strongest in their lives, a
kiss the like of which they would never have from a woman, undying
friendship and absolute certainty that their two hearts were henceforth
one for ever" (p. 388).[68]

Zola finds himself here at the point of no return: either he goes on to
show the consummation of this love affair or else he must find some
expedient to divert the characters' and the reader's attention/libido. It
should come as no surprise to those acquainted with a certain type of
erotic literature—where Sapphic love scenes are written by men for
men—that Zola chooses the second solution, that is, finds an expedient to
interrupt the natural course of events. That expedient is the introduction
of Henriette, Maurice's fraternal twin (and surrogate mother-protector).
When Maurice goes off to Paris, leaving the wounded Jean in the care of
Henriette (see above, segment 6), Jean simply transfers his feelings for
Maurice onto Henriette, who functions as a projection of Maurice's
feminine nature: "What was still striking was the likeness to her brother,
and yet all the profound difference between their natures showed clearly
at that moment. He was as highly strung as a woman" (*D*, p. 171; "Ce qui
restait frappant, c'était sa ressemblance avec son frère; et, cependant,
toute la différence de leurs natures s'accusait profonde, à cette minute:
lui, d'une nervosité de femme" [*R-M*, 5: 557]).

This transference is mutual, as Jean slowly takes Weiss's and Maurice's
place in Henriette's life. The affection that grows up between these two

widowed adults, catalyzed by Maurice, takes the form of a mutual indebtedness:

> They were one immediately when they talked about Maurice. She was devoting herself to him in this way because he was the friend, the brother of Maurice, his great help in time of need, and it was her turn to pay a debt of the heart. She was full of gratitude and of an affection which grew as she got to know how upright and wise he was and how reliable. And he, whom she cared for like a child, was also contracting a debt of infinite gratitude. (*D*, p. 398)[69]

Even this acceptable substitute union is not to be consummated, however; Jean's murder of Maurice makes it impossible, unthinkable, for Jean to marry Henriette: "Maurice's grave separated them for ever, like a bottomless abyss" (p. 506; "La tombe de Maurice les séparait, sans fond" [p. 909]). Once again, as in *Nana*, the sexual and social axes run parallel: the incestlike taboo—is not Jean referred to as "the brother of Maurice"? —which keeps Jean from Henriette not only averts a homosexual marriage by proxy, but attests to the profound class divisions which, according to Zola, produced the Commune and its bloody repression. Once again, as in *Le Ventre de Paris*, homosexuality and revolution are metaphors for each other: Jean's solitary setting off into the sunrise represents the restoration of order through repression on all levels. Maurice's murder is yet another variant on the founding sacrifice, but unlike the other surrogate victims, Maurice is perfectly lucid about the function of his death. The emphasis on amputation in the surgical sequence (part II, chapter VII) serves as a presage of Maurice's death, with the difference that the actual surgery has become symbolic and mere metonymy has given way to an extreme metaphor. As Maurice reminds Jean, using familiar imagery (what Genette would term "intra-diégétique"),[70] Jean had predicted Maurice's end: "'And you said, too, that if something had gone rotten somewhere, like a poisoned limb, it was better to see it hacked off and lying on the ground than to die of it like the cholera.... Well, I'm the rotten limb you have lopped off'" (pp. 503-4; "Et tu ajoutais que, lorsqu'on avait de la pourriture quelque part, un membre gâté, ça valait mieux de le voir par terre, abattu d'un coup de hache, que d'en crever comme d'un choléra.... Eh bien! c'est moi qui suis le membre gâté que tu as abattu" [pp. 906-7]).

This "living sacrifice" (*D*, p. 504) is considered necessary if the health of the body politic is to be restored. The righteous indignation voiced by Claude Lantier at the end of *Le Ventre de Paris* has no echo here; it is as though Maurice, Jean, and Henriette have all read Darwin. The "dreadful sacrifice" (p. 507) is accepted with stoic resignation by both Henriette and

Jean, as the inevitable prelude to a return of the Golden Age. The price of difference—the death of a beloved brother and cherished comrade-in-arms—is not considered exhorbitant.

3. The Ontological Axis: the Living/the Dead

Having arrived at this point in our analysis of Zola's double crowds, we can use the conclusions arrived at in the previous sections on *Nana* and *La Débâcle* as a springboard for our final inquiry. The question then becomes, Do we find the same breakdown of differences between the living and the dead as we found between male and female and friend and foe?

Fécondité, the first of the *Quatre Evangiles* cycle, provides the ideal test case, as the fierce, never-ending struggle between the forces of life and those of death is central to its conception, so to speak. In this hymn to fertility, centered around the Mathieu and Marianne Froment family or, rather, tribe (they have twelve children and countless grandchildren and great-grandchildren), Zola seeks to demonstrate on every level, didactic as well as mythic, the necessary triumph of life over death, the invincible strength in numbers. Crowds begin at home: "Never in the course of history has any progress been made without the many urging humanity forward. Tomorrow, like yesterday, will belong to the swarming crowd in its search for happiness" ("Il ne s'est pas fait, dans l'histoire, un seul pas en avant, sans que ce soit le nombre qui ait poussé l'humanité en sa marche. Demain, comme hier, sera conquis par le pullulement des foules, en quête du bonheur" [Mitt *OC*, 8: 499]).

Though death strikes the Froments twice, it cannot stop their march to victory, their imperialistic expansion. When Blaise Froment is murdered, his twin brother Denis immediately steps into his place: "What was the good of having killed Blaise, since Denis was there? When death mows down one of these soldiers of life, there is always another one to man the combat station left vacant" ("A quoi bon avoir tué Blaise, puisque Denis était là? Quand la mort fauche un de ces soldats de la vie, il y en a toujours un autre, pour prendre la place de combat restée vide" [Mitt *OC*, 8: 401]). Similarly, when Rose, the favorite daughter, dies, she is eventually replaced by, reincarnated in, another Rose. Proper names function here as empty squares to be filled.

Despite the relentless battle the Froments wage against death, however, it would be a misreading of the book to reduce it to a fertility vs. death opposition. The really operative opposition is indicated by Zola's

original title for the work, *Le Déchet*.[71] In the mythical universe of *Fécondité*, the opposite of life is not death but nonlife, the waste of potential life. It is the twilight zone between life and death and the survival struggle of the seed which fascinate Zola. *Fécondité* is a polemical affirmation of the right to life and a severe condemnation of all means by which potential life is destroyed, in particular, birth control, abortion, and wet nursing.

By far the most significant of these three is birth control, further confirmation of the preponderance of mythical inspiration over journalistic crusading in the writing of this novel. For not the least important of Zola's crowds are those which Canetti terms "invisible": on the one hand the *"invisible dead,"* on the other *"posterity."*[72] The invisible dead, Homer's "silent majority," are familiar characters in Zola's works. Not only his cemeteries, but his gardens, his rooms, his very cities (see *Rome*), are strangely animated by the palpable presence of the dead, and I use the word *animated* advisedly, because Zola believes in animism, in metempsychosis:

> The rose bushes that grow in cemeteries bring forth large flowers, some milk-white, some blood-red. Their roots plunge deep into the coffins, feeding on the pallor of virginal chests and the bloody brilliance of broken hearts. This white rose is the flowering of a young girl who died at sixteen, this red rose, the last drop of blood shed by a man who fell in battle.
>
> O bright flowers, vivid flowers, some part of our dead lives on in you![73]

One of the obvious consequences of this belief is that the dead never really die; they are always with us, about us. Hence the prominent role played by the dead in Zola's fiction: the dead buried in the Aire Saint-Mittre, those "invisible beings" ("êtres invisibles") who urge Miette and Silvère to consummate their passion ("the dead, the long dead, desired the marriage of Miette and Silvère" ["les morts, les vieux morts, voulaient les noces de Miette et Silvère"]);[74] the dead women whose specters haunt *La Faute de l'abbé Mouret, Le Ventre de Paris, Au bonheur des dames, Le Rêve,* and *Le Docteur Pascal;* the dead men whose cadavers, real or hallucinated, insistently return to separate the lovers in *Thérèse Raquin* and *Germinal.* The invisible crowd of the dead is one of the most active in Zola.

But *Fécondité* is concerned with yet another invisible crowd, not the direct binary opposite of the dead, that is, posterity—the Froment posterity is anything but invisible—but rather the invisible crowd that corresponds most closely to nonlife/nondeath, the billions of spermatozoa wasted nightly in Paris: "An invisible crowd which has always existed, but which has only been recognized as such since the invention of the microscope, is the crowd of *spermatozoa.* 200 million of these animalcules set out together on their way . . . They all have the same goal and, except

for one, they all perish on the way."[75] These remarks by Canetti could have been written by Zola. One of the major scenes in *Fécondité*, one which will mark a turning point in Mathieu's life, transforming him from a mere father of five into a practicing preacher of procreation, depicts the horrifying epiphany he has one voluptuous night while walking the teeming streets of Paris: "And that was the Paris that wanted to die: the complete waste of all the life lost in one Parisian night, the torrent of seed diverted from its legitimate use, fallen on the pavement where nothing grows—in short, a poorly sown Paris that would not produce the great and vigorous harvest it should have produced."[76]

The theme of waste will be reiterated in the passages dealing with the abortion mills. Abortion, like contraception, is classified as an unnatural act—and thus a reprehensible one—because it substitutes a negative valorization of life for a positive one; it inverts or perverts the conventional signs:

> In this sink of iniquity the sacredness of motherhood came to grief; the sublime act of giving life led to this cesspool.... The eternal river of sperm which flows through the world's veins, the seeds of mankind which swell wives' bellies like the good earth in spring, all forms of future life were transformed into a wretched and shame-stricken harvest, tainted before the fact.[77]

Extending his seed metaphor—generated as it were by the protagonist's name, Froment ("wheat")—Zola goes on to condemn yet another form of waste, that of sending infants to nearly certain death at the hands of mercenary provincial wetnurses:

> It was not just that human seed was squandered, spilled for pleasure's sake on the burning pavements; it was not just that the crop was poorly harvested, that there was the dreadful waste of abortions and infanticides: in addition, the surviving crop was poorly garnered, with the result that half of it was either destroyed, or crushed, or killed. The waste was endless: drawn by the smell of lucre, thieves and murderesses came from far and near and carried off all the new and babbling life their arms could hold in order to turn it into death.[78]

Zola's largest crowd is thus the invisible crowd of wasted human seed, a crowd which stands precisely midway between the living and the dead. We may conclude that whatever oppositional crowd structure Zola posits at the outset of one of his novels—whether male/female, friend/foe, the living / the dead—he always follows an identical trajectory, the very one Lévi-Strauss considers characteristic of mythical thought: "Mythical thought always works from the awareness of oppositions towards their progressive mediation."[79]

The Missing Axis

Perhaps the most telling confirmation of the preponderance of mythical thought patterns in Zola's fiction is not to be found in what is manifested, but rather in what is missing; and surely the most surprising aspect of Zola's double crowd structures is the conspicuous absence of a novel built on the opposition of two very important crowds: the rich and the poor. The class struggle between the bourgeois and the workers is not the stuff of myth. This bald, bold statement stands in need of immediate qualification and justification, for it raises a host of thorny questions, in particular that of the uneasy relationship between structural anthropology and Marxism. Responding to his Marxist critics, Lévi-Strauss reminds them that both Marx and Engels, working with the anthropological data of their times, recognized the existence of primitive societies "governed by 'blood ties' (which today we call kinship systems) and not by economic relationships"; "according to their views, in the non- and pre-capitalistic societies kinship ties played a more important role than class relations."[80]

One might usefully confront Marx and Freud on this point, equating primitive societies with infantile thought processes, for Freud remarks on several occasions that children have no realistic concept of money: "It is probable that the first meaning which a child's interest in faeces develops is that of 'gift' rather than 'gold' or 'money'. The child knows no money apart from what is given him—no money acquired and none inherited of his own."[81]

Zola's fictional universe—where kinship ties certainly play a more important role than class relations—is informed only by the most archaic mythical paradigms, which is not to say that we do not find "modern" oppositional structures (such as bourgeois vs. worker) *superimposed* on the mythical "infrastructure," because of course we do. But taking the term *crowd* literally and with the expanded meaning given it by the determinant *invisible*, not even *Germinal* is structured by the opposition of two *crowds* at either extreme of a social axis. The numerical disproportion between the miners and the bourgeois—cf. *Les Mystères de Marseille* and *La Fortune des Rougon*—symbolizes their relationship: a large, exploited mass working for a small, privileged group. In Zola's three "revolutionary" novels, real power is inversely proportionate to numerical strength; the disproportion or imbalance between the two "series" is extreme. There are, by definition it would appear, no rich crowds. And yet, in other novels, such as *La Curée* and *Son Excellence Eugène Rougon*, there are extensive descriptions of rich crowds. For heuristic purposes, it might be worthwhile violating the strict segregation confining each class-

crowd to a separate novel, thereby creating "experimentally" the missing confrontation.

As a prime example of a rich crowd, I have chosen one which Zola explicitly qualifies as such, the crowd gathered (by invitation only) in Notre-Dame to witness the baptism of the imperial prince in *Son Excellence Eugène Rougon:*

> And a rich crowd, shimmering with gold and alight with the sparkle of jewels, filled the church: at the far end, next to the altar, the clergy, the crosiered and mitered bishops, shone as brightly as one of those glories which reveal the heavens; surrounding the dais princes, princesses, and high dignitaries were marshaled with sovereign pomp... while delegations of all sorts crowded into the nave and the ladies in the galleries above leaned over to display the bright stripes of their light-colored dresses. A huge haze of blood-red steam hovered above. The faces of those arranged in tiers at the back, on the right, and on the left had the rosy hues of painted porcelain. The uniforms, the satin, the silk, the velvet, gleamed darkly as though they were about to burst into flame. All at once whole rows would catch fire. The depths of the Church were ablaze with the extraordinary radiance of a furnace.[82]

This is the ultimate crowd of "haves"; moments later the Emperor will rise and the portrait of the "Tout Empire" (the "Empire-that-matters") will be complete. What is most striking about this passage is the use of a hyperbolized light code, a splendor code, to communicate the opulence of the crowd. The redundant seme is brightness, as in these phrases: "shimmering with gold and alight with the sparkle of jewels," "shone as brightly," "the bright stripes of their light colored dresses," "gleamed darkly," "ablaze with the extraordinary radiance of a furnace." A superimposition of this passage on a like passage from *La Curée* should suffice to establish the wealth = brightness equation as an invariant of Zola's descriptions of rich crowds. The following is drawn from the opening scene of *La Curée*, a very elegant traffic jam, the late-afternoon return from the Bois de Boulogne:

> A thousand lively coruscations sprang up, quick flashes played among the wheels, sparks flew from the horses' harness. On the ground, on the trees, were broad reflections of trotting glass. This glitter of wheels and harness, this blaze of varnished panels glowing with the red gleam of the setting sun, the bright notes of colour cast by the dazzling liveries perched up full against the sky, and by the rich costumes projecting beyond the carriage-doors, were carried along amid a hollow, sustained rumbling sound, timed by the trot of the horses. (*K*, p. 3)[83]

La Curée makes explicit what *Son Excellence* does not, namely, that

the brightness surrounding the rich crowd emanates from its money, represents its gold. Whereas the poor hide their gold in order not to provoke envy—see the chainmaker Lorilleux and his wife in *L'Assommoir*—the rich indulge in conspicuous consumption, flaunting their wealth:

> On summer evenings, when the rays of the setting sun lit up the gilt of the railings against its white façade, the strollers in the gardens would stop to look at the crimson silk curtains draped behind the ground floor windows; and, through sheets of plate glass so clear that they seemed like the window-fronts of a big modern shop, arranged so as to display to the outer world the wealth within, the petty bourgeoisie could catch glimpses of the corners of chairs or tables, of portions of hangings, of patches of ceiling of a profuse richness, the sight of which would root them to the spot with envy and admiration, right in the middle of the pathways. (*K*, p. 15)[84]

The connection between signs of wealth—bright materials—and the gold they stand for is made dramatically in a tableau representing Plutus's cave, the high point of a play put on at the Saccards': "The silk simulating the rock showed broad threads of metal....On the ground...lay an avalanche of twenty-franc pieces, louis spread-out, louis heaped-up, a swarm of ascending louis" (*K*, p. 255; "La soie imitant le roc montrait de larges filons métalliques....A terre...il y avait un écroulement de pièces de vingt francs; des louis étalés, des louis entassés, un pullulement de louis qui montaient" [*R-M*, 1: 548]).

Let us turn now to the polar opposite of the rich crowd, the ultimate "have-nots"—the striking miners in *Germinal:*

> The women had come into sight, nearly a thousand of them, dishevelled after their tramp, in rags through which could be seen their naked flesh worn out with bearing children doomed to starve. Some of them had babies in their arms and raised them aloft and waved them like flags of grief and vengeance. Others, younger, with chests thrown out like warriors, were brandishing sticks, whilst the old crones made a horrible sight as they yelled so hard that the strings in their skinny necks looked ready to snap. The men brought up the rear: two thousand raving madmen, pit-boys, colliers, repairers in a solid phalanx moving in a single block, so closely packed together that neither their faded trousers nor their ragged jerseys could be picked out from the uniform earth-coloured mass. All that could be seen was their blazing eyes and the black holes of their mouths singing the *Marseillaise*, the verses of which merged into a confused roar, accompanied by the clatter of clogs on the hard ground. Above their heads an axe rose straight up amidst the bristling crowbars, a single axe, the banner of the mob, and it stood out against the clear sky like the blade of the guillotine. (*G*, pp. 333-34)[85]

Setting aside for reasons of economy and clarity certain very significant but nonpertinent (in this context) contrasts between the two crowds (e.g., passive vs. active), all of which pertain to the difference in what Canetti terms their "prevailing emotions" (reducible to love vs. hate),[86] we will consider only those elements relevant to the socioeconomic polarization. The extreme destitution of the miners is expressed by means of a redundant seme of deprivation, as indicated by the repetition of the prefix dé- in the French text: "dépeignés" ("dishevelled"), "décharnés" ("skinny"), "déteintes" ("faded"). In contrast with the lustrous cloths that cover the rich men and women's bodies, the miners' drab rags reveal theirs; in contrast with the excess of cultural artifacts surrounding the rich, the poor are characterized by an excess of natural attributes. Zola's emphasis throughout the passage is on the bodies of the strikers, bodies made not only insistently visible, but also audible in the French text by Zola's use of alliterative syntagma: "gorges gonflées de guerrières" ("chests thrown out like warriors"), "cordes de leurs cous" ("strings in their [skinny] necks"). In pathetic contrast with the splendor code of the rich crowd, all that burns in this passage are the miners' eyes. The only artifact which the miners display is a lone axe, symbol of their desperate need and their potential for violence. Here metonymy means lack of money: there is but one axe for the many miners.

This symbolic weapon, both metonym for the disarmed miners and metaphor for the guillotine (power of the people), raises the crucial question of point of view: through whose eyes do we see these two crowds, and how does this mediation affect or distort our reading? In the first example I have given, from Son Excellence Eugène Rougon, the observer is a sympathetic bourgeois, a member of Eugène Rougon's inner circle, Mme Correur. As she is forced to leave the church, she carries away an impression of admiration bordering on awe: "She then found herself in broad daylight, still dazed and convinced that she had seen some old painting like those crimson and gold ones in the Louvre which are glazed by the years and represent figures from a bygone era whom one is not likely to meet in the street" ("Alors elle se retrouva dans le plein jour, et elle resta ahurie, croyant avoir vu quelque vieux tableau, pareil à ceux du Louvre, cuit par l'âge, empourpré et doré, avec des personnages anciens comme on n'en rencontre pas sur les trottoirs" [R-M, 2: 102]). This commentary on the rich crowd is worth stopping over; to compare the scene in Notre-Dame to an old painting in the Louvre is to confer an extremely positive valorization on the rich crowd. The connotations implicit in this comparison fall under two headings: (1) aesthetics: patina

= preciousness; (2) politics: the Louvre = continuity and legitimacy of power. The temporal exoticism of these "personnages anciens" reemphasizes and confirms their great value; the rich crowd is otherworldly, not to be confused with the men in the street.

In *Germinal,* the number of observers, and hence, of commentaries, has multiplied, and these range from expressions of unmitigated to mitigated horror. The mitigated horror takes the form of an aesthetic appreciation (cf. King William in *La Débâcle*): "'Oh,' how wonderful!' whispered Lucie and Jeanne, whose artistic taste was deeply stirred by the *lovely horror* of it all" (*G*, p. 334; "—Oh! superbe! dirent à demi-voix Lucie et Jeanne, remuées dans leur goût d'artistes par cette *belle horreur*" [*R-M*, 3: 1436]). I emphasize this oxymoronic expression because it indicates the difference between the two crowd scenes: whereas the rich crowd is seen through the eyes of a sympathetic admirer, the poor one is seen through those of terrified class enemies. In other words, the observer figure—the writer's *persona*—remains unchanged; only the spectacle varies. Furthermore, Lucie and Jeanne, the most eccentric of the bourgeois spectators in *Germinal,* are impressed by the crowd's negative beauty, the beauty of the beasts. This painting of the decadent genre has no place in the Louvre.

The law governing point of view in Zola's crowd descriptions might be formulated as follows: if the observer and the crowd belong to the same class, there is admiration; if the observer is a bourgeois and the crowd poor, there is repulsion or, at best, a negative admiration, a fascination. The third possible permutation, poor observer and rich crowd, is not actualized.

Yet, it would be an oversimplification to reduce the problem to a rich crowd-poor crowd opposition, for as we discover in *Lourdes,* one of Zola's most important crowd-fictions—indeed, in the latter half of the nineteenth century, Lourdes and crowds are synonymous; Huysmans's title *Les Foules de Lourdes* is pleonastic—the bourgeois observers perceive the sick in exactly the same terms as they do the poor. The crowd of strikers marching by singing the "Marseillaise" can be superimposed squarely on the crowd of gravely ill worshippers winding their way to the grotto at Lourdes intoning the "Ave Maria." Similarly, the commentary of the omniscient narrator in *Germinal* can be superimposed on the reaction (which is implicit commentary) of the rich bourgeois bystanders in *Lourdes:*

> And what they saw was a red vision of the coming revolution that would inevitably carry them all off one bloody night at the end of this epoch. . . . Yes, it would be just like this, with the same rags, the same thunderous trampling

of heavy clogs, the same dreadful rabble with filthy bodies and *stinking breath,* sweeping away the old world like the onrush of a barbaric horde.... Yes, this was what was passing them by along the road like a force of nature, *they could feel its deadly blast blowing in their faces.* (*G,* pp. 334-35)

At the corner of Saint-Joseph street, in the vicinity of the Merlasse plateau, a family of tourists, people who had just come from Cauterets or Bagnères, stood rooted to the edge of the sidewalk in a state of deep astonishment. They must have been rich bourgeois; the father and mother were very proper, and the two grown daughters had the smiling faces of fortunate people enjoying themselves. But the group's initial surprise soon gave way to a growing sense of terror, as though they had just witnessed the opening of an old-time leper-house, the evacuation of one of those legendary hospitals after some great epidemic. The two young girls turned pale, and the mother and father remained frozen as they were confronted by the endless procession of so many horrors, *whose pestilential breath hit them full in the face.* My god! such ugliness, such filth, such suffering![87]

If the fear and repulsion experienced by the bourgeois observers in *Germinal* correspond to an incontrovertible reality—the strikers' threat of potential violence—the same feelings when experienced by the tourists in *Lourdes* seem at first less legitimate. What, in the eyes of the bourgeois beholders, constitutes the underlying unity (the invariant) of these two superficially dissimilar crowds? The answer is to be found in the French wording of the recurrent syntagm emphasized in the quotations above:

$$\textit{ils (en) recevaient le vent} \begin{cases} \textit{terrible} \\ \textit{empesté} \end{cases} \begin{cases} \textit{au visage} \\ \textit{à la face} \end{cases}$$

The foul smell common to both the poor and the sick is not just ordinary halitosis, for the etymological root of *empesté—la peste* ("the plague") —is activated by the comparison of the sick to escapees from "an old-time leper-house." Poverty, like the plague, is thought to be a highly communicable disease, and simple exposure to its carriers might prove fatal. The equation of poverty with disease is clearly enunciated in Zola's celebrated statement equating the body politic with the body: "The social *circulus* is identical with the vital *circulus:* in society, just as in the human body, there exists a form of solidarity which connects the different members, the different organs, so that if one organ decays, many others are affected, and a very complex disease develops."[88]

Both the poor crowds and the sick crowds force the bourgeois spectator(s) to confront the body in its naked and supremely offensive state. The mere excess of nature in *Germinal* has been transformed into

outright monstrosity in *Lourdes;* yet in terms of their effect on "innocent" bourgeois bystanders, la Mouquette's defiant exhibitionism and the miracle-seekers' grotesque parade of human suffering are equivalent:

> The main body had gone by and only the laggards were trailing on behind, when Mouquette appeared. She was dawdling in the rear, on the look-out for bourgeois at their garden gates or windows, and when she saw any, not being able to spit in their faces she showed them what was for her the supreme mark of contempt. She must have seen one now, for she suddenly lifted her skirt, proferred her buttocks and displayed her great fat behind, its nakedness lit up by the last gleams of sunlight. There was nothing obscene in this gesture, nothing laughable, it was terrible. (*G*, p. 335)

> Under the dazzling sky...the procession of the damned rolled by; there were those who suffered from skin diseases which ate away at their flesh, or from dropsy which caused them to swell up like goatskins; there were rheumatics and paralytics twisted with pain. And the hydrocephalous marched past, and the St. Vitus dancers, and the consumptive, the rickety, the epileptic, the cancerous, the goitrous, the insane, the idiots. "Ave, ave, ave, Maria!" The persistent lament surged up, accompanying the dreadful outpouring of human misery and suffering on its way to the Grotto, to the consternation and horror of the passers-by, who stood rooted to the spot, chilled by the sight of this nightmarish stampede.[89]

The class struggle is indeed an ass struggle; it is no coincidence that it is a female character who bares her behind: all the hideously deformed, sick marchers are, as the French text shows, of the feminine gender. The chain of equivalences is now complete: naked body $\simeq$ female body $\simeq$ diseased body. In Zola's fiction the opposition of the haves and the have-nots is subordinated to the Nature/Culture paradigm, *Nature* being the umbrella term covering all bodily functions and dysfunctions, including femininity. Now this projection of repressed instincts and anxiety-producing phobias onto the people is hardly peculiar to Zola; rather, it pervades nineteenth-century culture. This analysis by Borie, with reference to the shared assumptions of both Zola and Brunetière (his most representative critic), echoes analyses of other nineteenth-century authors by other critics articulating Freud and Marx (see Sartre on Flaubert):

> The identification of the popular with the natural clearly shows us that the bourgeois is ready to use the puritan façade of his self-imposed repression as either the justification or the expiatory compensation of the social exploitation he benefits from: he has earned the right to dominate the people because he has succeeded in mastering Nature within himself, or else he constrains himself, sacrifices himself, castrates himself and thus demonstrates that his position as leader is not usurped but legitimate, for he occupies it not to

derive any personal pleasure, but to serve the higher interests of social organization. In any case, the body and the people, those two repressed forces, will be very closely linked and will be able to function as metaphors for each other.[90]

Borie goes on to point out that, while imbued with the bourgeois ideology (and phraseology) of the age, Zola was a relentless crusader against Victorian prudery and hypocrisy, tirelessly exposing the universality of the (baser) instincts. Just as we find in his fiction examples of workers who sublimate their sexual energies—e.g., Goujet, the blacksmith in *L'Assommoir*—we also find depraved aristocrats (*Nana*) and promiscuous bourgeois (*Pot-Bouille*). Sublimation is not the birthright of a single class; sexual repression, just like its political equivalent, is a constant struggle.

The segregation of the rich and the poor crowds is neither gratuitous nor accidental. Nor is it peculiar to Zola: it is the fundamental hypothesis of all bourgeois political thought in the nineteenth century. This being said, what becomes significant are the diverse fictional universes (or, in another context, political ideologies) generated by this hypothesis: thus, Zola's "distribution" differs from Balzac's and seems to be motivated by idiosyncratic concerns, by a sort of literary hypochondria. The rigid compartmentalization which constitutes the ordering principle of the *Rougon-Macquart* is a prophylactic measure, a formal quarantine designed to bolster the insecure ramparts of repression. In order to avoid the spread of the people's plague, the people must be confined to certain novels. Zola is the Baron Haussmann of the novel.

Much remains to be written about Zola's iconography, a heterogeneous collection of blueprints (including maps, charts, floor plans, menus, family trees), but I will reproduce and discuss only one item culled from this graphic corpus, Zola's revealing rendering of his social vision, an early outline of the *Rougon-Macquart* series (Fig. 3). This particular blueprint is not all that easy to read: projected into space, Zola's sense of social organization develops along a vertical axis, but it is not clear whether the discrete "worlds" ranged along this axis are ranked in ascending or descending order of importance.

This document is worth stopping over for several reasons. First is its genetic importance; out of this initial classification will emerge the profession/class specific novels of the cycle. But second, and of more immediate concern to us, is the postulation of an independent category, the "world apart," a fifth and marginal estate. Considering two of the strange bedfellows we find under this rubric, drawn from opposite ends of the paradigmatic scale—the prostitute and the artist—we might very

There are four worlds

(initial novel)

People $\begin{cases} \text{worker} \\ \text{soldier} \end{cases}$

Merchants $\begin{cases} \text{Speculator in demolitions} \\ \text{and big business} \\ \text{(industry)} \end{cases}$

Bourgeoisie $\big\{$ sons of the newly rich

High society $\begin{cases} \text{official functionaries together} \\ \text{with members of high society,} \\ \textit{political} - \end{cases}$

And a world apart $\begin{cases} \text{prostitute} \\ \text{murderer} \\ \text{priest } (\textit{religion}) \\ \text{artist} - (\textit{art}) \end{cases}$

Figure 3

well ask, What is the invariant of this motley group? A common function, I would venture: both the prostitute and the artist (as well, of course, as the murderer and the priest) insure communication between the topologically separate classes. By virtue of their extraterritorial status, they enjoy a unique freedom to circulate in society. Thus, Nana, the "golden fly," transmits the virus picked up on the dung heaps below to the upper classes; thus, the author of the *Rougon-Macquart* exposes his bourgeois readers to those very aspects of themselves and society which they prefer to ignore.

The question then arises, Do the prostitute and the artist really constitute a classless society, do they really escape classification? Nana is after all the daughter of Gervaise, and Claude Lantier, the painter-hero of *L'Oeuvre*, her son. He is, however, adopted by a prosperous patron who leaves him a small income: a member of the working class by birth, he becomes a bourgeois by adoption. The prime artist figure in Zola is thus the perfect embodiment of the "déclassé," a man without a class, not because he belongs to none, but to two. The ambiguous status of the artist goes a long way towards explaining the difference between mythic and nonmythic polarizations. Whereas mythic oppositions progress towards mediation, that is, a form of synthesis, the nonmythic opposition of the bourgeoisie and the people results only in ambiguity, the very antithesis of true synthesis. Whereas in dealing with mythic paradigms such as male/female or the living/the dead, Zola can let himself be guided by

his imagination, his fantasies, in dealing with class conflict he can but reflect a verifiable external reality. The imaginary topography of Plassans, just like the real map of Paris (as redesigned by Haussman), is characterized by the strict segregation of the classes; each class, each crowd, is confined to a ghetto, from the "golden ghetto" of the aristocrats in *La Fortune des Rougon* to the golden-in-name-only ghetto of the poor in *L'Assommoir.* Through the language of fiction Zola could and did dramatize this state of affairs, but he could not change it.

Thus, Zola's crowds constitute a crucial thematic zone, one where the interplay of fantasy and fact is made visible, and where the limits of myth are revealed as mimesis. The question then becomes, Is there any form of mediation which obtains both within and without myth? It is to this question that we will address ourselves in the next and final chapter.

Chapter 4

Mediation

In his article "Individual and Group in the Novel," Michel Butor traces the evolution of this structuring relationship from the harmonious metaphoricity of medieval epics and *chansons de gestes* to the anguished metonymy of the naturalist novel:

> Whereas in the world of the epic, language flows from one end of the social scale to the other, with every noble able to communicate with the lowliest person in his domain . . . here the individual, who is noble in spirit but lost in the crowd, encounters a catastrophic gap. Everyone seems to speak the same language, and yet communication turns out to be impossible between the writer or his hero, who are turned in on themselves, and this threatening crowd. These people with whom the writer no longer gets along, yet whom he clearly perceives as the source of all power, are the novelistic subject par excellence; as a result, he will have to describe them as animals and, before long, as objects. This inclination of the naturalist novelist towards a position of complete exteriority, which is in the end nothing more than the critical moment of Romantic individualism, the moment in which its insufficiencies become blatantly obvious, will soon make him opaque even to himself. Obliged to recognize that despite his differences, he is one of these people, he will be devoured, as it were, by the quality of absolute strangeness he has attributed to them.[1]

To the extent that Zola was the direct heir to the tragic Romantic conflict between artist and society, to the extent that he considered himself to be an objective (hence exterior) observer of social phenomena, to the extent that he does often describe the crowd as animalistic, he resembles Butor's composite picture as though it were his portrait. Indeed, Butor's

remarks echo Zola's self-portrait; in his notes for *Paris*, he describes "the great Writer, the Man of the crowd" as "alone amidst all, a man apart who looks and judges" ("le grand Ecrivain, l'Homme des foules": "Il est seul au milieu de tous, le solitaire qui regarde et qui juge").[2]

But there are at least two Zolas (to paraphrase the title of J. H. Matthews's book[3]), and my concern is with the other Zola, the Zola who innovated literary devices which do reduce and, occasionally, momentarily abolish the "catastrophic gap" ("coupure catastrophique") of which Butor speaks. For, as Butor himself is aware—it is the gist of his essay—the problem of the I/C relationship *in the novel* is not so much ideological or psychological as it is structural. It is precisely this technical problem that the socialist-realist epic fails to solve: "As for socialist realism, it all too often stops at the simple juxtaposition of crowd movements with individual adventures, without managing to establish an authentic middle term between these two poles."[4] Here lies the secret of Zola's success: as the prime practitioner of the crowd-fiction, an updated form of the epic, Zola steered clear of the Scylla of excessive distanciation and the Charybdis of mere juxtaposition, the two dangers the author of a modern epic must avoid. Rather, he insured constant and necessary communication between individual protagonists and the crowd through the creation of a series of mediators; he did establish "an authentic middle term"; he did, to answer the question posed by Richard B. Grant, have an "intermediate vision."[5]

Before studying these mediators at some length, I would like to propose a reading of *La Bête humaine* as an allegory of the catastrophe that results from any attempt to set up unmediated contact between the individual and the crowd. The juxtaposition of tante Phasie, confined by paralysis to her armchair in the gatekeeper's cottage, and the crowd of passengers whizzing by daily before her window, constitutes a hyperbolization of the always already dysphoric individual/crowd separation. The excessive immobility of the individual (an enforced spectator) provides a painful and ironic contrast with the excessive mobility of the crowd (as driven as tante Phasie is riveted):

> And yet the thought of the crowd-flow which the ebb and the flood tides of the trains washed past her daily in the great silence of her solitude made her pensive....It seemed strange to her to be buried in this desert without a soul to confide in, when day and night, continually, so many men and women hurtled past, driven by the tempestuous trains....The torrent flowed on, leaving nothing behind in its wake. And what saddened her was to feel that beneath this continuous rumbling, this parade of well-being and money, this crowd which was always gasping and grasping did not know she was there in

danger of death, so much so that if one night her husband did her in, the trains would go on crossing each other next to her corpse, without even suspecting the crime committed in that desolate house.[6]

Tante Phasie suffers the same infernal, ironic torment as Tantalus: "Water, water everywhere and not a drop to drink," in the words of "The Ancient Mariner," or, to borrow from the French medieval tradition, "Je meur de soif auprès de la fontaine." Zola's reliance on an extended metaphor drawn from the liquid code (in the French, "flot de foule," "charriaient," "torrent coulait," "roulement") is here perfectly appropriate: the liquidity of the crowd stands in opposition to the aridity of tante Phasie's "desert." That tante Phasie's miserly husband, Misard, is slowly poisoning her by putting arsenic in her food only reinforces the central irony: Phasie's thirst is both figurative and literal, metaphysical and physical.

The persistence of the (dysphoric) association crowd ↔ train—their relationship is metonymic (contained/container)—is attested to by this passage from the exhibition scene in *L'Oeuvre:* "But what was astonishing, what caused people to look up, was the continuous din, the heavy trampling of the public on the gallery floor. The noise was deafening, a prolonged roar, as though an interminably long train going full speed had shaken the iron beams without cease" ("Mais ce qui surprenait, ce qui faisait lever la tête, c'était le fracas continu, le piétinement énorme du public sur le plancher des salles. Là, on en était assourdi, cela roulait démesurément, comme si des trains interminables, lancés à toute vapeur, avaient ébranlé sans fin les solives de fer" [*R-M*, 4: 305]). The crowd hurtling by like or in a train ranks highest on the scale of indifference to the individual bystander. Alfred de Vigny's poem "La Maison du Berger" bears witness to the place assigned trains in the mid-nineteenth-century imagination: the Train takes over the impassivity the Romantics had earlier ascribed only to Nature.

On two different occasions the extreme disjunction between tante Phasie and the crowd is suspended, and the passengers and the gate-keeper's family are brought face-to-face: once, when a snowstorm brings the train to a stop, forcing the stalled passengers to seek shelter in the gatekeeper's cottage, and a second time, when Flore, tante Phasie's daughter, causes a derailment out of jealousy. These dramatic meetings only serve to confirm the unbridgeable gap; instead of bringing the passengers and the gatekeepers closer together, these unmediated contacts take the form of either comedy or tragedy. First, the comic encounter:

During the five years they had lived there, how many trains had they seen

whizzing by at every hour of the day and night, in fair weather and foul!...The whole world, the crowd of humanity, hurtled past them, carried along at full speed, without their ever making out any more than a few faces glimpsed in a flash....And now, in the snow, a train landed at their door: the natural order was perverted; they stared at these unknown people thrown onto the tracks by an accident; they contemplated them like wide-eyed savages come rushing to a shore where Europeans had been shipwrecked.[7]

The shift from the tone of resignation conveyed in the first half of the passage to the comic absurdity of the second is signaled by the use of the word *débarquer* ("to land") in the sentence translated as "a train landed at their door." In its familiar use, *débarquer* has an anthropological connotation, so to speak: it is the word one uses to describe the recent arrival of a "hick" in the big city. Here the paradigm is reversed: it is the urban crowd that lands on the provincial doorstep. The complete incongruity of this long-awaited meeting is further indicated by the hyperbole: "the natural order was perverted," as if train schedules were part of a natural cycle. This hyperbole leads up to the final comic element, the comparison of the encounter between gatekeepers and passengers to that of savages and Europeans. The savages/Europeans opposition is particularly effective: it extends the metaphor of the gatekeepers' desert, which now becomes a desert island; it transcodes class differences into anthropological ones—the barrier that separates the savages and the Europeans is linguistic and cultural, not economic; and perhaps most important of all, it engenders a series of metaphors drawn from the two-different-worlds paradigm. Thus, as Flore examines the passengers at close range, she thinks: "As for the others, they seemed to her to be members of a different race, inhabitants of an unknown land, fallen from the sky, bringing into her home, her very kitchen, clothes, customs, ideas she had never thought she would see there" ("Quant aux autres gens, ils lui paraissaient être d'une race différente, des habitants d'une terre inconnue, tombés du ciel, apportant chez elle, au fond de sa cuisine, des vêtements, des moeurs, des idées, qu'elle n'aurait jamais cru y voir" [*R-M*, 4: 1178]).

The oppositions progress rapidly, in order of increasing polarization, going from two different races and continents to two different species and planets ("these people who had fallen from the moon" ["ces gens tombés de la lune" (p. 1184)]). Further along in the scene, Zola returns to his original paradigm—savages/Europeans—projecting it onto the syntagmatic axis, almost making it into a mininarrative:[8] "It was turning into a camp for castaways as wretched as a band of civilized men washed up on a desert island by a heavy sea" ("Cela tournait au campement de

naufragés, à la désolation d'une bande de civilisés jetés par un coup de mer dans une île déserte" [p. 1183]). Finally, as she watches the passengers reboard the train, tante Phasie understands that this meeting has at best satisfied her curiosity, but certainly established no communication; the crowd remains unknown and unknowing: "With the large, sunken eyes of an invalid, she stared at this unknown crowd, these passing members of a society on the march whom she would never see again and whom the storm had brought and was now taking away" ("Ses grands yeux caves de malade regardait cette foule inconnue, ces passants du monde en marche, qu'elle ne reverrait jamais, apportés par la tempête et remportés par elle" [p. 1188]).

The second and tragic encounter only corroborates the conclusions drawn from the first one; in death, the passengers remain as foreign and enigmatic as they were in life: "And Misard, like Flore, stared at these corpses as though hoping to recognize them from among the thousands and thousands of faces which over ten years had passed by them at full speed, leaving them only with the confused memory of a crowd come and gone in a flash. No! these were still nothing but the unknown multitudes of society on the march. In death, brutal and accidental, they remained anonymous."[9]

The chance encounter (brought on by "natural" causes) and the catastrophic confrontation (the result of premeditated murder) are two extremes of the I/C relationship which rejoin each other in their common failure to bridge the gap, to transcend juxtaposition. Mediation is, clearly, the only solution to this tragicomic aporia.

The Family

The very first words of the preface to La Fortune des Rougon set forth Zola's fundamental concept of the family as the prime mediating social group, situated as it is midway between the individual and society at large: "I want to explain how a family, a small group of human beings, act in a society by blossoming out and giving birth to ten or twenty individuals" ("Je veux expliquer comment une famille, un petit groupe d'êtres, se comporte dans une société, en s'épanouissant pour donner naissance à dix, à vingt individus" [R-M, 1: 3]).

As Zola continues to outline his project, it becomes apparent that although the family can act on society only through its individual members—hence each novel in the series, with the possible exception of the first, will focus on a single member of the family—the individuals are

subsumed to the family which they make up—hence the very conception of all three of Zola's novelistic cycles: "By solving the twin problems of temperament and environment, I will attempt to find and follow the thread which leads mathematically from one man to another. And when I hold all the threads in my hand, when I have an entire social group within my grasp, I will show this group performing as an actor in a historical epoch."[10]

Zola's choice of the family as the prime mediating agency can be explained in several ways. Zola's strongest conscious motivation is a will to difference: to study a single family sets him apart from Balzac, with his cast of three thousand characters: "I do not wish to depict contemporary society as a whole, rather a single family, showing the play of race modified by class [*milieu*]. If I accept a historical framework, it is solely to have an environment [*milieu*] which reacts; similarly, one's profession and place of residence constitute milieus."[11] To focus on a single family rather than a "heterogenealogical" microcosm of contemporary society is not only literarily and economically advantageous; it also permits Zola to pursue his scientific interest in the interaction of race and class.

Let us pause briefly to consider the ambiguous use of the word *milieu* in the previous quotation; as it is a key word in Zola's theoretical vocabulary, its polysemy is of special interest. Most often Zola uses it as an equivalent of class, as in the following note: "Properly speaking, the environmental and societal milieus determine the characters' class (worker, artist, bourgeois—my uncles and I, Paul and his father)" ("Les milieux proprement dit, milieu de lieu et milieu de société détermine la classe des personnages [ouvrier, artiste, bourgeois—moi et mes oncles, Paul et son père]").[12] This equivalence is in keeping with contemporary usage, according to Jean Dubois:

> The *vertical* representation is certainly the most common; it is in accordance with the evolution of the social groups themselves at the end of the Second Empire. But the representation can also be *horizontal;* the distinction is made between social groups considered to be somehow juxtaposed. The word *class,* whose usage is closely bound up with the hierarchical representation of society, is abandoned; the vague term *social groups* is used instead. . . . People begin to speak of "milieus," the term preferred by writers such as E. Zola in *La Fortune des Rougon* . . . or *La Curée,* or E. de Goncourt in his Journal.[13]

In his insistence on the family as the point of intersection of two determining factors, *race* (heredity) and *milieu* (class), Zola did more than echo and refine Taine's celebrated triad—*race, moment,* and *milieu;* he also anticipated more recent interdisciplinary attempts to demarcate the provinces of nature and nurture, or Freud and Marx. It is not so great a

leap from Zola's "natural and social history of a family" to Sartre's *L'Idiot de la famille* (*The Family Idiot*). Sartre's totalizing synthesis of psychoanalysis and Marxism, the organizing principle of his monumental study on Flaubert, is foreshadowed in an earlier passage dealing with Flaubert in the chapter entitled "The Problem of Mediations" in the *Critique de la raison dialectique* (*A Critique of Dialectical Reason*). Having taken orthodox Marxists to task for repudiating psychoanalysis and therefore the formative role played by the family in a child's class consciousness, which is first of all consciousness of his parents' class, Sartre goes on to say: "Existentialism, on the contrary, thinks it can adopt this method because it reveals the junction between man and his class, that is, the particular family as mediating agency between a universal class and the individual."[14]

But if in most contexts the word *milieu* is equivalent to "class," in the second half of Zola's note on the differences between Balzac and himself, Zola suddenly establishes a new and seemingly contradictory equivalence between *milieu* and "historical framework"; whereas in the previous sentence the *milieu* modified, here the *milieu* reacts, that is, is modified. Zola's vision takes the form of a spiral: first the individual is shaped by his milieu (his environment, his family's class, its place of residence, etc.); then through the family he in turn acts on the larger milieu, the contemporary scene. But whether active or passive, whether modified by the micromilieu or modifying the macromilieu, the individual's relation to society is mediated by the family. While it is easy to understand Zola's emphasis on the family's mediating role in the child/society relationship, it is perhaps less obvious why and how the family mediates the adult/society relationship. Here we touch on Zola's unconscious reason for writing first one, then two other "family romances." These reasons are already implicit in the preface to *La Fortune des Rougon*, but only become explicit in *Fécondité*.

In the preface, Zola writes: "The Rougon-Macquart, the group, the family I propose to study is characterized by the frenzy of desire, the great upheaval of our age, hell-bent on pleasure....Historically, they spring from the people, spread throughout contemporary society, rise to the highest positions...and by means of their individual dramas, they tell the story of the Second Empire."[15] The crucial word is "spread" ("s'irradient"); the cancerlike spread of the Rougon-Macquart throughout the body politic seems to foreshadow the locustlike invasion of the Snopses in Faulkner's fictional universe. Whereas an individual's impact on society is limited, a family's is multiplied in proportion to the number of its members; the extended family, in the manner of the Bonapartes or the

Rothschilds, to cite two examples which shaped nineteenth-century myths of success, is modern society's shortcut to power, replacing the diachronic power of the aristocracy with the synchronic power of nepotism. This very modern conception of power is inherent in the *Rougon-Macquart*, but for many leftist critics offensively advertised in *Fécondité*. Thus, Barthes remarks: "In Zola's *Fécondité*, the ideology is flagrant, especially sticky: naturism, family-ism, colonialism."[16] Zola's espousal of colonialism may shock and repel today's reader (though Zola's position was consonant with contemporary left-wing policies), but it should not surprise the attentive reader of the *Rougon-Macquart*, for Zola's imperialistic ideology is the inevitable outgrowth of an omnipotence fantasy which could only be satisfied by the creation of a personal army composed entirely of one's descendants.

The privilege granted the family by Zola also reflects the societal transformations that separate Balzac's "moment," to borrow Taine's term, from Zola's. The sanctification of the nuclear bourgeois family, one of the major social and political phenomena of the mid-nineteenth century, provided Zola with the source of difference between *La Comédie humaine* and the *Rougon-Macquart*. There was no need for Zola to invent an artificial difference: the epic of the bourgeois family is, in a sense, the product of the period in which Zola began to write, the only possible subject for a novelist working in the Balzacian tradition.

In *Fécondité* the family becomes openly and flagrantly what it was in fragmentary form in the *Rougon-Macquart:* the shock troops of imperialism. Mathieu Froment is but a Félicité Rougon who has come out of the closet. Whereas Félicité's fertility is repressed by her husband, Mathieu's is matched by his wife's, but both view their children as a means to fulfill their own ambitions:

> The young woman did not consider this brood a cause of ruin. On the contrary, she began rebuilding the crumbling fortune that was slipping through her fingers on her sons' heads. Hardly were they ten years old than in her dreams she was already banking on their future. Doubting that she would ever succeed on her own, she began to look to them to conquer inexorable fate. They would salve her disappointed pride; they would give her the coveted position of wealth she vainly sought after. From that time onwards, without ceasing to struggle for the firm, she devised a second set of tactics to ensure the satisfaction of her will to power. It seemed impossible to her that out of her three sons, not one was a great man who would make them all rich. She could feel it, she said. So she looked after the children with a passion that was one part a mother's strictness, one part a usurer's tenderness. She took loving pleasure in building them up like capital that would later yield high interests.[17]

Lest one be tempted to see in Félicité a textbook case of the mother who takes her son's penis for her own, one need only compare her to Mathieu, for whom making love is a form of making war; Mathieu has, as it were, beaten his plowshare into a sword: "And for a while it seemed that Mathieu sowed his dearly beloved children according to a rhythm, as though planting the fields with the seeds of future wheat harvests, multiplying them without stopping to count, *ad infinitum*, so that a small nation of sowers, born of his motion, would end up populating the earth."[18] The unbridled growth of the Froment family is repeatedly expressed in military code; their fertility is personified as aggressive, hostile, and victorious. Small wonder then that Nicholas, the Froment son who has not been provided for, should continue the imperialist tradition in the wilds of Africa:

> Today discovered and partially explored, the mystery of ancient Africa enticed him. He would first go to Senegal, then probably push on to Sudan, in the very heart of the virgin lands, where he dreamt of a new France, the huge colonial empire which would rejuvenate the aging race by giving it its share of the earth. That was where, by clearing vast tracts, he aspired to carve out his empire, to found together with Lisbeth another Froment dynasty, a Chantebled multiplied tenfold under the burning sun, peopled by the host of his children.[19]

Zola's dialectic of mediation is now clear: the child's relationship to the world is mediated by his family; then, when the child becomes an adult, the roles are reversed, and the parents' relationship to the world is mediated by their offspring. The question then becomes, What happens to the childless and power-hungry adult? How does Zola reconcile mediation and sublimation (not to say sterility)?

The Band

Eugène Rougon (*Son Excellence Eugène Rougon*) and Octave Mouret (*Au bonheur des dames*) are two Zola characters who come to mind immediately as needing some alternate form of mediation, for not only are they childless and power-hungry, but both have deliberately sublimated their sexuality by opting for marriages of convenience, Octave to the older but well-to-do Mme Hédouin, Eugène to the ageless but efficient Mlle Beulin-d'Orchère. Their sterility results from an ascesis designed to conserve their vital energies, in keeping with the theoretical model of the economy of desire repeatedly promoted by Balzac.[20] Vicarious satisfactions, power through reproduction, and the dynastic urge are antithetic

to their projects. Nevertheless, they cannot go it alone, neither conquer the crowd single-handedly, nor dominate it directly; they can do without sex and without children, but not without mediation. We come here to a little noted but very significant aspect of Zola's fictional social organization: midway between the crowd and the individual there exists a group of secondary characters who combine features of the collective with a certain degree of individuation. Sociologists call such a group a "primary" or "face-to-face" group; I am tempted to call it a surrogate family, an "artificial primary group" as opposed to the "natural primary group" constituted by a real family. Zola calls this hybrid social unit quite simply "la bande" ("the band").[21]

The characteristics that allow us to isolate the band, to abstract this social invariant, could be described as parameters of limitation: restrictions in the number of members and in meeting time and/or place. The number of members of a given band rarely exceeds ten, whether they be the ladies and gentlemen who gather in Mme Desforges's salon in *Au bonheur des dames*, or the soldiers of the squad in *La Débâcle*, but there may be more than one band in a given novel. *La Conquête de Plassans* consists entirely of the Abbot Faujas's careful maneuvering between two rival bands, the subprefecture band (supporters of the Second Empire) and the Rastoils' band (the legitimists); his final success in bringing the two bands together under his authority seals his conquest of Plassans. The band meets regularly and in a particular spot: nightly in the Rougons' "yellow salon" in *La Fortune des Rougon*, Thursday evenings in the Rougons' "green salon" in *La Conquête de Plassans*, Thursday and Sunday evenings after dinner at Eugène Rougon's in *Son Excellence*, Thursday evenings for dinner at Sandoz's in *L'Oeuvre*. This last example is of special interest because it invites us to add to our list yet another band, drawn not from Zola's bibliography, but rather from his biography; I am referring, of course, to the referential prototype for all these surrogate families, Zola's own—the "groupe de Médan," the band of young disciples who gathered periodically around their power-hungry and childless master.

Despite the inevitable monotony inherent in any recurrent feature, the band is remarkable for its versatility. In addition to the variables mentioned above (membership, time and place of meeting), there are others more directly connected with the band's mediating function, variables of a psychostructural order. As my readings of *Son Excellence Eugène Rougon* and *Au bonheur des dames* will reveal, there are two "poles" of variation, the leader and the crowd. Thus, the band can work for and/or against the leader; it can mediate his will to power both in a

linear and a triangular manner. Furthermore, the band can function either primarily as an extension of the leader or as a contraction of the crowd. In theory, all degrees of coextension are possible: (1) band = leader; (2) band $\simeq$ leader; (3) band $\simeq$ crowd; (4) band = crowd. In fact, variations 1 and 4, but especially 1, are possibilities almost never realized, and this is not a bad thing, for if variant 1 is the most gratifying for the leader's ego (i.e., to some extent, the author's), variant 4 represents the author's greatest technical triumph. These remarks, which may appear somewhat obscure in their schematic form, will become much clearer when fleshed out in the following pages.

Son Excellence Eugène Rougon

Eugène, like most men in positions of power, is surrounded by an entourage, a clique composed of his allies and his flunkies, those currying favor and those who do his dirty work. Ranging from the aristocratic marquis and marquise d'Escorailles to the common Gilquin, drawn from several if not all classes—the working class and the peasantry are most conspicuously absent—the members of the band constitute a cross section of contemporary bourgeois society, and incarnate that abstract entity over which Eugène seeks to and does exert his domination: France. Personification is, as we shall see throughout this chapter, synonymous with mediation. The metaphoric link which unites Eugène to the crowd through the band is actualized both on the narrative and the descriptive levels. When the band sets out to campaign actively for Eugène's return to power, Eugène is the spider to their web, the *deus absconditus* to their evangelism:

> It was a huge undertaking. Each of them had a role to play. Tacit under-
> standings were arrived at in the corners of Rougon's house itself, on Sundays
> and Thursdays. The difficult missions were apportioned. Every day people
> would launch out into Paris, determined to gain some influence. Nothing
> was disdained; the smallest successes counted. Everything was turned to
> account; something could always be derived from the slightest event, from
> the first morning greeting to the last handshake of the evening. Friends'
> friends became involved and their friends too. All of Paris was drawn into
> the plot. In remote corners of out-of-the-way neighborhoods there were
> people who yearned for Rougon's triumph without exactly knowing why.
> The band—ten or twelve people—held the city in its grip.[22]

The anaphoric repetition in the French text of the impersonal pronoun *on*—rendered here by the passive voice—corresponds to the

band's collective action. Rougon-like, the band radiates out from Eugène's salon, spreading its propaganda to the dimmest reaches of the city. This form of mediation is linear; the two poles—leader and crowd—are invisible to each other. The leader's apotheosis can thus take two forms: direct, unmediated contact with the crowd or indirect contact mediated by the band. But both the invisible and the visible leaders revel in the same euphoric experience: the inverse proportion of means and end. Just as Etienne makes three thousand hearts beat with a single word, Eugène controls all of Paris through his ten or twelve agents. The exaggeration inherent in both statements is the mark of the leader/author's omnipotence fantasy.

The web configuration barely disguises the strict hierarchy of a vertical power structure; and when Eugène and the crowd are brought face to face, this hierarchy becomes manifest. Never out of mind, the crowd does not always remain obligingly out of sight: in chapter IV, a crucial one for the student of Zola's crowds, all the important characters in the novel are brought together on the occasion of the crown prince's christening. Above the crowd, above Eugène, above the Emperor himself, there towers a symbolic image, an insistent reminder of the differences that structure Second Empire society:

> But what could be seen from all sides—from the embankments, from the bridges, from the windows—was a fresco, in the distance, of a gigantic grey frock coat painted in profile on the bare wall of a six-story building on the île Saint-Louis, with the left sleeve bent at the elbow, as though the garment had retained the posture and contours of a body now gone. In the sunlight, above the swarm of pedestrians, this monumental advertisement took on extraordinary significance.[23]

Lest anyone, member of the crowd or reader, should miss the pointed reference to Napoleon I, Zola has Gilquin call attention to it as the imperial family passes below the sign: "Gilquin noticed the frock coat just as it loomed over the two cars. He shouted: 'Look, over there—the uncle!'" ("Gilquin remarqua la redingote, au moment où elle dominait les deux voitures. Il cria: —Tiens! l'oncle, là-bas" [R-M, 2: 97]).

Just as Eugène controls the country by remote control—"The country quaked with a terror that emerged like a thunder cloud from the green velvet study where Rougon laughed by himself" ("Le pays tremblait, dans la terreur qui sortait, comme une fumée d'orage, du cabinet de velours vert, où Rougon riait tout seul" [p. 218])—Napoleon I continues to reign supreme through the mediation of the gigantic billboard. The image of the Emperor's empty clothes rises like an effigy of the dead leader, a modern version of the ancient Greeks' colossos: "By its function

as mediator between two opposite worlds, considered as a sign, the *colossos* exhibits aspects of tension and, so to speak, oscillation: now the visible, now the invisible aspect comes into the foreground."[24] The oversized sign serves as an enlargement, a magnified objective correlative of the band.

Throughout this key chapter, the band *does* nothing; its mediation does not shape events nor inflect the plotline. Rather, it operates as filter of the description. The band simultaneously mediates both the leader's and the reader's perception of the crowd, through the use of a technique which I shall term *superimposition*. Superimposition—a technique prevalent in Zola's crowd scenes—consists in overlaying the great anonymous mass of the crowd with a thin layer, a veneer, of familiar characters. Proceeding like a film director—Zola is to the novel what Eisenstein or D. W. Griffith are to film—Zola distributes members of the band along the parade route and inside Notre Dame and then, anticipating the camera's eye, alternates long shots and close-ups. Thus the opacity of both spectator-crowds is diminished, lightened by the recognition here and there of a known, identifiable face. This device, I hasten to add, functions quite independently of the feelings inspired by this recognition, as demonstrated by two symmetrical incidents involving Gilquin, the most obscure member of the band, and Eugène. In the first, having caught sight of Eugène's carriage, Gilquin attempts in vain to exchange salutations with the great man:

> "Look, Rougon!"
> And, standing, he saluted him with his gloved hand. Then, fearing he would not be seen, he took his straw hat and waved it. Rougon, whose senator's uniform was attracting a lot of attention, sank back quickly into a corner of the brougham. Next Gilquin called out to him, using his half-shut fist as a megaphone. Across from him, on the sidewalk, a crowd gathered, turning around to see whom this big fellow dressed in yellow twill was shouting at. Finally the driver was able to whip his horse, and the brougham plunged forward onto the Notre Dame Bridge.[25]

In the second, the now drunk and even more obstreperous Gilquin is once again brought face to face with Eugène. This time he manages an exchange with Rougon, reminding him in veiled terms of the services he has rendered; Eugène arranges to have Gilquin discreetly carted off. Eugène's refusal to acknowledge his recognition of Gilquin, the most popular member of the band, is consistent with the contemptuous distance he seeks to maintain from the crowd, but Gilquin's insistent salutations dramatize the crowd's refusal to be invisible, or, to be more specific, the refusal of one member of the band to return to the anonymity of the

crowd. What matters most is not the affective value of the contact, but that it occurs by means of the superimposition of a member of the band on the crowd.

Up to this point I have discussed mediation in its linear, one could almost say "transitive," manifestations: the band functioning as a conductor of current, a relay. But this narrow acceptation of mediation cannot in any way cover the polysemy, the overdetermination of this word in *Son Excellence*. Eugène's will to power is stated so baldly at times that it should and does arouse our suspicion that things are not so simple, indeed simplistic as they first appear, that there is more to mediation than meets the eye. Some examples of these explicit statements follow: "That was his ideal, to have a whip and to be in command, to be superior, stronger and more intelligent" ("C'était son idéal, avoir un fouet et commander, être supérieur, plus intelligent et plus fort" [*R-M*, 2: 42]); "He loved power for power's sake, free from any vain lust for wealth and honors" ("C'était chez lui, un amour du pouvoir pour le pouvoir, dégagé des appétits de vanité, de richesses, d'honneurs" [p. 131]).

Not surprisingly then, while he is out of power, Eugène entertains an old fantasy of running a model farm, in fact a kind of colonial empire or enclave on French soil (additional proof that Zola's espousal of extra-territorial imperialism in *Fécondité* is not a sign of senility, but rather perfectly consistent with the domestic policies outlined in *Son Excellence*):

> And he revived his cherished dream of being a great landowner, with herds of cattle to reign over. But, in the Landes his ambition grew; he became the conquering king of a new land; he had a people. He went into endless details. For two weeks, without mentioning it to anyone, he had been reading specialized works. He drained swamps, fought the rockiness of the soil with powerful machines, stopped the dunes' advance by planting pine trees, presented France with a miraculously fertile spot....
>
> "Huh! that's an idea!" he said. "I will give the city my name; I too will found a small empire."[26]

Since Borie has shown how much Zola's empire-building Oedipus complex and its "resolution" are colored by the fact that his father was an engineer whose most ambitious project (completed posthumously) was the Zola Canal near Marseilles,[27] we need not address ourselves to that level of the text. All the more so since our concern here is not with the Oedipus complex, Emile's or Eugène's, but rather with a more specifically literary form of mediated desire analyzed by René Girard in *Deceit, Desire, and the Novel* (*Mensonge romantique et vérité romanesque*).

Girard distinguishes two forms of mediation: *external mediation*, such as occurs in *Don Quixote*, *Madame Bovary*, and *The Red and the Black*,

where the mediators are books or historical figures, that is, legendary, remote from the desiring subject's world; and *internal mediation*, as in Proust or certain novels by Dostoievski, where the mediators are, on the contrary, so close to the subject as to become hated rivals. Of course, in novels as complex as *The Red and the Black* or *A Remembrance of Things Past*, both forms of mediation do appear, each relaying the other. If there is no incompatibility between external and internal mediation, the French title of Girard's book highlights the fundamental and irreducible opposition between two kinds of fiction: "In the future we shall use the term *romantic* for the works which reflect the presence of a mediator without ever revealing it and the term *novelistic* for the works which reveal this presence."[28]

While it would be absurd and vain to claim for Eugène Rougon anything approaching the psychological complexity of a Stendhalian or Proustian hero, *Son Excellence Eugène Rougon* is, to adopt Girard's terminology, novelistic. In no other novel does Zola so persistently attempt to demystify the hero's desire for power, to reveal the presence of the mediator(s). The most telltale indication of alienated desire is jealousy, for jealousy precisely reveals the essential role played by the Other—that is, the mediator—in making an object desirable to the subject; mediated desire is the desire of/for the Other's desire. Now Eugène's ambitions, his will to power, are fueled by jealousy, and his political mediator/rival is none other than the Emperor Napoleon III. It is no coincidence that it is during the crown prince's christening ceremony, at the very apogee of Napoleon III's reign, that Eugène entertains the following thoughts: "And, dreaming, he envied the emperor" ("Et, rêvant, il jalousait l'empereur" [*R-M*, 2: 105]). But at the same time as he is Eugène's hierarchical superior, the Emperor is in one crucial respect almost a double—the hyperbolic rival—for he too has a band. Staring up at the Emperor's lighted window during a visit to Compiègne, Eugène exclaims: "His band had made *him*" ("Sa bande l'a fait, lui" [p. 176]). Eugène's choice of Napoleon III as model/rival could be described as snobbish, for, as Girard points out, Proustian snobbism is desire twice mediated: "The mediator of a snob is himself a snob—a first copy."[29] Similarly, Eugène's model/rival is himself an imitator, not to say an impostor: Napoleon I is to Napoleon III as Napoleon III is to Eugène. The shadow of the "uncle," as we have already seen, looms over all; *fin de siècle* decadence consists perhaps in taking the degraded copy rather than the original for model.

Mediation also obtains in Eugène's sexual desire: when the beautiful Clorinde proposes to him, Eugène, despite his very real physical attrac-

tion to her, turns her down. Later, however, when she tells him of her affairs, he begs for her favors, and she responds: "You were so good, when I visited you on rue Marbeuf! And now you're in a state again because I am telling you dirty stories which I would never have imagined, thank god! Well! You're disgusting, my dear fellow!" ("Vous étiez devenu si sage, quand j'allais vous voir rue Marbeuf! Et vous voilà de nouveau en folie, parce que je vous raconte des saletés, dont je n'ai jamais eu l'idée, Dieu merci! Et bien! vous êtes propre, mon cher!" [p. 239]). Ultimately Eugène's sexual desire converges with his desire for power when Napoleon III becomes a syncretic mediator, the total rival—that is, Clorinde's lover:

> And never had he been more eaten up with that secret jealousy, felt the sting of the prideful envy he had occasionally experienced in the presence of the all-powerful Emperor. He would have preferred to see Clorinde on the arm of that coachman people spoke of in an undertone. It inflamed his old desires to know her beyond his grasp, at the very top, slave to a man whose word made people bow their heads.[30]

Whether the mediator appears as model or rival, whether the mediation is external or internal, Eugène's desires are clearly not spontaneous. At every step of the way his desire for power is mediated, and the band must be seen for what it is, the privileged link in a chain of mediators. The Individual/Band (hereafter abbreviated I/B) relationship is not static; it can shift from one form of mediation to another, from the linear to the triangular. It is only midway through the book, when Eugène is at the height of his power and in a neutral state vis-à-vis Napoleon III —"the Emperor had given him a free hand" ("il tenait de l'empereur une entière liberté d'action" [R-M, 2: 218])—that the band comes to the fore as the prime mediator. By attributing this role to a collective unit, Zola transforms the process to conform with his own preoccupations; his analysis of mediation by Others, as opposed to a singular Other, is his most original and authentic contribution to the subject. The following somewhat lengthy quotation admirably sets forth the specificity and the subtlety of this form of mediation:

> But Rougon's greatest pleasure was still to triumph in the eyes of his band. He would forget France, the functionaries at his feet, the crowd of petitioners besieging his door, to bask in the continuous admiration of the ten or fifteen members of his entourage. He opened his study to them at all hours, letting them hold sway there on the armchairs and even at his desk, claiming to be happy to find them constantly underfoot like faithful pets. He was not minister alone; they all were, for they were like appendages of himself. In victory, hidden forces were at work tightening the bonds between

them; he began to love them with a jealous affection, placing all of his strength in not being alone, feeling his chest expanded by their ambitions. He forgot his secret contempt for them and came to find them very intelligent, very strong in his image. Above all he wanted to be respected in them, defending them as heatedly as he would have defended the ten fingers of his hands. Their quarrels were his. He even ended up imagining that he owed them a great deal, smiling in recollection of the long propaganda campaign they had waged. And, having no needs of his own, he carved up rich prey for his band and in so doing enjoyed the personal satisfaction of seeing the grandeur of his fortune blazoned abroad.[31]

This passage is deceptively simple: read on the level of its manifest content, it seems to celebrate the joys of linear mediation. There is an accumulation of expressions which, taken together, constitute what A. J. Greimas terms an "isotope."[32] The band is described in rapid succession as "appendages," "in his image," and "the ten fingers of his hands." The members of the band are thus equated with children, confirming my hypothesis that the band is a surrogate family: "'Come, come children; it's bedtime,' said Rougon paternally" ("Voyons, mes enfants, il faut aller se coucher, dit paternellement Rougon" [R-M, 2: 144]). Read along this isotope, the I/B relationship signifies multiplication of the individual through the band (the word *ten* is repeated twice; Eugène is literally decupled by the band), aggrandizement of an already strong self: "feeling his chest expanded by their ambitions." But throughout the passage, there are sown hints of another level of meaning, of another form of I/B relationship, which is only the dialectical opposite of the first. The first such hint is the allusion to Eugène's "jealous affection" for the band. We have learned to be suspicious of jealousy, for it implies the existence, here only virtual, of a third party, a rival; it implies triangular mediation. Eugène's jealousy extends to the band; just as Clorinde's desirability derives from her desirability to others, so too does the band's. This statement is corroborated by a remark Zola makes earlier on, when Eugène is briefly abandoned by the band: "He needed to see them, to hold sway over them; his need was that of a *jealous master*, weeping in private over the slightest *infidelity*" ("Il avait le besoin de les voir, de régner sur eux; un besoin de *maître jaloux*, pleurant en secret des moindres *infidélités*" [p. 192; emphasis added]). We begin to sense the existence of a triangle involving Eugène (Subject) and the band (Object), but whose third member (Rival/Mediator) remains, at least for the moment, a function in search of a character.

The next hint is contained in the sentence which reads: "He even ended up imagining that he owed them a great deal." This sentence is

treacherous, for the point is that Eugène *does* owe the band a great deal, but not what is suggested. The fancied, conventional debt occults the real and less familiar one; the obviously absurd one distracts attention from the more costly. Eugène is not indebted to the band for their successful campaigning on his behalf: he is beholden to them for his very appetite for power. This contention may appear fanciful itself, but the text, or rather, the contradictions in the text, support it. Consider the remarks which immediately precede the passage under discussion: "To govern, to trample the crowd under foot—those were his immediate ambitions. The rest were merely minor circumstances he would always make the best of. His sole passion was to be superior" ("Gouverner, mettre son pied sur la nuque de la foule, c'était là son ambition immédiate; le reste offrait simplement des particularités secondaires, dont il s'accomoderait toujours. Il avait l'unique passion d'être supérieur" [p. 218]). Once again the message seems clear: Eugène loves power for power's sake. The fringe benefits, the prerogatives of his position, are indifferent to him; he enjoys them only because they please his entourage. Once again the Romantic mystique of the power-hungry superman is proclaimed, but this time the context suggests that the juxtaposition of Eugène's "immediate ambitions" and his "greatest pleasure" reflects the true order of priorities: having power *for* his *band* matters more to Eugène than having power *over* the *crowd*. One of the characteristics of mediated desire is that the order of events appears reversed, the cause masquerading as the effect. The subject is persuaded that his desire for the object antedates the arrival on the scene of the mediator, whereas, in fact, it is the presence of the mediator that precipitates the desire. The spontaneity of Eugène's will to power is illusory: it is the band which makes him prize political power (when it is not his mother or Napoleon III).

What fosters the illusion of spontaneity is the seeming absence of a rival. Unless the band's syncretic function as both mediator *and* rival can be demonstrated, the process of triangular mediation remains invisible, an interpretive construction without textual substantiation. To account for the peculiar, atypical functioning of triangular mediation in this novel, I propose the notion of "delayed rivalry." Indeed, in the latter part of the novel, the band, driven by an overwhelming desire for power and feeling that Eugène is not doing enough to satisfy it, abandons him and replaces him with one of their own, Clorinde's mediocre and spineless husband, Delestang. (It is no accident that Eugène's two chief political rivals—Delestang and Napoleon III—are sexually linked to Clorinde, for as we have repeatedly observed in Zola, the political and the sexual axes always run parallel.) A complete Greimasian actantial

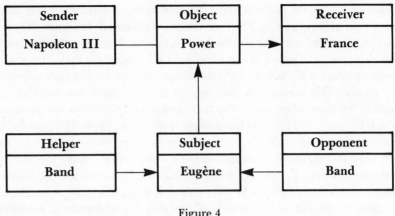

Figure 4

model allows for a graphic representation of the band's syncretism as shown in Figure 4. One might venture the hypothesis that the archactant produced by the syncretism of the helper and the opponent is in fact a second desiring subject—in other words, a rival for the possession of the object.

For the second-time-around reader (the critic), the band's betrayal of its leader is beautifully foreshadowed in our passage through Zola's use of animal imagery. At first the members of the band are described as "faithful pets," harmless little creatures to whom Eugène gives the run of his office. This metaphor translates Eugène's unchallenged supremacy over the band. But in the final sentence of the paragraph, Eugène's best friends appear in a new and ominous incarnation, as predatory beasts for whom Eugène must kill "rich prey" if he is to keep them satisfied, to keep them from devouring him. The expression "carve up rich prey" connects this passage to the most inclusive isotope running through the novel—the hunt—and more specifically, to the privileged moment in the hunt for Zola: the capture of the quarry ("La Curée"). The comparison which follows, between the hounds who devour a stag before the Emperor and his guests at Compiègne and the members of the band who devour Eugène, is as deliberate as it is effective: it turns on the ambiguity of the word *bande*, which can refer to both men and beasts, signifying as it does either group or pack.

And below, the dogs were finishing off their bones. They crawled all over each other, struggling frantically to reach the center of the heap. All one saw was a mass of rippling spines, black ones and white ones, setting up a terrible roar as they pushed and stretched and swirled like pools of blood. Voracious

jaws went to and fro at a rapid pace in a feverish attempt to eat everything. Brief squabbles ended with loud howls. A large and beautiful hound, angry at being on the outer edge, stepped back and sprang right into the midst of the pack. He worked himself into a good position and gulped down a shred of the stag's entrails.

He fell, sapped, ravaged, devoured by his band . . . . And in this dark hour he recalled his band's slow action, those sharp teeth daily nibbling away at his strength. They surrounded him; they climbed up to his knees, then his chest, then his neck, till they strangled him; they had taken everything from him, his feet to ascend with, his hands to steal with, his jaws to bite and swallow with; they inhabited his very limbs, drawing from them their joy and health, feasting on them without thought of the future.[33]

It is at this point in the band's activities that it best fits the description given by Canetti of the hunting pack, with one important difference: the band's prey is human:

> The truest and most natural pack is that from which the word derives, the hunting pack; and this forms wherever the object of the pack is an animal too strong and too dangerous to be captured by one man alone . . . If the slaughtered animal is very large, a whale or an elephant for example, its size means it can only be brought in and divided up by numbers of men working together, even if it was originally struck down by one or two individuals. Thus the hunting pack enters the stage of *distribution*.[34]

Eugène's fall is yet another reenactment of the initial sacrifice; in fact, the hunting imagery calls to mind a particular Greek variant of the sacrificial hunt, the myth of the hunter Acteon devoured by his own hounds.

The cannibalism perpetrated on Eugène by the band is a necessary step in the progression from mediation to conversion. Left for dead by the band, Eugène disappears for a period of three years. This "purgatory" calls to mind comparable exiles endured by other Zola characters: Etienne's imprisonment in the flooded mine in *Germinal*, Saccard's imprisonment in a real jail in *L'Argent*. In at least Eugène and Etienne's cases, these periods of living death pave the way for the final stage in their development, what Girard terms "conversion," the conclusion of all "novelistic" novels. Conversion consists quite simply in a repudiation of mediated, "metaphysical" desire and the accession to autonomy: "In renouncing divinity the hero renounces slavery. Every level of his existence is inverted, all the effects of metaphysical desire are replaced by contrary effects. Deception gives way to truth, anguish to remembrance, agitation to repose, hatred to love, humiliation to humility, mediated desire to autonomy, deviated transcendency to vertical transcendency."[35]

This new autonomy is complex, as it combines in unequal amounts two possible relations to others: for the previously solitary character, solidarity, for the previously gregarious character, solitude. In the concluding chapter of *Son Excellence*, Eugène returns to power without the band, pointedly reduced here to the rank of spectator; he appears solitary, self-sufficient. But if we pay close attention to the content of his lengthy speech to the legislators, we discover that, paradoxically, the severance of all ties with the band coincides with a redefinition of his relationship with the crowd. In the course of his exile, Eugène has undergone a political conversion; once the leading exponent of authoritarianism, he now presents himself as a prophet of the new liberalism, with its humane concern for individual freedom. But even more surprising than this political about-face is Eugène's final, dramatic affirmation of his faith in God and respect for the pope. This religious conversion confirms what is perhaps most controversial in Girard's conclusion: "Repudiation of a human mediator and renunciation of deviated transcendency inevitably call for symbols of vertical transcendency whether the author is Christian or not. All the great novelists respond to this fundamental appeal but sometimes they manage to hide from themselves the meaning of their response."[36] Zola certainly belongs to this self-deceptive family of novelists. By the use of hyperbole, Eugène's speech is made to appear as a parody of conversion, a calculated political ploy, rather than an authentic confession—but irony cannot completely negate the power of his words:

> "We have been accused of irreligion. That is a lie! We are the respectful children of the Church and we have the good fortune to be believers...Yes, gentlemen, faith guides and sustains us in the sometimes burdensome task of government. What would become of us if we did not place ourselves in the hands of Providence? We claim only to be the humble executors of [his] designs, the docile instrument of God's will. That is what permits us to talk loud and to do a little good...And, gentlemen, I am happy to take this occasion to kneel down here with all the fervor in my Catholic heart, before the sovereign pontiff, the august old man whose vigilant and devoted daughter France will remain."[37]

Perhaps the best proof that these words do carry their full weight is the fact that Zola twice attempts to undercut their effect: first through irony, second through out-and-out contradiction. The last paragraph of the novel is inspired once again by what Girard calls "romantic and Promethean individualism."[38] We have here in effect two conclusions, and the reader—like the spectator of Greek tragedies ending with the intervention of a deus ex machina—is left free to choose between the *novelistic* conversion ending and the *romantic* nonconversion ending:

When the session was over, Clorinde watched for Rougon. They had not spoken to each other for three years. When he appeared, looking younger and somehow lighter, now that in one hour he had cast off his entire political past, ready to gratify his tremendous appetite for authority under the guise of parliamentary government, she yielded to her enthusiasm and went towards him with outstretched hand and her eyes moist with tenderness, saying:

"I must say you're very good, you know."[39]

Au bonheur des dames

In *Son Excellence Eugène Rougon,* Zola's primary concern is the mediation by the band of Eugène's desire for power over the crowd. The earliest preparatory notes delineate the band's role strictly in terms of Eugène's psychological make-up: the band is his weakness, his tragic flaw. While obvious, the band's function as a representative cross section of the crowd is never commented on in either the notes or the final text. In sum, in that early novel the emphasis is on individual psychology, the psychology of the hyperbolic individual, the leader. Despite the family likeness which links Octave Mouret to Eugène Rougon, *Au bonheur des dames* is, at least within our narrow framework, the diametrical opposite of *Son Excellence Eugène Rougon;* as the very titles indicate, the preoccupation with the exceptional individual, the singular, so prominent in *Son Excellence,* has been displaced by a concern with the collective, the plural, in *Au bonheur.* Whereas the first title proclaims the leader's autonomy —His Excellency is not an elected official—the second announces the advent of a new power relationship: a dedication to pleasing the crowd. Indeed, though Octave's contempt for the crowd easily rivals Eugène's, he is totally dependent on it for the fulfilment of his ambitions. Octave cannot take his customers for granted; if his brilliant displays, his saturation advertising, do not drive his female customers into a frenzy of spending, his grandiose schemes of expansion will surely crumble, his business possibly fail. Eugène's attitude towards the crowd is, as we shall see in the next section, "masculine," whereas Octave's strategy is "feminine": the one seeks to subject, the other to seduce.

The difference between Eugène's situation and Octave's might best be illustrated by citing the difference in their relationships to their respective father figures: Napoleon III for Eugène and that pale, very attenuated carbon copy of the Emperor, the Baron Hartmann for Octave. (Just as Eugène and the Emperor are linked by Clorinde, Octave and the baron are brought together by their common mistress, Mme Desforges.)

Whereas Eugène's fate depends solely on the Emperor's determination, Octave's dealings with the baron are mediated by the crowd. The baron will back Octave only if Octave is already backed by the crowd: "'Well, I'll look into the matter...It will be settled if your Monday sale takes on the importance you predict'" ("—Eh bien! j'examinerai l'affaire... Elle est conclue, si votre vente de lundi prend l'importance que vous dites" [*R-M*, 3: 469]). Whereas Eugène thrives on governing by remote control, Octave wants not only to see the crowd, but to feel it. He is unique among Zola's leader figures in that he enjoys a physical, even sensual relationship with the crowd; he experiences an irresistible urge to plunge into the crowd, rather like a modern politician taking a "crowd-bath": "When she had ascended the staircase, Henriette searched in vain for Mouret, who had pushed Vallagnosc into the crowd, to make him quite dizzy. Overcome by the physical need to bathe in his success, he experienced a delicious sensation of breathlessness; it was as though all his limbs were held in a long embrace by his clientele."[40]

The differences in the I/C relationship cannot but entail a whole series of differences on other levels: Mouret's desire for direct contact with the crowd is paralleled by diminished dependency on the band as a go-between. Not only is the I/B relationship subsumed to the I/C, but both are subordinate to the newly prominent B/C relationship. We touch here on what constitutes Zola's major innovation in this novel: a significant shift away from the *psychology* of mediation to its *technique,* an explication and exploitation of the previously implicit B/C metonymic equivalence. As the crowd comes to the fore, Zola becomes increasingly preoccupied with the technical difficulties of presenting—that is, representing—it. Just as it is essential for Mouret to master techniques of crowd manipulation in order for his "machine" to function, Zola must devise methods of crowd presentation, specifically literary devices which will insure the proper functioning of his "machine," his novel.

In my reading of *Son Excellence,* I pointed out that in the large crowd scene of the crown prince's baptism, Zola resorts to a technique I termed superimposition. Had we the leisure to submit earlier crowd-fictions, such as *Les Mystères de Marseille* or *La Fortune des Rougon,* to close scrutiny in this same perspective, we could easily establish that Zola was from the first in possession of the rudiments of his technique of crowd presentation, but that it remained unrefined, "wild," so long as Zola focused his attention on the individual protagonists. *Au bonheur des dames* has rightly been termed one of Zola's "transitional novels,"[41] in that it constitutes the vital passage between the early crowd-fictions, where the crowd is only partially represented by the band, or a band, and the later novels, in particular *Germinal,* where the crowd is totally represented by the band.

As I shall not deal with *Germinal* in this section, I would like to indicate, however briefly, that from my point of view, as from so many others, it appears as the consummate elaboration of previous material. For example, the band (there are, of course, several, but our concern is with the one that surrounds the leader, that is, the Maheu) is coextensive with a family, thus reproducing in microcosm the very design of the *Rougon-Macquart;* furthermore, the leader is related to the band and the crowd not only metaphorically, but also metonymically, as they live and work in the same place. Etienne is one of them; there is no disjunction in the I/B/C relationship throughout the main events, and when a break does occur, the crowd is as instrumental in bringing it about as the individual. What Zola attains in *Germinal* is a classical equilibrium between component parts, an aesthetic harmony which informs and exceeds the social strife described.

We can now see just how *Au bonheur des dames,* that hymn to private enterprise, is *in its structure* a rehearsal for *Germinal,* that indictment of laissez-faire capitalism: Octave lies midway between Eugène and Etienne. Eugène, as I have amply demonstrated, lives a very secluded life, with minimal contacts with the outside world; when he does come face to face with the crowd, the crowd is always reduced to the position of spectator, whether lining a parade route, or listening to Eugène speak, in Niort or parliament. Octave, on the contrary, is constantly trying to see the crowd, even to merge with it. The measure of success Octave obtains in his quest to be at one with his largely female constituency—in order, of course, better to exploit it—is dramatically illustrated in the following remark: *"He was a woman;* they felt penetrated and possessed by the delicate sense he had of their innermost selves" (*"Il était femme,* elles se sentaient pénétrées et possédées par ce sens délicat qu'il avait de leur être secret" [*R-M,* 3: 468; emphasis added]). Etienne will go Octave one better, going down into the mine to work and suffer alongside the miners, leading them from within. (None of the above is meant to minimize the margin of difference, the distance between the leader and the crowd, which persists throughout Zola's fiction, but merely to stress the significance of its variations.)

Zola's preparatory notes for *Au bonheur des dames* provide an invaluable insight into and confirmation of his growing preoccupation with techniques of mediation. The words that recur most often are *personify, type* or *typical,* and *represent,* as in the following:

> Find a great figure of a man or rather of a woman through whom I will personify the death of small business.

> For clients I will start out with the women met, shown at the home of

Octave's mistress....But I will need five or six other women, named and known to the salesmen on sight, to personify the clientele....

As for the salesladies, they must represent all the varieties....Shadow them all and give each one a typical ending.[42]

Personification by synechdoche is the literary equivalent of miniaturization in modern technology; by taking the part for the whole, several typical individuals for an abstract class—one lonely shopkeeper for a doomed sector of the economy, ten customers for the clientele on a sale day, several salesgirls for a professional category—Zola seeks an economic means of presenting a large, unwieldy crowd. The notes pertaining to the clientele indicate that personification means personalization; the key words are "named" and "known to the salesmen on sight." The salesmen stand in for us, the readers; we too should be able to recognize and identify some faces in the crowd.

But personification cum personalization constitutes only the first step in Zola's two-step technique; the second is the one we have already seen at work: superimposition. This is the process implied in Zola's brief notations in the chapter outlines: "IV. Offering for sale of winter novelties....The unknown customers. The known customers, going from department to department" ("IV. Mise en vente des nouveautés d'hiver... Les clientes inconnues. Les clientes connues, allant de rayon en rayon" [*R-M,* 3: 1696]). These notes are, in fact, somewhat misleading, suggesting as they do a simple succession or juxtaposition of the known and unknown customers, whereas the actual process used is a bit more complex: personification (unknown → known) projected onto the syntagmatic axis, or personification + alternation.

That personification precedes alternation is indicated by the ordering of Zola's chapters: before going on to chapter IV, the first big crowd chapter, Zola takes the time to present the members of the band, assembled for the occasion in the intimate setting of Mme Desforges's salon. As Octave attempts to convince a sceptical Baron Hartmann of the viability of his ambitious projects, he deftly combines the presentation of the band with a representation ("mise en scène") of the band's genesis:

"No doubt the idea is appealing," he said. "Only it is the idea of a poet... Where would you find the clientele to fill such a cathedral?"

Mouret stared at him in silence for a moment, as if dumbstruck by his refusal. Was it possible? a man with such flair, who could smell money wherever it lay hidden! And, suddenly, he made a grand, eloquent gesture; he pointed to those women in the salon exclaiming:

"The clientele—why, there it is!"[43]

Farther along in the chapter general personification (band ≃ crowd)

gives way to particularization (individual members of the band $\simeq$ specific type of customer), as Zola describes "their particular shopper's temperament" ("leurs tempéraments particuliers d'acheteuses" [R-M, 3: 463]). There is Mme Marty, the indiscriminate shopper; Mme Guibal, the Platonic shopper; Mme de Boves, the frustrated shopper; Mme Bourdelais, the value-conscious shopper; and Mme Desforges, the selective shopper. With these thumbnail sketches, Zola has completed the preliminary step in his two-step method: the introduction of the nucleus of the "known" clients, those known to each other and then to Octave. In the course of the novel, these characters will become as familiar to the sales personnel as to the reader of *Au bonheur*.

If we compare the three large crowd chapters—IV, IX, and XIV —their constants and their variables stand out very clearly. If we assume at the outset that mediation through superimposition is the band's invariant function, what then are the modulations of the $\frac{B}{C}$ relationship?

Chapter IV   This chapter contains one of Zola's most fully elaborated "cyclical" crowd scenes, with its characteristic curve passing through five key points: emptiness, swelling, saturation, discharge, emptiness. At each critical moment in the cycle, from the moment the store opens its doors to the moment it closes them, Octave surveys the scene and the crowd from a vantage point. In sum, the emphasis throughout the chapter is on the very constitution of the crowd, the actual process of crowd formation. Now this process is remarkably reproduced on the level of the band; indeed, a minor leitmotif running through the chapter is the reconstitution of the band. The order of appearance of the members of the band is significant. It is cumulative, with Mme Desforges playing the role of pied piper, as it were: she is the first of the "known" clients to arrive, and as she slowly makes her way through the store, she encounters her friends along the way. Each meeting gives rise to a ritual exchange:

> As she was leaving, she recognized Mme Marty next to her, accompanied by her daughter Valentine....
> "Hullo! is that you, dear Madam?"
> "Why certainly, my dear...What a crowd, eh?"
> "Oh! don't mention it to me; it's suffocating. A success!...Have you seen the oriental room?"
> "Superb! extraordinary!"
>
> "So there you are!" said Mme Desforges, finding Mme Bourdelais settled in front of a counter.
> "Well, hello!" answered the latter, shaking the ladies' hands. "Yes, I came in to take a look."

"Isn't this display stupendous! It sets one dreaming...And the oriental room—have you seen the oriental room?"

"Yes, yes, extraordinary!"[44]

Finally the reconstituted band gathers briefly in the oriental room, almost as though it were driven by some instinct to recreate its original meeting place, Mme Desforges's salon.

Chapter IX   In chapter IX, the emphasis is no longer on the parallel crowd // band formation; significantly, the crowd appears full-grown in the early afternoon—that is, midway through the cycle, close to the point of saturation. What is stressed is the B/C relationship itself; whereas in chapter IV the band's explicit allusions to the crowd were limited to a few cliché sentences, chapter IX describes the band's growing awareness of the crowd. What is at stake here is the *integration* of the band, as evidenced by the recurrence in various guises of the following paradigms: outside/inside, repulsion/attraction, observation/participation.

The first members of the band to appear are Mme Marty and Mme de Boves and daughter. They are standing on the sidewalk, hesitating to join the crowd entering the store, when they find themselves irresistibly drawn in, carried by the crowd. We might describe this crucial passage as a case of "reluctant superimposition":

> The ladies, caught up in the current, could no longer retreat. Just as a river absorbs all the meandering rivulets in a valley, it seemed that the torrent of customers, flowing right through the entrance, drank in passersby off the street, sucked in people come from the four corners of Paris. They advanced very slowly, squeezed so hard they couldn't breathe and propped up by shoulders and stomachs whose soft warmth they could feel; and their satisfied desire took pleasure in this painful approach which whipped up their curiosity even more. It was a mishmash of ladies in silks, lower-middle-class women in shabby dresses, and hatless girls, all excited, all fired up by the same passion.[45]

The text reads like a demonstration of the painful process whereby an individual divests himself of his highly prized difference and autonomy to become a (mere) part of the collective. To enter the portals of this modern, profane temple,[46] one must renounce all the prerogatives of individualism, class differences in particular. This painful initiation rite is not, however, without its pleasurable compensation: the sexual gratification that so many frustrated female characters in nineteenth-century French fiction seem to seek and sometimes find in the temple of their

choice. Emma Bovary's case is, as always, exemplary: when the priest she turns to does not respond to her demand, she becomes the prey of the diabolical dry-goods merchant, Lheureux.

Once the "outsiders" have been drawn inside the store, the battle-ground shifts to within the store: as each member of the band appears, she reenacts the same scenario—resistance followed by capitulation. We might consider two examples of attempted resistance through distancing, or separation. The oriental room, which functioned primarily as a meeting place in chapter IV, turns up here in a new incarnation and serving a new function; it is the "reading room" ("salon de lecture"), where several members of the band meet by accident and not, as before, by prearrangement, not driven by female bonding instincts, but rather by mating instincts and, above all, by a need to escape the omnipresent crowd. The reading room is in every sense a refuge: "Next to the children, a lady was hidden from view by the pages of a magazine. It was Mme Guibal. She seemed upset at the meeting [with Mme Bourdelais]. But she immediately recovered and said that she had come upstairs to sit down a bit and escape the crush of the crowd" ("Près des enfants, une dame disparaissait entre les pages d'une revue. C'était Mme Guibal. Elle semblait contrariée de la rencontre. Mais elle se remit tout de suite, raconta qu'elle était montée s'asseoir un peu, pour échapper à l'écrasement de la foule" [R-M, 3: 624]). A difference in height, a vantage point, provides a similar shelter for Mme Desforges. Twice in the course of her store-wide expedition, she is briefly transformed from a participant into a spectator, a privileged observer of the crowd of which moments earlier she was a part: "Mme Desforges had just reached the second floor when a thrust somewhat more violent than the others brought her to a momentary standstill. Below her were spread out the ground floor depart-ments, the crowd of customers through which she had just made her way. It was a new spectacle, an ocean of foreshortened heads blotting out bodices, swarming like an anthill in turmoil."[47] But, just as Mme Marty and Mme de Boves are drawn into the store, just as Mme Guibal eventually leaves the haven of the reading room to return to the fray, Mme Desforges finds herself penetrated by the all-enveloping, ines-capable crowd: "But what astonished her most of all was that when, blinded by the bright patchwork of colors, she closed her eyes to rest, she felt the crowd's presence even more, because of the muffled sound it made—surging like a rising tide—and because of the human warmth it exuded."[48]

The chapter culminates in a series of superimpositions, timed to succeed each other as rapidly as a final bouquet of fireworks. The band

and the crowd are one, merged to the point of indistinction: the temporal counterpoint of chapter IV and the psychological and spatial distancing of the first part of chapter IX give way to total integration. Both the band and the crowd have invaded the store: "Then the ladies, still led by Denise, roamed about. They reappeared in all the departments. They were the only ones to be seen on the staircases and along the galleries" ("Alors, ces dames, toujours conduites par Denise, vagabondèrent. On les revit de nouveau dans tous les rayons. Il n'y avait plus qu'elles sur les marches des escaliers et le long des galeries" [R-M, 3: 639]); "the women reigned. They had taken the store by assault" ("les femmes régnaient. Elles avaient pris d'assaut les magasins" [p. 642]). The fundamental opposition between the ladies of the band and the all-female crowd has shrunk to grammatical proportions:

ces/les
demonstrative/article
individuals/category

Now each member of the band is immediately superimposed on the genus of customers she is meant to represent. The statistics in the following quotation attest to the lack of originality of "the ladies":

> Wishing to recover her expenditures, Mme Bourdelais had again led her three children over to the buffet. Now it was besieged by customers wild with hunger; even the mothers gorged themselves on malaga. Since the opening, eighty liters of syrup and seventy bottles of wine had been drunk....The fancy had taken Mme de Boves, who was followed by Blanche and Vallagnosc, to ask for a red balloon, although she hadn't bought anything....At the distribution center, they were starting on their forty thousandth balloon.[49]

Finally, in a typically Zolaesque use of symmetry, the first member of the band to arrive is the last to go. The "reluctant superimposition" of Mme Marty, early in the afternoon, is matched by her "reluctant de-superimposition" at closing time. Mme Marty turns out to be *primus inter pares*, the member of the band whose "shopper's temperament" best exemplifies that sale day's crowd:

> The clock struck five. Of all the ladies Mme Marty remained alone with her daughter in the climactic moments of the sale. Though dead tired she could not break away, held back by bonds so strong that, needing nothing, she kept retracing her steps, roaming through the departments driven by her unsatisfied curiosity. It was that hour of the day when the throng, which had been whipped up by all the advertisements went completely mad; the sixty thousand francs worth of newspaper ads, the ten thousand wall placards, the two hundred thousand catalogues launched into circulation, had first

emptied purses, then left excited female nerves in a state of shock....Mme Marty lingered in front of the bargain counters....The crowd was illuminated by the fiery five o'clock sun. Now Mme Marty's face was flushed and nervous like that of a child who had drunk a glass of pure wine....She had to struggle to get free of the constant crush at the door.[50]

Chapter XIV   The laws of symmetry determine the B/C relationship in this final chapter; his technique well-honed, Zola is content to repeat previous motifs and structural features with variations ranging in significance from the reversal of the order in which the "known" clients appear in chapter IV to the zeroing in on a different member of the band, Mme de Boves, the kleptomaniac. Just as each crowd chapter is set later and later in the day, farther and farther along in the crowd's "cycle," so there is a progression in the representation of the crowd, from its formative stage to its frenzied maturity, from Mme Desforges to Mme de Boves:

> The crush in the lace department was growing by the minute. The great linen display there scored a triumph with its most delicate and expensive whites. It was the violence of temptation, the frenzy of desire which drove all these women wild.
>
> Mme de Boves did not answer. Then the daughter, turning her languid face, saw her mother with her hands in the midst of the laces making off with Alençon flounces, which she hid in her coat sleeve.
>
> She stole with pockets full of money; she stole for the sake of stealing, just as one loves for love's sake: she was driven by the whiplash of desire, under the influence of the neurotic breakdown brought on by her unsatisfied appetite for luxury.[51]

In case the reader has missed the pointed personification of the crowd by Mme de Boves, Zola attributes these thoughts to Octave: "A vague connection arose in his mind: this poor woman's theft, the vanquished customers' final folly" ("Tout un rapport vague s'élevait dans son esprit: le vol de cette malheureuse, cette folie dernière de la clientèle conquise" [*R-M*, 3: 796]).

The chapter does not end on that didactic note, however. In a sort of recapitulation of all the previous superimpositions, Octave surveys the store and recognizes the members of the band disseminated throughout the departments. By a final twist of symmetry, his eyes focus on the first privileged member of the band, his former mistress, Mme Desforges. Beyond Mme de Boves, who embodies the crowd's insanity, stands Mme Desforges, who incarnates the crowd's submission to Octave's will:

Mme Marty and her daughter, swept up to the top floor, wandered through the furniture. Held back by her youngsters, Mme Bourdelais could not tear herself away from the fancy goods. Then came the band: Mme de Boves as always on Vallagnosc's arm and followed by Blanche, stopping in every department, still daring to look at the fabrics with her stately air. But in this huddled crowd, this sea of warm breasts beating with desire,...he came to focus on the bare bodice of Mme Desforges, who, together with Mme Guibal, had stopped at the glove counter. Despite her rancorous jealousy, she too way buying; and for the last time he felt he was the master; under the glare of the electric lights they groveled at his feet as though they were cattle from which he had drawn his fortune.[52]

Doubtless the band, that hybrid social/structural invariant, must figure as Zola's most personal contribution to the psychology and technique of mediation, but it is by no means the exclusive mediating agency operative in his fiction. There are at least two other important categories of mediators: the leader's love-object and a number of nonhuman agents.

The Love-Object

Eugène and Octave, those paragons of sublimation, both endure the test of temptation: a deep attraction to a woman who threatens their principles of erotic ascesis. However, each responds differently to the challenge: Eugène by hard-won resistance, Octave by hard-fought submission. These differing sexual responses are consistent with the previously explored differences in their I/B/C relationships. Indeed, it is my contention that throughout Zola's crowd-fictions—from "Celle qui m'aime" to *Travail*—the male/female relationship (M/F) is intimately linked with the I/C; my initial working hypothesis—to be refined in the next few pages, is that this correlation might be formulated as follows:

$$I : C : : M : F$$

Not the least interesting consequence of this theorem is its corollary: $C = $ or, better yet, $\simeq$ F. The crowd as female is, of course, a cliché of late-nineteenth-century crowd representation. To read Gustave Le Bon's classical work *The Crowd* (1902) is to discover that the crowd-female equivalence is only a fragment of a far longer chain of equivalences, which links up that period's "minorities": crowd $\simeq$ women $\simeq$ children $\simeq$ savages. What Zola does, then, is to take ready-made associations and generate fiction from these stereotyped matrices.

In *Son Excellence Eugène Rougon,* a single, rather tenuous element connects Clorinde and the crowd—the signifier "whip" ("fouet"). In

Eugène's fantasies of omnipotence over the crowd, he pictures himself as a sort of lion-tamer: "That was his ideal: to have a whip and be in command....he spoke of the animals as he would have spoken of men, saying that crowds like the stick" ("C'était son idéal, avoir un fouet et commander....il parla des bêtes comme il aurait parlé des hommes, disant que les foules aiment le bâton" [R-M, 2: 42]). Similarly, in one of his first erotic encounters with Clorinde, while she is posing for a sculptor, the same fantasy is pressed into service to reassure Eugène of his superior strength; in both fantasies the instrument is the same, the future victims interchangeable: "In his blurred vision Clorinde loomed ever larger, blocking out the entire bay with her monumental proportions. But when he blinked, he found that she was much smaller than he, but standing on the table. Then he smiled; if he had wanted to, he could have whipped her like a little girl, and he remained surprised at his momentary fear."[53]

But the similarities end there, for whereas Eugène succeeds in dominating the crowd, he fails to subjugate Clorinde. In fact, in the seduction scene (chapter V), it is very emphatically Clorinde who wields the whip. From the moment Clorinde drops in on Eugène, attired in full riding habit, to the moment she rebuffs his advances in the stable, the whip and the whole semantic network it commands increasingly become the dominant image, functioning on both the figurative and the literal levels of language, organizing the action: "She still held her riding whip, a very fine riding whip with a delicate silver handle" ("Elle avait gardé sa cravache à la main, une cravache très fine, à petite manche d'argent" [R-M, 2: 110]); "His big body lumbered like that of a bear about to pounce" ("Son grand corps avait des mouvements ralentis d'ours rêvant quelque traîtrise" [p. 115]); "It was like a whiplash. She stood up" ("Ce fut comme un coup de fouet. Elle se mit debout" [ibid.]). All these mentions of the paraphernalia of whipping lead up to the sequence in the stable where the roles are completely reversed: the would-be sadist revels in masochism, as the whipper in fantasy becomes the whipped in reality; the lion-tamer becomes a dancing bear:

> Crimson and wild with anger, Rougon was a terrifying sight as he rushed at her, panting like a runaway bull. As for her, she was so happy to strike him that a glimmer of cruelty lit up her eyes. Silent in turn, she moved away from the wall and advanced majestically into the middle of the stable; then, spinning on herself, she lashed out repeatedly, keeping him at bay, hitting him in the legs, the arms, the stomach, and the shoulders, while stunned, he danced like a huge beast under his trainer's whip.[54]

In *Son Excellence* there is a significant disparity between the leader's fantasies and the events that belie them. Contrasting Eugène's public

power with his private impotence, Zola sets up a paradigm for the novels to follow, *Nana* as well as *Au bonheur;* the Emperor's chamberlain grovelling at the courtesan's feet will become the fabulously successful department store owner begging for the favors of his humblest employee: "He watched the torrent flow in and reflected that he was one of those masters of the common weal; the fate of French manufacture was in his hands, and he could not even buy a kiss from one of his saleswomen" ("Il regardait ce torrent tomber chez lui, il songeait qu'il était un de ces maîtres de la fortune publique, qu'il tenait dans ses mains le sort de la fabrication française, et qu'il ne pouvait acheter le baiser d'une de ses vendeuses" [*R-M*, 3: 708]). Nonetheless, the male-female dialectic is not frozen once and for all in chapter V of *Son Excellence;* after this crucial episode of role reversal, Eugène regains his self-control and refuses to give in to Clorinde and marry her. Finally, after several more duels, Eugène triumphs simultaneously over the crowd and Clorinde, who signifies her submission by celebrating Eugène's power (see above, p. 153). Ultimately then, sublimation prevails; the M/F relationship is brought back into line with the I/C, thereby restoring the initial situation.

Whatever the variations introduced, the opposition of the leader's supremacy over the crowd and his lack of power over a woman appears to be a distinctive feature of Zola's crowd-fictions. The counterpoint between the I/C and the M/F relationships constitutes an essential structural device, designed to create tension and insure suspense. If this is so, it would appear that my preliminary equivalence between the crowd and the love-object is in need of some qualification, not to say reconsideration. I must now add an ingredient omitted from the initial hypothesis: time. The discrepancies or contradictions between the I/C and the M/F relationships are always temporary. And never more so than in *Au bonheur,* where the very word *mediation* takes on another of its possible meanings: the Christian meaning of "intercession."

Denise is as different from Clorinde as Octave is from Eugène. Whereas in *Son Excellence,* the connection between the love-object and the crowd exists only in the leader's mind, in *Au bonheur* the love-object's mediating function exists before her appearance on the scene. The coming of a woman who will avenge all those Octave has exploited is predicted by his associate Bourdoncle: "They will have their revenge . . . There will be one woman who will avenge the others; it's bound to happen" ("Elles se vengeront . . . Il y en aura une qui vengera les autres, c'est fatal" [*R-M*, 3: 419]). Denise has no life of her own; she exists to personify and to avenge not just the female customers Octave manipulates, but also the

sales personnel he exploits and the surrounding small businesses he destroys.

But Denise's revenge is a peaceful one, for she intercedes for all of Octave's victims. Slowly she encourages him to enact all sorts of reforms, to improve the lot of his workers, to make the store a more pleasant place to work and shop. In a first movement, she vindicates her co-workers—a segment of the crowd—thus earning their respect, going from rejection to apotheosis:

> And, from that moment on, she became popular. People knew they owed her certain of the comforts that they enjoyed, and they admired her strength of will. She was the woman who put a knife to the boss's throat, avenging them all because she knew how to extract something other than promises from him. So she had come at last, the one who insured a measure of respect for the poor devils that they were![55]

Denise's mediating function does not cease, however, until it encompasses the whole crowd. As long as Octave is engaged in his ruthless empire-building, Denise refuses his offers. It is only in the final pages of the novel, after Octave has scored the greatest triumph of his career, passing the million-franc mark on one sale day, that he decides to submit totally to Denise and marry her. To marry Denise, to accept the higher order of values she represents, is to accede at the same time to the crowd's will, to give back what he has taken. Denise's ultimate victory symbolizes the completion of her predestined mission of mediation. Both the initial refusal scene—closely patterned on the stable scene in *Son Excellence*—and the final acceptance scene attest to the inseparability of individual and collective destinies; there is no moment, however intimate, in Octave's courtship of Denise where the crowd she represents is not present, if only by metonymy. Despite the fact that their important meetings take place behind the closed doors of Octave's office, the couple is never, in effect, alone. The sounds of the store penetrate into the inner sanctum, and the crowd, functioning as an ancient chorus, punctuates and participates in the conversation, miming defeat, roaring approval: "Silence reigned anew. Beyond the closed doors one could still make out the faint hum of stock-taking. It was like a dying note of triumph, a discreet accompaniment to the master's defeat"; "A last faint murmur rose from the *Bonheur des dames,* the crowd's distant acclamation."[56]

Thus, mediation, whatever its acceptation, implies a *telos,* and that *telos* is the resolution of the contradiction between the I/C and the M/F relationships. Whether the novel ends in the crowd's and the female's submission to the leader, as in *Son Excellence,* or in the leader's capitula-

tion to the female and the crowd, as in *Au bonheur*, the equivalence between the crowd and the female is fundamental and, posited at the outset, must always be restored in the end.

From Zola's earliest crowd-novel, *Les Mystères de Marseille*, to one of his last, *Travail*, the female love-object is always charactĕrized by a mediating function. As the following passages show, as the crowd represented by the female grows in size and the male leader's project goes from wreaking revenge on the rich to succoring the poor, the personification/mediation becomes more explicit. The first quotation is from *Les Mystères de Marseille* and deals with the doomed love of Philippe Cayol (adventurer) for Blanche de Cazalis (heiress):

> Philippe's love had turned to fury. Constantly obliged to flee, his dreams of wealth threatened by the harsh punishment he faced, the young man was roused to indignation, and he took his anger out on Blanche by clasping her to his breast as if to crush her. The child's abandon was his revenge; he possessed her like an irate master....His pride developed into a profound and constant source of pleasure. He, the son of the people, held at last in his arms a daughter of those proud and powerful men whose carriages had sometimes splattered him with mud. And he remembered local legends, harassment by the nobles, the martyrdom of the people, the repeated cowardice of his ancestors in the face of the nobles' cruel whims. Then he would smother Blanche in an even closer embrace.[57]

Though on the surface Philippe's violent love/hate for Blanche bears little resemblance to the apostle Luc's very Freudian desire to redeem the fallen mother/whore Josine through marriage, if we look closely, we can see that both men's libido is directed at a class, not at a woman. In *Travail*, the negative mediation of *Les Mystères* has been positivized, but the woman's function as a means by which the male leader can reach and act on the collective remains unchanged:

> In her he loved the long-suffering people; it was she he wanted to save from the monster. He had chosen her because she was the most miserable and the most wronged, brought down so low that she was about to fall into the gutter. With her poor, work-injured hand she represented the whole race of victims, of slaves who sacrificed their bodies either to labor or to pleasure. When he had redeemed her, he would have redeemed the whole race.[58]

Other instances of women as "class-objects" could be cited: Josine immediately calls to mind Catherine Maheu (*Germinal*), of whom she is but a more extreme version, as the proliferation of superlative qualifications—"the most...the most"—indicates. But perhaps the most revealing or instructive example is Nana, for she syncretizes two functions which

have so far appeared mutually exclusive: she is both mediator and leader. The question then becomes, What is the fate reserved for a character who is both female and in a position of power?

As the "golden fly" ("la mouche d'or"), Nana avenges the poor, carrying her heritage of corruption into the highest spheres of society. Qualified as an avenger, she is related to Philippe (leader) on the one hand, and Denise (mediator) on the other. Or, Nana : Muffat : : Phillipe : Blanche, but also, Nana : Crowd : : Denise : Crowd. Nana, unwittingly of course, avenges one class of victims by victimizing another class:

> She had grown up in the slums, in the gutters of Paris; and now, tall and beautiful, and as well made as a plant nurtured on a dungheap, she was avenging the paupers and outcasts of whom she was the product. With her the rottenness that was allowed to ferment among the lower classes was rising to the surface and rotting the aristocracy. She had become a force of nature, a ferment of destruction, unwittingly corrupting and disorganizing Paris. (*N*, p. 221)[59]

Nana's "monstrosity" — Zola describes her as "like those monsters of ancient times" (p. 452; "comme ces monstres antiques" [*R-M*, 2: 1470]) — is her doubleness: to be both leader and mediator makes Nana a terrifying exception to the rule and makes her death not only inevitable, but also necessary. If order is eventually to be restored in the land, Nana must die. Indeed, Nana's death is the direct consequence of her monstrous syncretism. The carrier, the "golden fly," becomes her final and most spectacular victim; the scorpion poisons itself: "It was as if the poison she had picked up in the gutters, from the carcases left there by the roadside, that ferment with which she had poisoned a whole people, had now risen to her face and rotted it" (p. 470; "Il semblait que le virus pris par elle dans les ruisseaux, sur les charognes tolérées, ce ferment dont elle avait empoisonné un peuple, venait de lui remonter au visage et l'avait pourri" [p. 1485]).

To kill off a character is in some sense to interpret him: by inflicting on Nana an end worthy of an eighteenth-century moralist, Zola does more than judge and condemn his main protagonist; he also traces the limits of mediation by the love-object. In essence the mediator and leader functions are incompatible because the leader is defined by *his* will to power and the mediator by *her* passivity; Nana, as Zola repeatedly emphasizes, exercises her considerable power over men involuntarily, unwittingly: "And while, as it were, her sex rose in a halo of glory and blazed down on her prostrate victims like a rising sun shining down on a

field of carnage, she remained as unconscious of her actions as a splendid animal, ignorant of the havoc she had wreaked, and as good-natured as ever" (*N*, p. 453)[60]

In Nana, the "feminine" functions dominate the "masculine," making the conclusion inescapable that mediation is a distinctively female feature. To mediate is to serve as a means, a substitute—in other words, to be deprived of autonomy and initiative. Denise, in this respect, is no different from Nana: "Today she was the moving spirit of this universe, so all-important that a single word from her could stimulate or stay the giant fallen at her dainty feet. And yet she had not wanted this; she had presented herself simply and guilelessly, endowed only with the charm of her sweetness."[61] It appears, further, that female mediation consists in resisting the leader's sexual advances. Otherwise, death ensues: Blanche dies of cholera, Nana, of smallpox, Catherine, of inanition. Clorinde survives by never giving in; Denise's marriage occurs off stage. Only Josine, in the utopian setting of *Travail*, manages to combine mediation and sexual union with the leader. In Zola's crowd-fictions, mediation by a female love-object supposes sublimation.

Not the least interesting aspect of the $F \simeq C$ equivalence is that it marks the end of intimacy for the couple; two is a crowd. The invasion of the boudoir by the "street," a metonym for the crowd, spells the end of the psychological novel, focused on the couple and based on a definite distinction between inside and outside. As Borie argues, the breakdown of architectural barriers spatializes a corresponding breakdown in social mores:

> The world is divided between a fortress-like enclosure and an irresistible openness.... This opposition seems to manifest itself here with such strength for the first time in the tradition of the novel in France.... The boudoir of a great Balzacian lady is a charming place...open to the select friends (male and female) granted the privilege of close intimacy.... There are no boudoirs in Zola, but the "alcoves" and "dressing rooms" which in some way take their place exude drama, and not tender and easy abandon.[62]

In each of the novels we have been examining, the private becomes public. Clorinde keeps an "open house" and briefly holds her salon in a restaurant. Octave actively solicits the invasion of his store-home by the crowd: "Had he found a way, he would have had the street pass through his house" ("S'il en avait découvert le moyen, il aurait fait passer la rue au travers de sa maison" [*R-M*, 3: 614]). And Nana, once again the exception that confirms a rule, throws open the door to her bedroom: "This bedroom had become a veritable public place" (*N*, p. 439; "Cette chambre devenait un carrefour" [*R-M*, 2: 1458]).

Finally, the drama that unfolds in the alcove is the final permutation of the dialectical relationship between the leader, the love-object, and the crowd. Instead of acting as the intercessor between a despotic leader and a servile crowd, the love-object becomes the protector of the pharmakos, the leader against whom the volatile crowd has turned or the would-be leader rejected by the ignorant mob. The situation I am alluding to is, in effect, the reversal of the initial paradigm, public power/private impotence, that is, public failure/private success. The crowd's presence in the bedroom, via the medium of sound, goes from being euphoric (applause) to dysphoric (laughter). The mediation of desire by the crowd —Nana is desirable to her individual lovers because she is desirable to all men—goes from a positive rivalry to a negative one: the victim, spurned by the crowd, is comforted by his mistress.

Nowhere is this type of mediation more fully explicit than in *L'Oeuvre.* Claude Lantier paints a revolutionary portrait of his girlfriend, Christine. When this painting, entitled *Plein Air,* is placed on exhibition at the Salon des Refusés, it is greeted with unanimous hilarity by the bourgeois public. Independently of Claude, Christine too witnesses this scene of public humiliation, in which she shares as the model of the painting. She rushes back to Claude's studio and, to console him, gives herself to him for the first time:

> She went on to tell of her violent desire to see the painting and her running off to the salon: she was met with a storm of laughter, the jeers of a multitude. *She* was being hissed in this manner, these people were spitting upon *her* nude figure, and it was the brutal exposure of her nakedness to the mockery of Paris which had made her gasp as soon as she entered. And wild with fear, mad with suffering and shame, she had run away, as though she had felt the lash of this laughter whipping her bare skin to the blood. But now she forgot herself and thought only of him, deeply troubled by her sense of what his anguish must be like, infusing the bitterness of this failure with all of her female compassion, brimming over with a tremendous charitable impulse.[63]

A detail allows us to link this scene to a similar scene in *Travail:* both Christ*ine* and Jos*ine* comfort their injured lovers with bouquets of flowers. Since, as we established in Part I, public mockery is a symbolic form of lapidation, it follows that in Zola's idiolect, flowers = nonstone. This equation is in keeping with and refers to two common French expressions—*jeter une pierre à quelqu'un* ("to attack someone") and *jeter des fleurs à quelqu'un* ("to laud someone").

What is remarkable about this episode is that it cumulates an interlocking series of mediations. Christine's need to buffer the crowd's

rejection of Claude places her in the position of a mediator, but at the same time, the crowd acts as a go-between which brings Claude and Christine together, so much so that the child they conceive that fatal evening is symbolically fathered by the crowd—"it would be the child of suffering and pity, cursed at conception by the stupid laughter of the crowd" ("ce serait l'enfant de la souffrance et de la pitié, souffleté à sa conception du rire bête de la foule" [R-M, 4: 152]). Finally, there is the mediation by a nonhuman agent, that is, the painting *Plein Air*.

The Nonhuman Mediators

The use of a painting as an *analogon* for both the painter and his model, while accountable to the mimesis of a painter's life, should be viewed in a broader context, as an instance of Zola's predilection for nonhuman mediators. In discussing the Emperor Napoleon I's empty riding coat earlier, I described it as a mediator, a *colossos*. Other examples could be adduced, but perhaps the best occurs in *Nana*, in a scene which is in many ways the symmetrical opposite of the opening of the salon—the celebrated day at the races. In both scenes the contact between the main protagonist and the crowd is mediated by a nonhuman double: the painting *Plein Air* for Claude and Christine, the filly Nana for Nana. In *L'Oeuvre*, the analogon is jeered, in *Nana*, cheered, but in both cases the effect derived from this device is the transformation of the subject into a spectator of his own relation to the crowd, thereby doubling his humiliation or his triumph:

> Now that he had judged his work, he listened to and looked at the crowd. The explosion continued, turning into a crescendo of uncontrollable laughter. As they entered he saw the visitors' jaws drop, their eyes narrow, their faces widen; and he heard the wheezing of fat men, the rusty rasp of thin men, and the sharp, flutelike sounds of the women.
>
> There came a sound like the roar of a rising tide: "Nana! Nana! Nana!" the cry rolled along, swelling with the violence of a storm, and gradually filling the horizon, from the depths of the Bois to Mont Valérien, from the prairies of Longchamps to the plain of Boulogne. . . .
> At that, Nana, standing tall and erect on the seat of her landau, imagined that it was she whom they were applauding. For a moment she had stood motionless, stupefied by her triumph, gazing at the course as it was invaded by such a dense flood of people that the grass was hidden from sight beneath a sea of black hats. . . .
> "God, it's me, you know!. . .God, what marvellous luck!" (*N*, pp. 376-77)[64]

Needless to say, Nana's delight at the confusion between the filly and

herself is matched by Claude's sense of relief at the lack of any visible connection between his canvas and himself: "Averting his glance from the crowd, Claude stared at [Fagerolles] in silence. He had not flinched; the laughter had only made him turn pale and his lips tremble with a slight nervous tic. No one knew him; only his work was insulted" ("Claude, en silence, détournant les yeux de la foule le [Fagerolles] regarda. Il n'avait point faibli, pâle seulement sous les rires, les lèvres agitées d'un léger tic nerveux: personne ne le connaissait, son oeuvre seule était souffletée" [R-M, 4: 130]).

The superimposition of *Nana* on *L'Oeuvre* reveals some curious aspects of the analogon. The analogon is a detachable extension of the character whose name it bears. When the crowd approves it, the character valorizes the association; when the crowd rejects it, the character de-valorizes the association. Thus, the analogon bears all the earmarks of a child-substitute. Lest this remark appear fantastic, not to say fantasmatic, in its own right, let us return to the texts. The connection between the analogon—the imaginary child—and the character's real child is made in both *Nana* and *L'Oeuvre*. Immediately following the passage quoted above, where Nana congratulates herself on having a winning namesake, at a loss for a means to express her joy, she suddenly grasps her sickly son Louiset to her bosom: "And not knowing how to give expression to her overwhelming joy, she hugged and kissed little Louis, whom she had just discovered high in the air on Bordenave's shoulder" (*N*, p. 377; "Et, ne sachant comment traduire la joie qui la bouleversait, elle empoigna et baisa Louiset qu'elle venait de trouver en l'air, sur l'épaule de Bordenave" [R-M, 2: 1405]). The implicit contrast between the glorious namesake and the sickly offspring is eloquent.

Like Nana, Claude has a sickly son, Jacques, who dies a premature death. However, unlike Nana's, Claude's imaginary child cannot compen-sate for his real one. In a second and final scene of public humiliation, Claude endures the total indifference of the salon public, when he places on exhibit the tragic portrait of his dead son, *L'Enfant mort*. In this painting the real child and the imaginary one are fused into one analogon; the difference between the real child/imaginary child relationship in *Nana* and *L'Oeuvre* is equivalent to that between simile and metaphor. *L'Enfant mort*, materializing as it does the metaphoric process, functions as a sort of metaphor of metaphor. On this occasion, Claude draws no comfort from the separateness of the painting from his person; on the contrary, he is rooted to the spot, his former stoical manner replaced by tears:

> But Claude heard only the dull beat of his heart, saw only *The Dead Child*, way up in the air next to the ceiling. He never took his eyes off it, under a

fascination that rooted him to the spot against his will. The crowd, dizzy with fatigue, milled about him; his feet were stepped on; he was jostled, carried along; and, like an inert object, he let himself go, floated, found himself in the same place, without lowering his head, unaware of what was going on below, living only up there with his work, with his little Jacques, swollen in death. Two big teardrops hovering on his eyelids prevented him from seeing clearly. It seemed to him that he would never have time to see enough.[65]

In a sense, we have come full circle, following the variations on mediation from the family as mediator to the nonhuman mediator, which brings us back to the family, since the analogon is an imaginary child. I have given the word *mediation* full play, a necessary liberty if we are to account for the many modulations in mediation of the I/C relationship in Zola's fiction.

Beyond Mediation; or, toward Utopia

To say, as I do above, that "I have given the word *mediation* full play" is somewhat misleading, since the word *mediation* never appears as such in Zola's texts: it is a pure metatextual construct. Yet we do find in certain Zola novels, particularly those written in the latter half of his life, a signifier chosen from the same paradigm: *intermediary*. The choice of this word is significant, for whereas the word *mediator* has nothing but positive connotations, the word *intermediary* can have or has come to have certain pejorative connotations. Hence these pertinent remarks by Giraudoux:

> The word *intermediary,* which is one of the most beautiful in the human lexicon—the bee is the intermediary between honey and flower, music, the intermediary between sounds and ear—has become a shameful word in the French lexicon. The role of intermediary, which in modern civilization is equal to that of a creator,...in our country barely corresponds to that of a door-to-door salesman or a procurer.[66]

Taken as a category, the intermediary is widespread in Zola's fiction; the intermediary is anyplace or anyone that might be described as "in between." Under this rubric, we might include Félicité's salon, a social no-man's-land; the numerous hermaphrodites; the sexually unclassified. Perhaps the best single example of the intermediary is Sidonie Rougon, "the procuress with a hundred shady trades."[67] But no intermediary comes in for as much attention and criticism as the economic intermediary. Thus, in *Au bonheur des dames,* Denise speaks out in favor of the

gradual withering away of the middlemen in commerce; at this stage, her inflammatory remarks are couched in the reassuring guise of a joke: "And a discussion began. Denise pretended to speak in jest, all the while adducing solid arguments: the intermediaries—factory agents, travellers, buyers—would disappear, which would contribute greatly to lowering the prices" ("Et une discussion s'engagea. Denise affectait de plaisanter, tout en apportant des arguments solides: les intermédiaires disparaissaient, agents de fabrique, représentants, commissionnaires, ce qui entrait pour beaucoup dans le bon marché" [R-M, 3: 574]).

In *Travail,* the utopian genre facilitates the expression of wishes and fantasies without resorting to humor as an alibi. As an essential preliminary to the institution of cooperatives, middlemen—those parasites of capitalism (see *L'Argent*), "the intermediaries, the idlers, and the thieves—all those who once lived off other people's work without producing anything themselves" ("les intermédiaires, les oisifs et les voleurs, tous ceux qui vivaient jadis du travail d'autrui, sans rien produire eux-mêmes" [Mitt *OC*, 8: 928])—are condemned to extinction. But in *Travail,* the word *intermediary* appears in another, less predictable context—the physical. Both Luc and Jordan, the apostle and the scientist, are convinced from the foundation of their utopia that in order for the factory and the community to thrive, the mediation of the boiler in the energy chain must be done away with. The boiler is the last of Zola's nonhuman mediators, the "hungriest" of his mechanical ogres: "Yes, the steam engine should be done away with, as well as the boiler, which is the awkward intermediary between the coal extracted and the electricity produced. In a word, the thermal energy contained in coal should be transformed directly into electrical energy, bypassing mechanical energy."[68]

The concern with streamlining the production of electricity becomes an obsession with Jordan and generates some of the most arresting pages in the novel: those recounting the scientist's trial-and-error progression toward a solution of the problem. To analyze these pages of science fiction is to return to the mythical substructure of Zola's novels, first unearthed in the Aire Saint-Mittre. The gradual transformation of the Aire Saint-Mittre, first into the Côte-Verte in *Germinal,* then finally into La Crêcherie in *Travail,* attests to a constant, unconscious, imaginative effort to understand, eliminate, or at least limit mediation.

In the Aire Saint-Mittre the basic opposition between Life and Death is mediated by a combination of two complex processes, *fertility* (Nature) and *revolution* (Culture). What was not brought out earlier, because it was not pertinent to our inquiry, is that both these forms of mediation share a

common, negative side effect: both entail loss, through either death or destruction. In the long years separating *La Fortune des Rougon* from *Travail,* Zola's imagination returned constantly to the scene of the crime, the cemetery where the body is buried, in a desperate effort to turn it into a place where life breeds life, without a mediating loss, or rather, without any loss in the mediation. Let us recall that the Aire Saint-Mittre is the scene of a very specific crime, the sacrifice of the founding victim. Now as Marcel Mauss and Lévi-Strauss after him have pointed out, the sacrificial victim is defined as an intermediary between Man and God:

> One sees what the distinctive trait of consecration in sacrifice is: it is the fact that the thing consecrated serves as an intermediary agent between the sacrificer, or the object which is to receive the useful effects of the sacrifice, and the deity to whom the sacrifice is generally addressed. Man and god are not in direct contact.[69]

> In sacrifice, the series of natural species (continuous and no longer discontinuous, oriented and no longer reversible) plays the part of an intermediary between two polar terms, the sacrificer and the deity, between which there is initially no homology nor even any sort of relation.[70]

Therefore, Zola's efforts to do away with mediation could be interpreted as an attempt to deny the origins of his fiction, to rewrite the history of his own literature, to purge the cemetery once and for all of its dreadful secret—the sacrifice of the surrogate victim, the original intermediary.

If we begin by superimposing the description of the cemetery/Aire Saint-Mittre outlined in Chapter 1 on that of the Tartaret/Côte-Verte, the direction of Zola's enterprise begins to emerge:

> Le Tartaret was a piece of wild moorland on the edge of the forest, sterile volcanic rock beneath which a coal mine had been burning for generations. It went back to legendary times, and the local miners told a story about it. The fire from heaven had fallen on this Sodom in the bowels of the earth where long ago pit girls committed untold abominations, and it had fallen so swiftly that they had not had time to come up, so that to this very day they were still burning down in this hell. . . . And it was here that, like a miracle of eternal spring in the midst of the accursed moor of Le Tartaret, the Green Hill stood forth with its grass for ever green, the leaves of its harvests ripened. It was a natural hothouse, warmed by the burning strata below. Snow never settled there. Beside the bare trees of the forest the great clump of verdure flourished on this December day, and the frost had not even nipped its edges. (*G,* pp. 291-92)[71]

The two modes of mediation operative in the Aire Saint-Mittre reappear here with significant variations.

Revolution   Just as in the comparable passage from *La Fortune des Rougon,* revolution is not mentioned explicitly here. But just as the desecration of the sacred burying ground implies the French Revolution, the destruction of the mine by celestial fire prefigures the coming (second) revolution. Indeed, throughout *Germinal* there is a constant association of fire and *fin de siècle* apocalypse. For Souvarine, the anarchist, there is no question but that the world should and will end in fire; only a total conflagration will usher in a new and better world: "'Don't talk to me about evolution! Raise fires in the four corners of cities, mow people down, wipe everything out, and when nothing whatever is left of this rotten world perhaps a better one will spring up'" (*G,* p. 144; "Fichez-moi donc la paix avec votre évolution! Allumez le feu aux quatre coins des villes, fauchez les peuples, rasez tout, et quand il ne restera plus rien de ce monde pourri, peut-être en repoussera-t-il un meilleur" [*R-M,* 3: 1255]). At first Etienne is shocked by the violence of Souvarine's system, but by the time he makes his major speech in the forest clearing, Etienne has been completely won over to the anarchist's rhetoric, and fire and revolution are synonymous: "Gone were the scruples of his human feeling and common sense, and nothing seemed simpler than the realization of this brave new world: he had foreseen everything and he referred to it as though it were a machine he could fix up in a couple of hours, and neither fire nor blood counted" (*G,* pp. 275-76).[72] Finally, this vision is shared by the bourgeois spectators who watch in terror as the miners march by: "And what they saw was a red vision of the coming revolution that would inevitably carry them all off one bloody night at the end of this epoch....Fires would blaze and not a single stone would be left standing in the cities" (*G,* pp. 334-35; "C'était la vision rouge de la révolution qui les emporterait tous, fatalement, par une soirée sanglante de cette fin de siècle....Des incendies flamberaient, on ne laisserait pas debout une pierre des villes" [*R-M,* 3: 1436-37]).

   In both *La Fortune* and *Germinal,* revolution functions as the prime cultural form of mediation. In *La Fortune* it is situated in a mythic past, a pre-text; in *Germinal* it is projected into an equally mythic future, into a future text, a sequel: *La Débâcle,* where Paris does burn, set on fire by the Communards.[73]

Fertility   The invariant in this category is the determinant *excessive,* as both the Aire and the Green Hill are remarkable for their overabundant fertility. The variable is the source of this fertility (see Table 6). The passage from *La Fortune* to *Germinal* is marked by the convergence of two

Table 6

Work	Locus	Source
La Fortune des Rougon	Cemetery/Aire Saint-Mittre	Below : chthonian : Dead
Germinal	Green Hill	Below : chthonian : Dead (noological)
		Above : celestial : Fire (cosmological)

mechanisms: the increased complexity of the source of fertility (dead vs. dead + coal + fire), inextricably linked with the hyperbolization of the chtonian component:

> CONTAINED: dead → dead sinners
> CONTAINER: underground → hell

Fertility has yet another variable: extension in time. In *La Fortune*, fertility is cyclical, seasonal: "Every spring the former cemetery had purged itself" ("l'ancien cimetière s'était épuré à chaque printemps" [*R-M*, 1: 5]). In *Germinal*, the seasonal cycle has all but been eliminated. The Green Hill is likened to "a miracle of eternal spring," the vegetation is evergreen, the crops multiplied. Yet this apparent miracle has a disastrous side effect: the excessive sterility of the Tartaret. Whatever has been gained in or over time is lost in space; if the underground fires produce eternal spring on the one hand, on the other, they produce eternal winter. The problem of loss in mediation appears insurmountable.

The quest for mediation *without* loss culminates in the Parc de la Crêcherie, literally, the Nursery Park:

> The dwelling-house was a nondescript, rather narrow brick structure built by Jordan's grandfather under the reign of Louis XVIII on the site of the former castle, which had burned down during the Revolution. It was set against the slope of the Bleuses Mountains, a huge, sheer wall jutting out where the Brias Gorge opened out onto the great plain of Roumagne. And the park, sheltered as it was from the north winds and enjoying southern exposure, seemed to be a natural hothouse where spring reigned eternally. Hardy vegetation covered this craggy wall thanks to the many streams which fell from it in crystalline cascades, while goat paths hewn in the rock wound their way up among the climbing plants and evergreen shrubs. Then the streams came together in a river which flowed gently through the whole park, watering broad lawns and clumps of the stateliest and sturdiest tall trees.[74]

The superimposition of this text on the two analyzed above reveals

the persistence of destructive mediation below the cosmetic variations of the surface. The substitution of beneficial sunlight for the celestial fire of *Germinal*, of crystal clear waterfalls from above for the hell fires below, the complete disappearance of all telltale corpses, cannot hide or diminish the original destruction, the traumatic lesion: the burning of the first castle. The triple reiteration of this event on the same page as the passage quoted above, associating fire and revolution, attests to its importance: "The former castle, which had burned down during the Revolution" ("l'ancien château, brûlé pendant la Révolution" [Mitt *OC*, 8: 627]); "their castle in flames" ("leur château en flammes" [ibid.]); "built on the ashes of the castle" ("construire, sur les cendres du château" [ibid.]). Furthermore, the Nursery, like the Green Hill before it, is an island of fertility surrounded by sterile lands: "A thousand hectares of barren rock, blasted heath, a great wide strip of the high plateau of the Bleuses Mountains" ("mille hectares de roches nues, de landes stériles, toute une large bande du haut plâteau des monts Bleuses" [ibid.]). On both the cultural and natural levels, the quest that began in the Aire Saint-Mittre ends in the Parc de la Crêcherie in complete failure.

But, la Crêcherie does keep the promise of its name: for on its grounds are located Jordan's laboratory, where he spends an entire lifetime perfecting the production of cheap and abundant electricity. Here, too, the factory fueled by this new form of energy: "The factory was built at the very foot of the slope of the Bleuses Mountains, in that part of the former park with southern exposure which the sun had long since turned into a paradise overflowing with fruit and flowers" ("L'usine était construite au pied même de la rampe des monts Bleuses, dans cette partie de l'ancien parc exposée en plein midi, et dont l'astre faisait autrefois déjà un paradis débordant de fruits et de fleurs" [p. 947]).

The presence of the "machine in the garden"[75]—the construction of the laboratory on the site of the former castle and of the factory on the site of the former park—signifies the replacement of revolution by science as the privileged means of cultural mediation, in keeping with Zola's stated latter-day ideology. This changeover from destructive to peaceful mediation does not, however, automatically solve the initial problem; indeed, if anything, the painfully slow progress of Jordan's research serves to dramatize the magnitude of the obstacles impeding the final resolution. Jordan, nothing daunted, pursues his goal relentlessly, yet each improvement uncovers a new difficulty; mediation without loss eludes him like the proverbial pot of gold at the end of the rainbow. In a first stage of his work, he does away with all the intermediaries between coal and electricity:

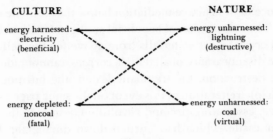

CULTURE   NATURE

energy harnessed: energy unharnessed:
    electricity   lightning
    (beneficial)   (destructive)

energy depleted: energy unharnessed:
    noncoal   coal
    (fatal)   (virtual)

Figure 5

First he had strained his ingenuity to do away with the cartage by burning the coal under the boilers as it came out of the pits, and by bringing, via cable, the electrical energy thus obtained to each factory *with minimal loss.* Then he had conceived the long-sought device permitting him to transform the thermal energy contained in coal directly into electrical energy, bypassing mechanical energy. This meant *the elimination of the boiler,* a considerable improvement, a savings of more than fifty per cent.[76]

Jordan cannot satisfy himself with this solution, however, because he is haunted by the threat of a loss that would undo all that he had accomplished: the depletion of world coal resources. At this point in his work, he is confronted by four possibilities, as shown in Figure 5. Thus, in a second stage, his research is directed at discovering an inexhaustible source of energy, one which can never be depleted. For Jordan, that source is the sun. If one places sun where coal is in Figure 5, under the heading "energy unharnessed," the opposite category, "energy depleted," is cancelled out. In a remarkable paragraph dealing with Jordan's sun worship, Zola makes the crucial point that sun and coal are not in comparable positions in the paradigm of potential sources of energy, for coal is itself a product of the sun—that is, already a mediator:

> And, in that case, why wouldn't the sun continue or complete its work? After all, for thousands of years it had stored its beneficent heat in the plants and trees of which coal was made. For thousands of years coal had been, so to speak, distilled in the bowels of the earth, keeping in reserve for our needs that immense store of heat, restoring it to us in the end as a priceless gift at a time when our civilization was destined to find in it a new splendor.[77]

Reduced schematically:

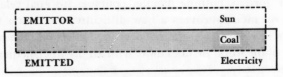

EMITTOR   Sun

                                                   Coal

EMITTED   Electricity

Figure 6

Just as the boiler must be eliminated, so too must coal. Having dropped this last intermediary in the energy chain, Jordan can address himself to the original source of all energy: "Thus, the problem which cropped up was both simple and formidable: it was a matter of *dealing directly with the sun*, of collecting solar energy and transforming it with the help of special equipment into electricity, of which huge stocks would have to be kept in leakproof reservoirs."[78]

In the third and final stage of his quest, Jordan succeeds in the first two goals he sets for himself, but the problem of conservation without loss pursues him literally until his dying day: "But a troublesome flaw persisted: the huge reservoirs leaked a good deal. There was thus a final improvement to be made: to achieve the perfect conservation of the winter reserves, accumulating enough sunlight to light another sun above the city during the long December nights."[79] Once the problem is solved —and Zola is unusually silent as to the means—Jordan dies, mission accomplished.

Whereas the notion that poets pun on their names has long been accepted, the notion that novelists do the same has only recently claimed critical attention. With its complementary emphases on the structuring role of "the Father's Name" ("le Nom du Père") and on the insistent inscription of the signifier in the unconscious, Lacanian psychoanalysis has inspired new readings of such authors as Balzac, Proust, and now Zola, which dwell not so much on their works as on their signatures. For it appears that these novelists—and they are surely not the only ones—wove intricate fantasies around their surnames or even initials, encoding them in their fiction through various devices, ranging from anagrams to translations.[80]

In the case of Zola, what we have is not so much the father's name as the Fathers' names. *Zola* is, of course, first and foremost Zola's father's surname, carrying with it connotations of exoticism and absence. But I would suggest that for Zola, his surname was also, and perhaps more importantly, an anagram of the two paternal imagos that presided over his writing destinies. It is Sandoz, Zola's pseudonymous persona in *L'Oeuvre*, who provides the derivation of *Zola*, etymology functioning here as a form of spiritual autobiography. Speaking to Claude about their common and burdensome Romantic heritage, Sandoz "bemoaned the fact that he had been born at the point of intersection of Hugo and Balzac" ("[lui aussi] se lamentait d'être né au confluent d'Hugo et de Balzac" [*R-M*, 4: 48]). Even Freud, who, in *The Interpretation of Dreams*, was the first to decode the pseudonym *Sandoz*, reconstructing its genesis, misses this precious revelation:[81] when Zola looks at his name, he sees it as a syncretic anagram of B*ALZ*ac + Hug*O*. Zola's Oedipus is grounded

in literary history; like many mythological heroes, he has not one but three fathers, though one, Balzac, overshadowed the others.

When one considers what great lengths Zola went to to differentiate himself from Balzac, to have the two key letters of Balzac's surname, *a* and *z*,[82] disseminated in his own could only have been regarded as a mixed blessing. This ambivalence results largely from the letter *z*'s contradictory connotations. If, as Jean Paris suggests, *z* is regarded, because of its rarity, as "the very sign of genius,"[83] then the homography could be welcomed as a sign of election. If, however, *z*, because of its cutting edge, is regarded as a "bad letter,"[84] signifying castration and death, then the homography appears as a curse, a stigma to be exorcised. Whether perceived as beneficial or fatal, the striking similarities between Balzac and Zola's surnames make the essential peculiarity of Zola's patronym all the more perceptible: it exists in defiance of the alphabet —that is, the law that orders Western civilization. It is one thing to have the letter *z* inscribed in the middle of one's name, quite another to have it for one's initial, especially with the letter *a* in final position. To put *z* before *a* is to begin at the end, for whatever else one can say about the letter *z*, it is not, as *a*(lpha) is, a "founding letter."[85] Zola's unusual patronym informs his entire work: Jordan's obsessive quest is Zola's, to go from *z* to *a*, from the final link in the chain of mediators back to the first, the source. Such a quest can meet with success only in Utopia; indeed, Utopia might be defined here as the place beyond mediation. Zola's latter-day Utopias are not, as has long been held, the aberrations of a senescent writer, but rather the logical conclusion to a lifetime project: the "scientific" subtitle of *La Fortune des Rougon,* "the *Origins,"* could serve as well for *Travail.* The desire to recover a lost origin, to go from *z* to *a*, leads from the Aire Saint-Mittre to la Crêcherie—that is, from the cemetery to the nursery. Only in a futuristic Utopia, where what is projected into the future is nothing but a regression into an archaic past, can the illusion that the Son can capture the Sun be entertained, however briefly. For even in Utopia, where the omnipotence of thought reigns supreme, the reality principle obtains: as Jordan's death signifies, there is no life beyond mediation.

Notes

Before and After

1. Edward W. Said, *Beginnings: Intention and Method* (New York: Basic Books, 1975), p. xiii.

2. Emile Zola, *Les Rougon-Macquart,* ed. Henri Mitterand, 5 vols. (Paris: Pléiade, 1960-67), 5: 1736-37.

3. As evidenced by this self-addressed warning: "Be careful above all not to portray too often the same nervous fellow (Claude, Daniel, Guillaume). Find diverse temperaments" (ibid., p. 1742).

4. Zola as quoted by Henry Massis in *Comment Emile Zola composait ses romans* (Paris: Fasquelle, 1906), p. 99. Cf. the chapter entitled "The Romantic Survival," in F. W. J. Hemmings, *Emile Zola* (Oxford: Oxford University Press, Oxford Paperbacks, 1970).

5. Zola, *Les Rougon-Macquart,* 1: 3.

6. Martin Turnell, *The Art of French Fiction* (New York: New Directions, 1959), p. 123.

7. Among Zola scholars this trend is best represented by Henri Mitterand in "Corrélations lexicales et organisation du récit: Le Vocabulaire du visage dans *Thérèse Raquin,*" *Nouvelle Critique,* special issue: *Linguistique et littérature* (1968): 21-28; "Système des personnages dans *Germinal,*" *Cahiers de l'association internationale des études françaises* 24 (1972): 155-66; and "Fonction narrative et fonction mimétique: Les Personnages de *Germinal,*" *Poétique* 16 (1973): 477-90; and by Philippe Hamon, who, in his forthcoming Doctorat d'Etat—"Le Personnage et les personnages dans *Les Rougon-Macquart* d'Emile Zola"—uses Zola's texts to anchor and elaborate a new theory of characters in fiction. Many of his preliminary conclusions are contained in his "Pour un statut sémiologique du personnage," in *Poétique du récit* (Paris: Seuil, Points, 1977).

Chapter 1

1. Gustave Flaubert, *Oeuvres complètes,* vol. 16, *Correspondance* (Paris: Club de l'Honnête Homme, 1975), p. 322.

2. See Guy Robert, *"La Terre" d'Emile Zola: Etude historique et critique* (Paris: Les Belles Lettres, 1952), pp. 383-87; Philip Walker, "Prophetic Myths in Zola," *PMLA* 74 (1959): 444-52; Jean Borie, *Zola et les mythes* (Paris: Seuil, 1971); and Michel Serres, *Feux et signaux de brume: Zola* (Paris: Grasset, 1975).

3. Northrop Frye, *Anatomy of Criticism* (Princeton: Princeton University Press, 1957), p. 192.

4. Claude Lévi-Strauss, *Introduction to a Science of Mythology*, vol. 1, *The Raw and the Cooked*, trans. John Weightman and Doreen Weightman (New York: Harper & Row, Harper Torchbooks, 1970), p. 6.

5. *R-M*, 1: 4. The French text reads "de son titre scientifique: *Les Origines.*" Thus Zola doubly emphasizes the word "origins", through a combination of capitals and italics.

6. Frye, *Anatomy*, p. 367.

7. Ibid., p. 341.

8. James George Frazer, *The Golden Bough* (New York: Macmillan Co., Macmillan Paperbacks, 1963), p. 638.

9. Ibid., pp. 667-68.

10. René Girard, *Violence and the Sacred*, trans. Patrick Gregory (Baltimore: The Johns Hopkins University Press, 1977), p. 20. All subsequent references to this work are included in the text.

11. Roger Caillois, *Man and the Sacred*, trans. Meyer Barash (Glencoe, Ill.: The Free Press, 1959), pp. 60-127.

12. Cf. an important note Caillois appends to his first use of the word *festival:* "It is pointless to emphasize that this theory of the festival is far from an exhaustive account of its different aspects. In particular, it would have to be correlated with a theory of sacrifice. In fact, the sacrificial victim seems to be a kind of privileged character at the festival. It is akin to the inner mechanism that sums it up and gives it meaning. . . . For want of being able to stress this intimate connection (a choice had to be made), I tried to indicate the sacrificial atmosphere of the festival in the hope that it would thus become meaningful to the reader, just as the dual dialectic of the festival reproduces the dialectic of sacrifice" (ibid., p. 185, n. 22).

13. Ibid., p. 96.

14. Ibid., pp. 179, 172.

15. Frye, *Anatomy*, p. 109.

16. Lévi-Strauss, *The Raw and the Cooked*, p. 6. Cf. Lévi-Strauss's remarks on Freud and the Oedipus myth: "We define the myth as consisting of all its versions. . . . Therefore, not only Sophocles, but Freud himself, should be included among the recorded versions of the Oedipus myth on a par with earlier or seemingly more 'authentic' versions" (*Structural Anthropology*, trans. Claire Jacobson and Brooke Grundfest Schoepf [Garden City, N.Y.: Doubleday & Co., Anchor Books, 1967], p. 213).

17. Mircea Eliade, *Aspects du mythe* (Paris: Gallimard, Idées, 1963), pp. 15, 33, and 35.

18. Bronislaw Malinowski, *Argonauts of the Western Pacific* (New York: E. P. Dutton & Co., A Dutton Paperback, 1961), pp. 300-301.

19. Gérard Genette, *Figures III* (Paris: Seuil, 1972), pp. 139-40.

20. Roland Barthes, *S/Z*, trans. Richard Miller (New York: Farrar, Strauss, and Giroux, Hill and Wang, 1974), p. 31.

21. There are, however, important exceptions to this rule, as I argue in my article, "Le Sourire du sphinx: Zola et l'énigme de la féminité," *Romantisme* 13-14 (1976): 183-95. When the enigma proposed is femininity itself, at least in nineteenth-century French fiction, the answer remains suspended *sine die*. In these cases the "hermeneutic code" is replaced by a "hieratic code": woman ≃ stone statue ≃ indecipherable text. Cf. Barthes's remarks on "the pensive text" in *S/Z*, pp. 216-17.

22. Barthes, *S/Z*, pp. 209-10 et passim.

23. See the supplement "Arbres généalogiques des Rougon-Macquart (Etats de 1878 et de 1893)" in *R-M*, vol. 5. Two unrelated remarks: first, it is interesting to note that in the earliest extant version of the family tree (1869), Zola is still groping his way toward this

important coincidence of personal and national destinies. Second, it should be pointed out that this is not the only instance where the family tree provides a *supplement* of information; a study comparing the family trees among themselves on the one hand, and to the novels on the other, would be well worth undertaking.

24. Lévi-Strauss, *Structural Anthropology,* p. 207.

25. Ibid., p. 226.

26. For this key quotation I refer the reader to a different translation of the text quoted above—"The Structural Study of Myth," in *Myth: A Symposium,* ed. Thomas A. Sebeok (Bloomington: Indiana University Press, Midland Books, 1965), p. 99.

27. "Une des *curiosités* de ce champ était alors des poiriers aux bras tordus, aux noeuds *monstrueux,* dont pas une ménagère de Plassans n'aurait voulu cueillir les fruits *énormes.* Dans la ville on parlait de ces fruits avec des grimaces de *dégoût"* (*R-M,* 1: 5-6).

"Ce qui a achevé de donner à ce coin perdu un caractère *étrange,* c'est l'élection de domicile que, par un usage traditionnel, y font les bohémiens de passage. . . . il y a toujours là quelque bande aux allures *singulières,* quelque troupe d'hommes fauves et de femmes horriblement séchées, parmi lesquels on voit se rouler à terre des groupes de beaux enfants. Ce monde vit *sans honte, en plein air,* devant tous, faisant bouillir leur marmite, mangeant des choses sans nom, étalant leurs nippes trouées, dormant, se battant, s'embrassant, puant la saleté et la misère" (p. 8). Emphasis added.

28. See Robert L. Füglister, "Baudelaire et le thème des bohémiens," *Etudes baudelairiennes* 2 (1971): 99-143.

29. "La route de Nice. . .était bordée, en 1851, d'ormes séculaires, vieux *géants,* ruines *grandioses* et pleines encore de *puissance,* que la municipalité proprette de la ville a remplacés, depuis quelques années, par de petits platanes" (*R-M,* 1: 17).

"En tête, venaient de *grands* gaillards, aux têtes carrées, qui paraissaient avoir une *force* herculéenne et une foi naïve de *géants"* (p. 29). Emphasis added.

30. "Cet arbre, un jeune peuplier apporté des bords de la Viorne, s'était desséché peu à peu, au grand désespoir des ouvriers républicains qui venaient chaque dimanche constater les progrès du mal, sans pouvoir comprendre les causes de cette mort lente. . . .L'arbre mort, la municipalité déclara que la dignité de la République commandait de l'enlever. . . .La société du salon jaune s'était mise aux fenêtres. Quand le peuplier craqua sourdement et s'abattit dans l'ombre avec la raideur tragique d'un héros frappé à mort, Félicité crut devoir agiter un mouchoir" (*R-M,* 1: 91).

The horticultural politics of the municipality of Plassans have a celebrated precedent —those of the municipality of Verrières, in the second chapter of *Le Rouge et le noir.*

31. "Le matin et l'après-midi, quand le soleil est tiède, le terrain entier grouille, et *au-dessus* de toute cette turbulence, *au-dessus* des galopins jouant parmi les pièces de bois et des bohémiens attisant le feu sous leur marmite, la silhouette sèche du scieur de long monté sur sa poutre se détache en plein ciel, allant et venant avec un mouvement régulier de balancier, comme pour régler la vie ardente et nouvelle qui a poussé dans cet ancien champ d'éternel repos" (*R-M,* 1: 9). Emphasis added.

32. Jacques Lacan, "Seminar on 'The Purloined Letter,'" trans. Jeffrey Mehlman, *Yale French Studies* 48 (1972): 55.

33. "Il y avait là, dans l'angle, une vieille pierre tombale, oubliée lors du déménagement de l'ancien cimetière, et qui, posée sur champ et un peu de biais, faisait une sorte de banc élevé. La pluie en avait émietté les bords, la mousse la rongeait lentement. On eût cependant pu lire encore, au clair de lune, ce fragment d'épitaphe gravé sur la face qui entrait en terre: *Cy-gist. . . Marie. . . morte. . .* Le temps avait effacé le reste" (*R-M,* 1: 10-11; Zola's emphasis).

34. "Elle eut un soir l'étrange fantaisie de vouloir que Silvère retournât la pierre pour voir ce qu'il y avait dessous. Il s'y refusa comme à un sacrilège, et ce refus entretint les rêveries de Miette sur le cher fantôme qui portait son nom. Elle voulait absolument qu'elle

fût morte à son âge, à treize ans, en pleine tendresse. Elle s'apitoyait jusque sur la pierre, cette pierre qu'elle enjambait si lestment, où ils s'étaient tant de fois assis, pierre glacée par la mort et qu'ils avaient réchauffée de leur amour. Elle ajoutait: — Tu verras, ça nous portera malheur... Moi, si tu mourais, je viendrais mourir ici, et je voudrais qu'on roulât ce bloc sur mon corps" (*R-M*, 1: 208).

    35. See Serres, *Feux et signaux*, pp. 59-60, 63, 67, and especially, Gilles Deleuze, "Zola et la fêlure," *Logique du sens* (Paris: 10/18, 1969), pp. 424-36. According to Deleuze, "what is designated by the crack [*fêlure*], or rather what this void is, is Death: the Death instinct" (p. 429).

    36. Borie, *Zola*, p. 43; cf. idem, *Le Tyran timide* (Paris: Klincksieck, 1973), p. 71: "Zola's landscapes are in fact connected to the origin myth of which they are a reflection."

    37. Girard, *Violence*, p. 307. Cf. Auguste Dezalay, "Ordre et désordre dans les *Rougon-Macquart:* L'Exemple de *La Fortune des Rougon*," *Travaux de linguistique et de littérature* 11 (1973): 71-81. Dezalay emphasizes the Roman aspects of Plassans's topography; however, he does take note of certain Greek elements also present in the novel (pp. 77-79). Our "archeologies" are in no way incompatible: I have simply "unearthed" a Greek base underlying the surface Roman superstructure (one enters the town through the *porte de Rome*, the Roman gate).

    38. Some time after having written this sentence, I read in Serres: "The entire cycle proceeds from these open and emptied tombs" (*Feux et signaux*, p. 327). Thus, following independent trajectories, our readings converge on the Aire Saint-Mittre, but — and for this very reason the point must be stressed — the difference between my singular ("tomb"/"stone") and Serres's plural ("tombs") is more than diacritical; it is critical.

    39. "Dans la vie de terreur qu'il menait, sa pensée délirait et montait jusqu'à l'extase du génie; la maladie en quelque sorte morale, la névrose dont tout son être était secoué, développait en lui un sens artistique d'une lucidité étrange; depuis qu'il avait tué, sa chair s'était comme allégée, son cerveau éperdu lui semblait immense, et, dans ce brusque agrandissement de sa pensée, il voyait passer des créations exquises, des rêveries de poète" (Mitt *OC*, 1: 629).

    40. Note that in *Thérèse Raquin*, the murderers and the crowd are only juxtaposed; the sacrifice is collective only by metonymy.

    41. "Il y a des années et des années... Le Paradou appartenait à un riche seigneur qui vint s'y enfermer avec une dame très belle.... — Quand le seigneur s'en alla, il avait les cheveux blancs. Il fit barricader toutes les ouvertures, pour qu'on n'allât pas déranger la dame... La dame était morte dans cette chambre" (*R-M*, 1: 1355).

    42. "Il avait sur lui une jeune femme, en chapeau rose, dont le châle glissait, découvrant une guimpe plissée à petits plis. Au-dessus de la gorge, dans la guimpe, deux balles étaient entrées; et, lorsqu'il repoussa doucement la jeune femme, pour dégager ses jambes, deux filets de sang coulèrent des trous sur ses mains. Alors il se releva d'un bond, il s'en alla, fou, sans chapeau, les mains humides. Jusqu'au soir, il rôda, la tête perdue, voyant toujours la jeune femme, en travers sur ses jambes, avec sa face toute pâle, ses grands yeux bleus ouverts, ses lèvres souffrantes, son étonnement d'être morte, là, si vite. Il était timide; à trente ans, il n'osait regarder en face les visages de femme, et il avait celui-là, pour la vie, dans sa mémoire et dans son coeur" (*R-M*, 1: 610-11).

    43. "The barrel of the weapon struck Rengade violently in the face and put out his right eye. Blood flowed and gore spurted onto Silvère's hands" ("Le canon de l'arme alla frapper violemment Rengade au visage et lui creva l'oeil droit. Le sang coula, des éclaboussures jaillirent sur les main de Silvère" [ibid., p. 156]).

    44. The composite figure one arrives at if one assembles all these characters is a character who, having encountered failure in one place — "ailleurs" (elsewhere) — moves to a new community to begin anew the search for fame and fortune. Gervaise, Faujas, and

Etienne are all, like Florent, fugitives, fleeing their respective authority figures: Gervaise, her father who beats her (*R-M*, 2: 388-89); Faujas, his hierarchical superior, with whom he does not get along (1: 904); Etienne, the foreman whom he slaps (3: 1135, 1170). The stranger's quest is always conquest—conquest of independence first and of power second.

45. "Les deux femmes, ayant habité la même maison, rue Pirouette, étaient des amies intimes, très liées par une pointe de rivalité qui les faisait s'occuper l'une de l'autre, continuellement. Dans le quartier, on disait la belle Normande, comme on disait la belle Lisa. Cela les opposait, les comparait, les forçait à soutenir chacune sa renommée de beauté. En se penchant un peu, la charcutière, de son comptoir, apercevait dans le pavillon, en face, la poissonnière, au milieu de ses saumons et de ses turbots" (*R-M*, 1: 674).

46. "La rivalité de la belle Lisa et de la belle Normande devint alors formidable. La belle Normande était persuadée qu'elle avait enlevé un amant à son ennemie, et la belle Lisa se sentait furieuse contre cette pas grand-chose qui finirait par les compromettre, en attirant ce sournois de Florent chez elle" (*R-M*, 1: 740).

"Mais la véritable victime des deux femmes était Florent. Au fond, lui seul les avait mises sur ce pied de guerre, elles ne se battaient que pour lui" (p. 743).

47. "Et vous, donc! vous êtes un Maigre surprenant, le roi des Maigres, ma parole d'honneur....En principe, vous entendez, un Gras a l'horreur d'un Maigre, si bien qu'il éprouve le besoin de l'ôter de sa vue, à coups de dents, ou à coups de pieds. C'est pourquoi, à votre place, je prendrais mes précautions. Les Quenu sont des Gras, les Méhudin sont des Gras, enfin vous n'avez que des Gras autour de vous. Moi, ça m'inquiéterait" (*R-M*, 1: 805).

48. Charles Baudelaire, "Abel and Cain," trans. Kenneth O. Hanson in *The Flowers of Evil*, selected and ed. Mathiel Mathews and Jackson Mathews (London: Routledge & Kegan Paul, 1955), pp. 168-69.

49. "Au cri de la victime, je vis les créatures se disperser sous le vent de l'effroi....

"Alors passa devant moi l'éternelle fuite. L'épervier fondit sur l'hirondelle, l'hirondelle dans son vol saisit le moucheron, le moucheron se posa sur le cadavre. Depuis le ver jusqu'au lion, tous les êtres se sentirent menacés. Le monde se mordit la queue et se dévora éternellement" (Mitt *OC*, 9: 70).

"Cette nuit-là, Denise ne dormit guère. Une insomnie, traversée de cauchemars, la retournait sous la couverture. Il lui semblait qu'elle était toute petite, et elle éclatait en larmes, au fond de leur jardin de Valognes, en voyant les fauvettes manger les araignées, qui elles-mêmes mangeaient les mouches. Etait-ce donc vrai, cette nécessité de la mort engraissant le monde, cette lutte pour la vie qui faisait pousser les êtres sur le charnier de l'éternelle destruction?...Oui, c'était la part du sang, toute révolution voulait des martyrs, on ne marchait en avant que sur des morts" (*R-M*, 3: 747-48).

50. "La douceur enfantine du lit était toute tachée d'un paquet d'écharpes rouges qui pendaient jusqu'à terre. Sur la cheminée, entre les boîtes dorées et les vieux pots de pommade, des brassards rouges traînaient, avec des paquets de cocardes qui faisaient d'énormes gouttes de sang élargies....Lisa fit le tour, examina les guidons, les brassards, les écharpes, sans toucher à rien, comme si elle eût craint que ces affreuses loques ne l'eussent brûlée" (*R-M*, 1: 860-61).

51. Serres, *Feux et signaux*, p. 116. Cf. Michel Butor, "Emile Zola, romancier expérimental, et la flamme bleue," *Critique* 239 (1967): 407-37; F. W. J. Hemmings, "Fire in Zola's Fiction: Variations on an Elemental Theme," *Yale French Studies* 42 (1969): 26-37.

52. Serres, *Feux et signaux*, p. 118.

53. "Au Corps législatif, l'émotion fut si grande, que le centre et la droite oublièrent cette malencontreuse loi de dotation qui les avait un instant divisés, et se réconcilièrent, en votant à une majorité écrasante le projet d'impôt impopulaire, dont les faubourgs eux-mêmes n'osaient plus se plaindre, dans la panique qui soufflait sur la ville" (*R-M*, 1: 892).

54. "Et me permettez-vous d'être franc? Eh bien! si je vous aime, vous, c'est que vous

m'avez l'air de faire de la politique absolument comme je fais de la peinture. Vous vous chatouillez, mon cher.

"Et comme l'autre protestait: —Laissez donc! vous êtes un artiste dans votre genre, vous rêvez politique....Enfin, vous vous chatouillez avec vos idées de justice et de vérité. Cela est si vrai que vos idées, de même que mes ébauches, font une peur atroce aux bourgeois" (*R-M*, 1: 849).

55. "Puis, les livres ne lui parlaient que de révolte, le poussaient à l'orgueil, et c'était d'oubli et de paix dont il sentait l'impérieux besoin. Se bercer, s'endormir, rêver qu'il était parfaitement heureux, que le monde allait le devenir...il arrangeait des mesures morales, des projets de loi humanitaires, qui auraient changé cette ville souffrante en une ville de béatitude" (*R-M*, 1: 644-45).

"...elle n'était qu'une Macquart rangée, raisonnable, logique avec ses besoins de bien-être, ayant compris que la meilleure façon de s'endormir dans une tiédeur heureuse est encore de se faire soi-même un lit de béatitude" (p. 648).

56. "Il lui semblait que son frère Quenu rapetissait, qu'ils se trouvaient encore tous les deux dans la grande chambre de la rue Royer-Collard. Sa joie, son rêve secret de dévouement, était de vivre toujours en compagnie d'un être jeune, qui ne grandirait pas, qu'il instruirait sans cesse, dans l'innocence duquel il aimerait les hommes" (*R-M*, 1: 725).

57. In *Zola before the "Rougon-Macquart"* (Toronto: University of Toronto Press, 1964), John Lapp writes: "Despite the preponderance of female heroines in the *contes*, the chief characters in three of the stories are males whose relationship was to remain of lasting importance in Zola's works. The central figure is in each case the object of wonder and admiration of a smaller, weaker man" (p. 21). See also pp. 22 and 138.

58. Sigmund Freud, *The Standard Edition of the Complete Psychological Works of Sigmund Freud*, ed. James Strachey and trans. James Strachey, Anna Freud, Alix Strachey, and Alan Tyson, 24 vols. (London: Hogarth Press, 1953-74), 18: 232.

59. Freud, *Standard Edition*, 13: 144.

60. "Pour un statut sémiologique du personnage," *Littérature* 6 (1972): 105.

Chapter 2

1. Gérard Genette, *Figures III* (Paris: Seuil, 1972), pp. 122-44.

2. With reference to the *Ebauche* of *Nana*, Mitterand writes: "The four stages of this career match the four stages of Eugène Rougon's...with one discrepancy: Rougon falls at the beginning of the novel bearing his name, and at the end sets out again for new triumphs; Nana's 'star' 'rises' at the outset of her story, and the novel ends with her final disappearance. If *Son Excellence Eugène Rougon* is a novel open at both ends, *Nana* is closed, at least in its conclusion" (Mitterand, *R-M*, 2: 1665).

3. Gustave Flaubert, *Oeuvres*, 2 vols. (Paris: Pléiade, 1963-66), 2: 449.

4. This is a paraphrase of Philippe Hamon, "Pour un statut sémiologique du personnage," in *Poétique du récit* (Paris: Seuil, Points, 1977), p. 140. Cf. A.-J. Greimas, *Sémantique structurale* (Paris: Larousse, 1966); idem, *Du sens* (Paris: Seuil, 1970); idem, "Les Actants, les acteurs et les figures," in *Sémiotique narrative et textuelle*, ed. Claude Chabrol (Paris: Larousse, 1973), pp. 161-76; and idem, *Maupassant: La sémiotique du texte* (Paris: Seuil, 1976).

5. "Cependant le *passage* du prêtre, au milieu du salon, avait causé un étonnement. Une jeune femme, ayant levé brusquement la tête, eut même un geste contenu de terreur, en apercevant cette masse noire devant elle. L'impression fut défavorable: il était *trop grand*, trop carré des épaules; il avait la face trop dure, les mains trop grosses. Sous la lumière crue du lustre, sa *soutane* apparut *si lamentable*, que les dames eurent une sorte de honte, à voir un abbé si mal vêtu. Elles ramenèrent leurs éventails, elles se remirent à chuchoter, en affectant

de tourner le dos. Les hommes avaient échangé des coups d'oeil, avec une moue significative" (*R-M*, 1: 949).

"...au moment où la belle société de Plassans s'écrasait dans le salon vert des Rougon, l'abbé Faujas *parut* sur le seuil. Il était *superbe*, grand, rose, vêtu d'*une soutane fine* qui luisait comme un satin....Autour de lui, c'était une ovation flatteuse, un chuchotement de femmes ravies....Le maire, le juge de paix, jusqu'à M. de Bourdeu, lui donnèrent des poignées de main vigoureuses" (pp. 1020-21). Emphasis added.

6. "Serge raconta à son tour que plusieurs fois, en rentrant du collège, il avait accompagné de loin l'abbé Faujas, qui revenait de Saint-Saturnin. Il traversait les rues sans parler à personne; il semblait ne pas connaître âme qui vive, et avoir quelque honte de la sourde moquerie qu'il sentait autour de lui" (*R-M*, 1: 921).

"Au bout du cours Sauvaire, lorsque Mouret passa devant le cercle de la Jeunesse, il retrouva les rires étouffés qui l'accompagnaient depuis qu'il avait mis les pieds dans la rue" (p. 1120).

7. "Imaginez-vous qu'à tort ou à raison je passe pour un républicain....Eh bien! j'ai là, à droite, chez les Rastoil, la fine fleur de la légitimité, et là, à gauche, chez le sous-préfet, les gros bonnets de l'Empire. Hein! est-ce assez drôle? mon pauvre vieux jardin si tranquille, mon petit coin de bonheur, entre ces deux camps ennemis. J'ai toujours peur qu'ils ne se jettent des pierres par-dessus mes murs... Vous comprenez, leurs pierres pourraient tomber dans mon jardin" (*R-M*, 1: 933).

8. The use of insane asylums as alternate prisons for the politically undesirable is not a recent invention, nor the exclusive product of totalitarian regimes. In *La Politique de la folie* (Paris: Stock, 1974), Bernard Cuau and Denise Zigante reprint documents showing that in nineteenth-century France the legislation setting up insane asylums, promulgated in 1838 and 1874, coincided with periods of political unrest and repression; 1874 is the date of publication of *La Conquête de Plassans*.

9. "Mais, au moment où elle allait descendre, le fou, qu'elle n'avait pas vu, sauta sur l'abbé Faujas, qu'il lui arracha des épaules. Sa plainte lugubre s'achevait dans un hurlement tandis qu'une crise le tordait au bord de l'escalier. Il meurtrissait le prêtre, l'égratignait, l'étranglait.

"—Marthe! Marthe! cria-t-il.

"Et il roula avec le corps le long des marches embrasées; pendant que Mme Faujas, qui lui avait enfoncé les dents en pleine gorge, buvait son sang" (*R-M*, 1: 1200).

10. If the imperatives of historical accuracy dictated the leader/victim disjunction, the same constraints do not apply to Zola's remarkable and revealing choice of a crime equivalent to treason: the homosexual rape and murder of a young boy by an assailant entering through the window of the boy's room. Much could be written about this transcoding of a political crime into a sexual one, as well as about the thematic reinvestment of Zola's obsessive locus, the window. See my article "Zola: From Window to Window," *Yale French Studies* 42 (1969): 38-51.

11. "Aussi cette foule, nourrie des contes du *Petit Beaumontais*, encore secouée par l'horreur du crime, poussa-t-elle des cris, dès qu'elle aperçut l'instituteur, le juif maudit, le tueur de petits enfants, qui avait besoin pour ses maléfices de leur sang vierge, encore sanctifié par l'hostie" (Mitt *OC*, 8: 1063).

12. "Tout ce que ses concitoyens lui jetaient de salissant et d'amer, il le rendait en douceur, en bonté, en sacrifice. Il s'efforçait tendrement de faire les enfants meilleurs que les pères, il ensemençait l'exécrable présent de l'heureux avenir, rachetant le crime des autres au prix de son propre bonheur" (Mitt *OC*, 8: 1184).

13. "Cependant, Marc ayant marché à la rencontre de Simon et de David, que Delbos avait rejoints, les quatre hommes se trouvèrent un instant ensemble, au seuil même de la maison. Et ce fut alors un redoublement de passion heureuse, un véritable délire de cris et de gestes, à les voir tous les quatre ainsi côte à côte, aux bras les uns des autres, les trois

défenseurs héroïques et l'innocent qu'ils avaient sauvé des pires tortures. "D'un grand élan, Simon se jeta au cou de Marc, qui lui rendit son étreinte. Tous les deux sanglotaient" (Mitt *OC,* 8: 1463).

14. "Ces gens-là, c'était la France, la grande foule pesante, inerte, beaucoup de braves gens sans doute, mais une masse de plomb qui clouait la nation au sol, incapable de vie meilleure, incapable d'être libre, juste, heureuse, puisqu'elle était ignorante et empoisonnée" (Mitt *OC,* 8: 1054).

"Et il avait voulu cela, c'était son oeuvre qui s'accomplissait, la délivrance d'un peuple par l'école primaire, tous les citoyens tirés de l'iniquité où ils croupissaient, en stupide troupeau, devenus enfin capables de vérité et et de justice" (p. 1449).

15. Victor Brombert, *The Intellectual Hero* (Chicago: University of Chicago Press, Phoenix Books, 1964), pp. 72-73.

16. Victor Hugo, *Les Misérables,* trans. Isabel F. Hapgood (London: Walter Scott Publishing Co, 1908), p. 168. Emphasis added.

17. Jean Borie, *Zola et les mythes* (Paris: Seuil, 1971), pp. 224-25.

18. "Il y a, au-dessus des foules, je ne sais quelle angoisse, quelle immense tristesse, comme s'il se dégageait de la multitude un souffle de terreur et de pitié. Jamais je ne me suis trouvé dans un grand rassemblement de peuple sans éprouver un vague malaise. Il me semble qu'un épouvantable malheur menace ces hommes réunis, qu'un seul éclair va suffire, dans l'exaltation de leurs gestes et de leurs voix, pour les frapper d'immobilité, d'éternel silence" (*Contes à Ninon,* in Mitt *OC,* 9: 57).

19. Edouard Toulouse, *Emile Zola: Enquête médico-psychologique sur les rapports de la supériorité intellectuelle avec la névropathie* (Paris: Société d'éditions scientifiques, 1896), pp. 165-66.

20. "Peu à peu, je ralentis le pas, regardant cette joie qui me navrait. Au pied d'un arbre, en plein dans la lumière jaune des lampions, se tenait debout un vieux mendiant, le corps roidi, horriblement tordu par la paralysie. . . . Les jeunes filles, fraîches et rougissantes, passaient en riant devant ce hideux spectacle" (Mitt *OC,* 9: 57).

21. "Un singulier phénomène moral s'était produit là, cette sorte d'action lente d'un maître sur un disciple d'abord révolté, ramené et absorbé ensuite. Certes, chez Mignot, personne autrefois n'aurait soupçonné l'étoffe du héros qu'il devenait aujourd'hui. Il s'était montré très louche dans l'affaire, chargeant Simon, songeant surtout à ne pas se compromettre. . . . Et Marc était venu, et dans la tragique histoire, il s'était trouvé l'homme, l'intelligence et la volonté, qui devaient décider de cette conscience, l'embellir, la hausser à la vérité et à la justice. Ainsi la leçon éclatait, lumineuse, certaine: il suffisait de l'exemple, de l'enseignement d'un héros, pour faire lever d'autres héros, du sein obscur et vague de la foule moyenne" (Mitt *OC,* 8: 1271-72).

22. Sigmund Freud, *The Standard Edition of the Complete Psychological Works of Sigmund Freud,* ed. James Strachey and trans. James Strachey, Anna Freud, Alix Strachey, and Alan Tyson, 24 vols. (London: Hogarth Press, 1953-74), 18: 115.

23. Ibid., p. 113.

24. Ibid., p. 134.

25. "Mon sujet était l'action et la réaction réciproque de l'individu et la foule, l'un sur l'autre" (Zola, *Correspondance: 1872-1902,* p. 636, in Lebl *OC*).

26. Etienne, it will be recalled, emerges white-haired from his entrapment in the flooded mine: "When they brought Etienne up at last. . . he was a skeleton with hair as white as snow" (*G,* p. 487; "Lorsqu'on le sortit enfin. . . Etienne apparut décharné, les cheveux tout blancs" [*R-M,* 3: 1580]). According to Vladimir Propp's terminology, set forth in *Morphologie du conte* (Paris: Seuil, Points, 1970), Etienne's white hair is the "mark" (p. 65) which the hero receives during his trial ("épreuve").

27. "Alors, Etienne se tint un instant immobile sur le tronc d'arbre. La lune, trop basse

encore à l'horizon, n'éclairait toujours que les branches hautes; et la foule restait noyée de ténèbres, peu à peu calmée, silencieuse. Lui, noir également, faisait au-dessus d'elle, en haut de la pente, une barre d'ombre" (*R-M,* 3: 1377).

28. "Ce furent des satisfactions d'amour-propre délicieuses, il se grisa de ces premières jouissances de la popularité: être à la tête des autres, commander, lui si jeune et qui la veille encore était un manoeuvre, l'emplissait d'orgueil, agrandissait son rêve d'une révolution prochaine où il jouerait un rôle" (*R-M,* 3: 1281).

29. Jean-Pierre Vernant, "Ambiguïté et renversement: Sur la structure énigmatique d'*Oedipe-Roi,"* in Jean-Pierre Vernant and Pierre Vidal-Naquet, *Mythe et tragédie en Grèce ancienne* (Paris: Maspéro, 1972), p. 126.

30. Peter Hambly, "La Pensée socialiste dans les *Rougon-Macquart"* (thèse de Doctorat d'Université, Paris, 1960), p. 78.

31. Aimé Guedj, "Les Révolutionnaires de Zola," *Cahiers naturalistes* 36 (1968): 135. Emphasis added.

32. Claude Bremond, *Logique du récit* (Paris: Seuil, 1968), p. 249.

33. Ibid., p. 263.

34. "Il se souvenait d'avoir, sous les hêtres, entendu trois mille poitrines battre à l'écho de la sienne. Ce jour-là, il avait tenu sa popularité dans ses deux mains, ce peuple lui appartenait, il s'en était senti le maître. Des rêves fous le grisaient alors. . . . Et c'était fini! il s'éveillait misérable et détesté, son peuple venait de le reconduire à coups de briques" (*R-M,* 3: 1520-21).

35. "Le soir, Luc s'enferma, voulut être seul dans le pavillon qu'il habitait toujours. . . . Pendant ses rares heures de défaillance, il préférait s'enfermer étroitement, il buvait sa souffrance jusqu'à la lie, pour ne reparaître que guéri et vaillant. Et il avait donc verrouillé portes et fenêtres, en donnant l'ordre absolu de ne laisser entrer personne" (Mitt *OC,* 8: 729-30).

36. "Un dimanche, comme il mettait le pied hors de chez lui, il aperçut, sur le trottoir de la rue Balande, Rose, qui causait vivement avec la bonne de M. Rastoil. Les deux cuisinières se turent en le voyant. . . . Lorsqu'il fut arrivé à la place de la Sous-Préfecture, il tourna la tête, il les retrouva plantées à la même place. . . .

" . . . Derrière lui, il laissait toute une agitation; des groupes se formaient, des bruits de voix s'élevaient, mêlés de ricanements. . . .

" . . . Arrivé au marché, il hésita un moment, puis s'engagea résolument au milieu des marchandes de légumes. Mais là sa vue produisit une véritable révolution" (*R-M,* 1: 1116-17).

37. "'Je marche trop vite, elles se moquent de moi,' pensa Mouret" (*R-M,* 1: 1116).

"Lui, hâtait toujours le pas, cherchant à se dégager, ne pouvant croire décidément qu'il était la cause de ce vacarme" (p. 1117).

Il lui semblait que les boutiquiers de la rue de la Banne, les femmes du marché, les promeneurs du cours, les jeunes messieurs du cercle, les Rougon, les Condamin, tout Plassans, avec ses rires étouffés, roulaient derrière son dos, le long de la pente raide de la rue" (p. 1121).

38. Sophocles, *Sophocles,* vol. 1, *Oedipus the King,* trans. David Greene (Chicago: University of Chicago Press, 1954), p. 53.

39. The complete text of "Histoire d'un fou" is reprinted in the notes to *La Conquête de Plassans* (*R-M,* 1: 1641-44).

40. "Histoire d'un fou" is situated midway between *Thérèse Raquin,* in which the lovers do murder the husband, and *La Conquête,* in which the couple that stands to gain the most by Mouret's internment, Marthe Mouret and Abbot Faujas, are not lovers and do not act in concert. If "Histoire d'un fou" is linked to *Thérèse Raquin* by the triangular configuration of the characters, the mode of disposal of the unwanted third party calls to mind another Zola

short story, "La Mort d'Olivier Bécaille." The sane man interned is a variant of the live man buried.

41. "On s'est beaucoup occupé des aliénés ces derniers temps. Il y aurait eu, paraît-il, d'audacieuses séquestrations; des hommes sains d'esprit se seraient vu garrotter et jeter dans les cabanons pour avoir commis le seul crime de gêner certaines personnes. Je crois qu'une enquête a été provoquée. Dieu me garde de fouiller ces infamies; mais je crois pouvoir raconter sans danger l'histoire d'un fou, que les préoccupations présentes viennent de réveiller dans ma mémoire" (*R-M*, 1: 1641).

42. Zola, *Correspondance: 1872-1902*, p. 637, in Lebl *OC*.

43. David Shapiro, *Neurotic Styles* (New York: Basic Books, Harper Torchbooks, 1965).

44. Freud, "Preface to Reik's *Ritual: Psycho-Analytic Studies*," *Standard Edition*, 17: 260-61.

45. Sarah Kofman, *L'Enfance de l'art* (Paris: Payot, 1970), p. 195.

46. Freud, "Construction in Analysis," *Standard Edition*, 23: 268. In my article on Salvador Dali's "paranoia-criticism" ("Dali's Freud," *Dada/Surrealism*, no. 6 [1976], pp. 10-17) I attempt to deal with one of Freud's celebrated paranoiac-critical constructions (in *Leonardo da Vinci and a Memory of his Childhood*).

47. "Les deux cuisinières se turent en le voyant. Elles l'examinaient d'un air tellement singulier, qu'il s'assura si un bout de son mouchoir ne pendait pas d'une de ses poches de derrière" (*R-M*, 1: 1116).

"Mouret, intimidé, n'osait plus se retourner; il était pris d'une vague inquiétude, tout en ne comprenant pas nettement qu'on parlait de lui. Il marcha plus vite, fit aller ses bras d'un air aisé. Il regretta d'avoir mis sa vieille redingote noisette, qui n'était plus à la mode" (p. 1117).

"Il ôta son chapeau, le regarda, craignant que quelque gamin ne lui eût jeté une poignée de plâtre; il n'avait non plus ni cerf-volant ni queue de rat pendu dans le dos" (p. 1118).

48. "Un ancien chapelier du faubourg, qui avait examiné Mouret depuis son noeud de cravate jusqu'au dernier bouton de sa redingote, s'était finalement absorbé dans le spectacle de ses souliers. Le lacet du soulier gauche se trouvait dénoué, ce qui paraissait exorbitant au chapelier; il poussait du coude ses voisins, leur montrant, d'un clignement d'yeux, ce lacet dont les bouts pendaient. Bientôt tout le banc n'eut plus de regards que pour le lacet. Ce fut le comble. Ces messieurs haussèrent les épaules, de façon à montrer qu'ils ne gardaient plus le moindre espoir" (*R-M*, 1: 1120).

49. Marie Henri Beyle [Stendhal], *The Red and the Black*, trans. C. K. Scott-Moncrieff (New York: Modern Library, 1929), p. 231.

50. A term I have proposed to describe a character who interprets, in an essay entitled "Fiction as Interpretation / Interpretation as Fiction," to appear in *The Reader in Fiction*, ed. Inge Crossman and Susan Suleiman (Princeton: Princeton University Press, forthcoming).

51. Freud, *The Interpretation of Dreams*, in the *Standard Edition*, 4: 345. Subsequent references to the *Interpretation of Dreams* will be included in the text.

52. In his article "The Purveyor of Truth," trans. Willis Domingo et al., *Yale French Studies* 52 (1975): 31-113, Jacques Derrida comments extensively on precisely this category of dreams; see in particular pp. 34-39. The perspective or context is, of course, quite different, but Derrida's analysis is pertinent to my reading of Zola's reworking of this dream material.

53. "Et voilà comme quoi une troupe de gamins a rencontré un jour Edouard Manet dans la rue, et a fait autour de lui l'émeute qui m'a arrêté, moi passant curieux et désintéressé. J'ai dressé mon procès-verbal tant bien que mal, donnant tort aux gamins, tâchant d'arracher l'artiste de leurs mains et de le conduire en lieu sûr. Il y avait là des sergents de ville—pardon, des critiques d'art—qui m'ont affirmé qu'on lapidait cet homme parce qu'il avait outrageusement souillé le temple du Beau" (Mitt *OC*, 12: 845).

54. Cf. Pierre Vidal-Naquet, "Chasse et sacrifice dans l'*Orestie* d'Eschyle," in Vernant and Vidal-Naquet, *Mythe et tragédie en Grèce ancienne,* in particular p. 140, where Vidal-Naquet explains that the hunt and the "classical Olympian sacrifice" are, generally speaking, antithetical, but that occasionally this binary opposition is mediated by a sacrificial hunt: e.g., Pentheus (*The Bacchae*) is the victim of just such a hunt.

55. "Ils [les gamins] se jetèrent de côté, riant, hurlant, s'échappant *à quatre pattes.* Mouret, très rouge, se sentit ridicule. . . . Ce qui l'épouvantait, c'était de traverser la place de la Sous-Préfecture, de passer sous les fenêtres des Rougon, avec cette suite de vauriens qu'il entendait grossir et s'enhardir *derrière son dos.*

". . . Les enfants tapaient des pieds, glissaient sur les pavés pointus, faisaient un vacarme de *meute* lâchée dans le quartier tranquille" (*R-M,* 1: 1120-21).

"Bientôt, ce fut une fuite, chaque maison le huait au passage, on *s'acharnait sur ses talons* . . . . Il sortit du coron, blême, affolé, galopant, avec cette bande hurlante *derrière son dos"* (*R-M,* 3: 1519).

"Depuis la salle où les rires l'avaient souffleté, il les entendait le poursuivre comme une *meute aboyante,* là-bas au Champs-Elysées, puis le long de la Seine, puis à présent encore chez lui, *derrière son dos"* (*R-M,* 4: 140). Emphasis added.

56. "S'il tombait, la *meute* se jetterait sur lui, il serait dévoré" (Mitt *OC,* 8: 722).

"Ah! cette montée de la rue de Brias, avec cette bande grossissante d'ennemis *sur les talons.* . . . il la [la ville entière] sentait derrière cette bande qui *aboyait à ses trousses"* (pp. 727-28).

"Il sentit le galop qui se rapprochait, il fit face une dernière fois, quand il eut sur la nuque le souffle ardent de cette *meute* qui le poursuivait" (p. 729). Emphasis added.

57. "Un caillou enfin l'atteignit, lui déchira l'oreille droite, tandis qu'un autre le frappait à la main gauche, dont il coupait la paume, comme d'un coup de couteau. Et le sang coula, tomba en larges gouttes rouges" (Mitt *OC,* 8: 728-29).

58. "Il s'était fait l'apôtre de demain, d'une société de solidarité et de fraternité. . . . Il avait donné un exemple, cette Crêcherie où la Cité future était en germe, où régnait déjà le plus de justice et le plus de bonheur possible. Et cela suffisait, la ville entière le considérait comme un malfaiteur" (Mitt *OC,* 8: 727-28).

59. Victor Hugo, *La Légende des siècles* (Paris: Pléiade, 1967), pp. 524-25.

60. Ibid., p. 526.

61. Zola gives vent to these negative feelings in his article on Victor Hugo, included in *Documents littéraires* (Mitt *OC,* 12: 301-25). In what is, from my point of view, the most interesting section of this study, Zola contrasts the fates of his two literary paternal imagos: "I have often pondered the very different destinies of Balzac and Victor Hugo. . . . We know about Balzac's long obscurity, about his struggles and his death at the very moment when he was at last gaining fame and fortune. Always misunderstood, he was a fighter to the end. . . . *Balzac died lapidated and crucified,* as though he were the Messiah of the great school of naturalism. . . . As for Hugo, he has enjoyed so much glory in his lifetime, that were he to die tomorrow a forgotten man, he would have no cause for complaint" (pp. 322-23; emphasis added). As written or rewritten by Zola, the literary history of nineteenth-century France reads like the twenty-first volume of the *Rougon-Macquart.*

62. Blaise Pascal, *Pensées,* in *Oeuvre* (Paris: Pléiade, 1941), p. 862.

63. John Lapp, *Zola before the "Rougon-Macquart"* (Toronto: University of Toronto Press, 1964), p. 160.

64. See, for example, Philippe Hamon, "Zola, romancier de la transparence," *Europe* 468-69 (1968): 385-91; idem, "Du savoir dans le texte," *Revue des sciences humaines* 160 (1975): 489-99.

65. "Mon cerveau est comme un crâne de verre, je l'ai donné à tous, et je ne crains pas que tous viennent y lire" (Mitt *OC,* 12: 707).

66. "Une langue nette, quelque chose comme une maison de verre laissant voir les idées à l'intérieur" (Mitt *OC*, 11: 92).

67. According to one Genealogical Tree (1878) it occurs in 1851; according to another (1893), in 1831.

68. "Tenez! madame, ils sont là, sur la table. Donnez-les-moi, que nous en fassions un paquet, et vous les emporterez, vous emporterez tout... Oh! je vous appelais, je vous attendais! Mes papiers perdus! toute ma vie de recherches et d'effort anéantie!" (*R-M*, 5: 391).

69. "Et, dans une crise d'enragé désespoir, il ramassa les papiers épars sur le lit, il les déchira, les broya, comme s'il avait voulu anéantir tout ce travail imbécile et jalousé, qui lui avait tué son frère" (*R-M*, 5: 395).

70. This essentially Kleinian notion of art as the nexus of guilt and reparation informs such psychocritical (de)constructions as Serge Doubrovsky's *La Place de la madeleine* (Paris: Mercure de France, 1974) or Jacques Trilling's "James Joyce ou l'écriture matricide," *Etudes Freudiennes*, nos. 7-8 (1973), pp. 7-70.

71. "D'un geste large, elle montra l'armoire vide, la cheminée où se mouraient des étincelles.

"'Maintenant, c'est fini, notre gloire est sauve, ces abominables papiers ne nous accuseront plus, et je ne laisserai derrière moi aucune menace... Les Rougon triomphent'" (*R-M*, 5: 1202).

72. That is, Serres's neologism appears in the context of remarks about the circular structure of *Le Docteur Pascal*: "A text framed by two messages to be decoded" (Michel Serres, *Feux et signaux de brume: Zola* [Paris: Grasset, 1975], p. 96).

73. "Mais, pour elle, à mesure qu'elle les examinait, un intérêt se levait de ces phrases incomplètes, de ces mots à moitié mangés par le feu, où tout autre n'aurait rien compris....Et chaque débris s'animait, la famille exécrable et fraternelle renaissait de ces miettes, de ces cendres noires où ne couraient plus que des syllabes incohérentes" (*R-M*, 5: 1215).

74. Marcel Proust, *The Captive*, trans. C. K. Scott-Moncrieff (New York: Random House, 1970), p. 110.

75. Hugo, *Les Misérables*, p. 280.

76. Jacques Derrida, *Of Grammatology*, trans. Gayatri Chakravorty Spivak (Baltimore: The Johns Hopkins University Press, 1976), p. 112.

77. Ibid., p. 124.

78. Ibid., p. 125.

79. "L'enfant était venu, le rédempteur peut-être....Que serait-il, quand elle l'aurait fait grand et fort, en se donnant toute? Un savant qui enseignerait au monde un peu de la vérité éternelle, un capitaine qui apporterait de la gloire à son pays, ou mieux encore un de ces pasteurs de peuple qui apaisent les passions et font régner la justice? Elle le voyait très beau, très bon, très puissant. Et c'était le rêve de toutes les mères, la certitude d'être accouchée du messie attendu; et il y avait là, dans cet espoir, dans cette croyance obstinée de chaque mère au triomphe certain de son enfant, l'espoir même qui fait la vie" (*R-M*, 5: 1218).

80. "Du reste, Maheu coupa la parole au directeur. Maintenant, il était lancé, les mots venaient tout seuls. Par moments, il s'écoutait avec surprise, comme si un étranger avait parlé en lui. C'étaient des choses amassées au fond de sa poitrine, des choses qu'il ne savait même pas là, et qui sortaient, dans un gonflement de son coeur" (*R-M*, 3: 1320).

"L'on fut surpris d'apercevoir, debout sur le tronc, le père Bonnemort en train de parler au milieu du vacarme....Sans doute il cédait à une de ces crises soudaines de bavardage, qui, parfois, remuaient en lui le passé, si violemment, que des souvenirs remontaient et coulaient de ses lèvres, pendant des heures" (*R-M*, 3: 1382).

81. "Ce qui faisait son influence sur les ouvriers des fosses, c'était la facilité de sa parole, la bonhomie avec laquelle il pouvait leur parler pendant des heures, sans jamais se lasser. Il ne risquait aucun geste, restait lourd et souriant, les noyait, les étourdissait" (*R-M*, 3: 1346).

"Il parla. Sa voix sortait, pénible et rauque; mais il s'y était habitué, toujours en course, promenant sa laryngite avec son programme. Peu à peu, il l'enflait et en tirait des effets pathétiques. Les bras ouverts, accompagnant les périodes d'un balancement d'épaules, il avait une éloquence qui tenait du prône, une façon religieuse de laisser tomber la fin des phrases, dont le ronflement monotone finissait par convaincre" (p. 1347).

82. "Il s'agissait de compter celui qui, pendant une heure, répéterait le plus de fois la phrase de son chant.... Et les pinsons étaient partis, les 'chichouïeux' au chant plus gras, les 'batisecouics' d'une sonorité aiguë, tout d'abord timides, ne risquant que de rares phrases, puis s'excitant les uns les autres, pressant le rythme, puis emportés d'une telle rage d'émulation, qu'on en voyait tomber et mourir" (R-M, 3: 1266).

83. "On l'applaudissait, il triomphait. Son grand corps emplissait la tribune. Ses épaules, balancées, suivaient le roulis de ses phrases. Il avait l'éloquence banale, incorrecte, toute hérissée de questions de droit, enflant les lieux communs, les faisant crever en coups de foudre. Il tonnait, il brandissait des mots bêtes. Sa seule supériorité d'orateur était son haleine, une haleine immense, infatigable, berçant les périodes, coulant magnifiquement pendant des heures, sans se soucier de ce qu'elle charriait" (R-M, 2: 364).

"Peu à peu, Etienne s'échauffait. Il n'avait pas l'abondance facile et coulante de Rasseneur. Les mots lui manquaient souvent, il devait torturer sa phrase, il en sortait par un effort qu'il appuyait d'un coup d'épaule. Seulement, à ces heurts continuels, il rencontrait des images d'une énergie familière, qui empoignaient son auditoire; tandis que ses gestes d'ouvrier au chantier, ses coudes rentrés, puis détendus et lançant les poings en avant, sa mâchoire brusquement avancée, comme pour mordre, avaient eux aussi une action extraordinaire sur les camarades. Tous le disaient, il n'était pas grand, mais il se faisait écouter" (R-M, 3: 1378-79).

84. Jacques Derrida, "La Pharmacie de Platon," in La Dissémination (Paris: Seuil, 1972), p. 89.

85. "Elle ne disait pas un mot, même les auteurs lui avaient coupé une réplique, parce que ça gênait; non, rien du tout, c'était plus grand, et elle vous retournait son public, rien qu'à se montrer.... Paris la verrait toujours comme ça, allumée au milieu du cristal, en l'air, ainsi qu'un bon Dieu" (R-M, 3: 1476).

86. "Etourdi, il ne fuyait plus, il leur faisait face, cherchant à les calmer avec des phrases. Ses anciens discours, si chaudement acclamés jadis, lui remontaient aux lèvres. Il répétait les mots dont il les avait grisés, à l'époque où il les tenait dans sa main, ainsi qu'un troupeau fidèle; mais sa puissance était morte, des pierres seules lui répondait" (R-M, 3: 1520).

87. Zola, Correspondance: 1858-1871 in Lebl OC, p. 298. Emphasis added.

Chapter 3

1. "Et, dans les coups de soleil qui tombaient entre deux nuées, tout flambait brusquement, la pelouse peu à peu emplie d'une cohue d'équipages, de cavaliers et de piétons, la piste encore vide" (R-M, 2: 1376).

"En faisant le tour des rayons, il venait de les trouver vides.... Sans doute, onze heures sonnaient à peine; il savait par expérience que la foule n'arrivait guère que l'aprèsmidi" (R-M, 3: 477).

"Mais la peur qu'il gardait du public fameux de cette solennité, lui fit ramener ses regards sur la foule peu à peu grossie.... Des espaces restaient vides" (R-M, 4: 283).

2. "Cependant, la pelouse s'emplissait.... on n'entendait plus que le brouhaha de la foule croissante, des cris, des appels, des claquements de fouet, envolés dans le plein air" (R-M, 2: 1379).

"C'était enfin la poussée attendue, l'écrasement de l'après-midi....Et il ne se trompait plus aux bruits qui lui arrivaient du dehors, roulements de fiacres, claquement des portières, brouhaha grandissant de la foule" (R-M, 3: 482).

"Et, quand il retomba dans le salon d'honneur, la cohue y avait grandi rapidement, on commençait à y marcher avec peine" (R-M, 4: 283).

3. "Cependant, ce coup de pluie avait brusquement empli les tribunes. Nana regardait avec sa jumelle. A cette distance, on distinguait seulement une masse compacte et brouillée, entassée sur les gradins" (R-M, 2: 1386).

"Ce n'était plus chose facile que de gagner l'escalier. Une houle compacte de têtes roulait sous les galeries" (R-M, 3: 491).

"Après d'autres courses lointaines, il retomba pour la troisième fois dans le salon d'honneur. On s'y écrasait maintenant. Le Paris célèbre...les hommes de cercle...les femmes de tous les rangs...montaient en une houle accrue sans cesse" (R-M, 4: 284-85).

4. Elias Canetti, Crowds and Power, trans. Carol Stewart (New York: Viking Press, Compass Books, 1966), p. 17.

5. See John Lapp, Zola before the "Rougon-Macquart" (Toronto: University of Toronto Press, 1964), pp. 73, 84-86, 118, and 152.

6. "C'était l'heure où la cohue, fouettée de réclames, achevait de se détraquer....Cette fièvre, depuis le matin, avait grandi peu à peu, comme la griserie même qui se dégageait des étoffes remuées....Maintenant, Mme Marty avait la face animée et nerveuse d'une enfant qui a bu du vin pur" (R-M, 3: 643-44).

"C'était l'étouffement embrasé de cinq heures, lorsque la cohue, épuisée de tourner le long des salles, saisie du vertige des troupeaux lâchés dans un parc, s'effare et s'écrase, sans trouver la sortie....Et il n'y avait plus, flagellant ces milliers de têtes, que ce dernier coup de la fatigue qui délabrait les jambes, tirait la face, ravageait le front de migraine" (R-M, 4: 306-7). Emphasis added.

7. Sigmund Freud, The Standard Edition of the Complete Psychological Works of Sigmund Freud, ed. James Strachey and trans. James Strachey, Anna Freud, Alix Strachey, and Alan Tyson, 24 vols. (London: Hogarth Press, 1953-74), 18: 15.

8. Jacques Lacan, Ecrits (Paris: Seuil, 1966), p. 575.

9. Canetti, Crowds, pp. 63-64.

10. Charles Baudelaire, Oeuvres complètes (Paris: Pléiade, 1961), pp. 247-49. As the Baudelaire prose poem was published in 1861, and "Celle qui m'aime" was written sometime between 1862 and 1864, it is quite probable that Zola had read the Baudelaire text. This possible direct influence makes the marked differences between text and intertext all the more significant. For a structural analysis of Zola's conte, see André Bellatorre, "Analyse d'un conte de Zola: 'Celle qui m'aime,'" Cahiers naturalistes 47 (1974): 88-97.

11. "Je laissai retomber le rideau et me trouvai dans le temple. C'était une sorte de chambre longue et étroite, sans aucun siège, aux murs de toile, éclairée par un seul quinquet. Quelques personnes, des filles curieuses, des garçons faisant tapage, s'y trouvaient déjà réunies. Tout se passait d'ailleurs avec la plus grande décence: une corde, tendue au milieu de la pièce, séparait les hommes des femmes.

"Le Miroir d'amour, à vrai dire, n'était autre chose que deux glaces sans tain, une dans chaque compartiment, petites vitres rondes donnant sur l'intérieur de la baraque" (Mitt OC, 9: 54).

12. "Ainsi les curieux se succédaient devant la vitre....O vision de la bien-aimée! quelles rudes vérités tu faisais dire à ces yeux grands ouverts! Ils étaient les vrais Miroirs d'amour, Miroirs où la grâce de la femme se reflétait en une lueur louche où la luxure s'étalait dans la bêtise.

"Les filles, à l'autre carreau, s'égayaient d'une plus honnête façon. Je ne lisais que beaucoup de curiosité sur leurs visages; pas le moindre vilain désir, pas la plus petite méchante pensée" (ibid., p. 55).

13. "En bas, dans le grand vestibule dallé de marbre, où était installé le contrôle, le public commençait à se montrer.....Des roulements de voiture s'arrêtaient court, des portières se refermaient bruyamment, et du monde entrait, par petits groupes, stationnant devant le contrôle, montant, au fond, le double escalier, où les femmes s'attardaient avec un balancement de taille. Dans la clarté crue du gaz, sur la nudité blafarde de cette salle dont une maigre décoration Empire faisait un péristyle de temple en carton, de hautes affiches jaunes s'étalaient violemment, avec le nom de Nana en grosses lettres noires. Des messieurs, comme accrochés au passage, les lisaient; d'autres, debout, causaient, barrant les portes" (R-M, 2: 1096-97).

14. Edouard Toulouse, *Emile Zola: Enquête médico-psychologique sur les rapports de la supériorité intellectuelle avec la névropathie* (Paris: Société d'éditions scientifiques, 1896), p. 241.

15. "Un tapage de voix montait, dans lequel le nom de Nana sonnait avec la vivacité chantante de ses deux syllabes. Les hommes qui se plantaient devant les affiches, l'épelaient à voix haute...tandis que les femmes, inquiètes et souriantes, le répétaient doucement, d'un air de surprise" (R-M, 2: 1100).

16. "C'étaient des signes d'appel, des froissements d'étoffe, un défilé de jupes et de coiffures, coupées par le noir d'un habit ou d'une redingote. Pourtant, les rangées de fauteuils s'emplissaient peu à peu; une toilette claire se détachait, une tête au fin profil baissait son chignon, où courait l'éclair du bijou. Dans une loge, un coin d'épaule nue avait une blancheur de soie. D'autres femmes, tranquilles, s'éventaient avec langueur, en suivant du regard les poussées de la foule; pendant que des jeunes messieurs, debout à l'orchestre, le gilet largement ouvert, un gardénia à la boutonnière, braquaient leurs jumelles du bout de leurs doigts gantés" (R-M, 2: 1102-3).

17. I use the term "male bonding" as in Lionel Tiger, *Men in Groups* (New York: Random House, Vintage Books, 1970). With reference to female bonding, Tiger remarks: "In a subsequent publication it will be suggested that all-female groups differ structurally from all-male groups, are generally less stable over time, and considerably less common for a variety of reasons. A serious deficiency of the present project is its relative inattention to the phenomenon of female aggregation" (p. xiii, n. 2).

18. See Nancy Miller, "Gender and Genre" (Ph.D. diss., Columbia University, 1974), in particular chap. 3.

19. "Un instant, elle fut intéressée par un jeune homme, aux cheveux courts et bouclés, le visage insolent, tenant en haleine, pendue à ses moindres caprices, toute une table de filles, qui crevaient de graisse. Mais, comme le jeune homme riait, sa poitrine se gonfla. —Tiens, c'est une femme! laissa-t-elle échapper dans un léger cri" (R-M, 2: 1301).

20. "—Jamais il ne séchera, il va s'enrhumer, dit Nana, en voyant Georges pris d'un frisson.

"Et pas un pantalon d'homme! Elle était sur le point de rappeler le jardinier, lorsqu'elle eut une idée. Zoé, qui défaisait les malles dans le cabinet de toilette, apportait à madame du linge pour se changer, une chemise, des jupons, un peignoir.

"—Mais c'est parfait! cria la jeune femme, Zizi peut mettre tout ça. Hein? tu n'es pas dégoûté de moi... Quand tes vêtements seront secs, tu les reprendras et tu t'en iras vite, pour ne pas être grondé par ta maman... Dépêche-toi, je vais me changer aussi dans le cabinet.

"Lorsque, dix minutes plus tard, elle reparut en robe de chambre, elle joignit les mains de ravissement.

"Oh! le mignon, qu'il est gentil en petite femme!" (R-M, 2: 1236).

21. "Et le soir, lorsque, étourdie par sa journée vécue au grand air, grise de l'odeur des feuilles, elle montait rejoindre son Zizi, caché derrière le rideau, ça lui semblait une escapade de pensionnaire en vacances, un amour avec un petit cousin qu'elle devait épouser, tremblante au moindre bruit, redoutant que ses parents ne l'entendissent, goûtant les tâtonnements délicieux et les voluptueuses épouvantes d'une première faute" (R-M, 2: 1244).

22. Cf. Marcel Proust, "La Confession d'une jeune fille," in *Les Plaisirs et les jours* (Paris: Gallimard, 1924), pp. 135-53.

23. "Je la voyais encore, —et c'est cette image qui devrait épouvanter toutes les mères, —je la voyais s'égarer dans les coins avec une élève plus grande qu'elle; elle l'appelait sa petite maman, elle se laissait prendre par la taille, baiser sur les lèvres; et toutes deux s'en allaient derrière les lilas, comme deux amoureux pâmés par les senteurs tièdes du printemps" (Zola, in *L'Atelier de Zola: Textes de journaux, 1865-1870,* ed. Martin Kanes [Geneva: Droz, 1963], pp. 220-21). Zola's fantasy should be viewed in the context of a long tradition of male polemic against convent education; cf. in particular the chapter entitled "Des pensionnats" in Honoré de Balzac, *Physiologie du mariage* (Paris: Garnier-Flammarion, 1968).

24. Gustave Flaubert, *Dictionnaire des idées reçues,* ed. Lea Caminiti (Paris: A. G. Nizet, 1966), p. 162; Pierre Larousse, *Grand Dictionnaire universel du XIXe siècle* (Paris: Larousse et Boyer, 1866-90).

25. "Quand il jouait avec elle, qu'il la tenait dans ses bras, il croyait tenir un garçon" (Mitt *OC,* 1: 531); "Lazare, dès le premier jour, l'avait acceptée comme un garçon, un frère cadet" (*R-M,* 3: 838).

26. See A. E. Carter, *The Idea of Decadence in French Literature: 1830-1900* (Toronto: University of Toronto Press, 1958).

27. Henri Mitterand, "Fonction narrative et fonction mimétique: Les Personnages de *Germinal,*" *Poétique* 16 (1973): 483.

28. Ralph Ellison, *Invisible Man* (Harmondsworth: Penguin Books, 1965), p. 337.

29. "Il fallait l'entendre. Les agents, pour avoir des gratifications, arrêtaient le plus de femmes possible; ils empoignaient tout, ils vous faisaient taire d'une gifle si l'on criait, certains d'être soutenus et récompensés, même quand ils avaient pris dans le tas une honnête fille. L'été, à douze ou quinze, ils opéraient des rafles sur le boulevard, ils cernaient un trottoir, pêchaient jusqu'à des trentes femmes en une soirée....Nana écoutait ces choses, prise de frayeurs croissantes. Elle avait toujours tremblé devant la loi, cette puissance inconnue, cette vengeance des hommes qui pouvaient la supprimer, sans que personne au monde la défendît" (*R-M,* 2: 1314-15).

30. "On servait le rôti. Les deux femmes se lancèrent dans leurs souvenirs. Ça les prenait par crises bavardes; elles avaient un brusque besoin de remuer cette boue de leur jeunesse; et c'était toujours quand il y avait des hommes, comme si elles cédaient à une rage de leur imposer le fumier où elles avaient grandi. Ces messieurs pâlissaient, avec des regards gênés" (*R-M,* 2: 1365).

31. "Il n'y avait plus une protestation. Au milieu de ces messieurs, de ces grands noms, de ces vieilles honnêtetés, les deux femmes, face à face, échangeant un regard tendre, *s'imposaient* et régnaient, avec le tranquille abus de leur sexe et leur mépris avoué de l'homme. Ils applaudirent" (*R-M,* 2: 1368). Emphasis added.

32. "Du haut en bas, on se roulait. Eh bien, ça devait être du propre, dans Paris, de neuf heures du soir à trois heures du matin; et [Nana] rigolait, elle criait que, si l'on avait pu voir dans toutes les chambres, on aurait assisté à quelque chose de drôle, le petit monde s'en donnant par-dessus les oreilles, et pas mal de grands personnages, ça et là, le nez enfoncé dans la cochonnerie plus profondément que les autres" (*R-M,* 2: 1314).

33. "Cependant, en face du fauteuil où la mère du comte était morte, un fauteuil carré, au bois raidi et à l'étoffe dure, de l'autre côté de la cheminée, la comtesse Sabine se tenait sur une chaise profonde, dont la soie rouge capitonnée avait une mollesse d'édredon. C'était le seul meuble moderne, un coin de fantaisie introduit dans cette sévérité, et qui jurait" (*R-M,* 2: 1144-45).

34. "...elle a beau être comtesse, c'est une pas grand-chose... Vous savez, j'ai l'oeil, moi. Maintenant, je la connais comme si je l'avais faite, votre comtesse... Voulez-vous parier qu'elle couche avec cette vipère de Faucherey?... Je vous dis qu'elle y couche! On sent bien ça, entre femmes" (*R-M,* 2: 1252).

35. Leyla Perrone-Moisès, "Le Récit euphémique," *Poétique* 17 (1974): 37.

36. Cf. in Toulouse, *Emile Zola,* Zola's free association with the word *virility:* "a male member" ("une verge d'homme"), which, he specifies, is a "visual image" (p. 239).

37. Roland Barthes, *S/Z,* trans. Richard Miller (New York: Farrar, Strauss, and Giroux, Hill and Wang, 1974), p. 36.

38. Mitterand, "Etude," in *R-M,* 5: 1378, 1391.

39. See Paul Lidsky, *Les Ecrivains contre la Commune* (Paris: Maspéro, 1970), pp. 63-67.

40. Tiger, *Men in Groups,* pp. 202, 241.

41. "N'était-ce point la fraternité des premiers jours du monde, l'amitié avant toute culture et toutes classes, cette amitié de deux hommes unis et confondus, dans leur commun besoin d'assistance, devant la menace de la nature ennemie?" (*R-M, 5:* 521).

"La fraternité qui avait grandi entre ce paysan et lui, allait au fond de son être, à la racine même de la vie. Cela remontait peut-être aux premiers jours du monde" (p. 663).

42. Canetti, *Crowds,* p. 68.

43. Ibid., p. 53.

44. "'J'étais montée à une fenêtre qui donne sur la rue et sur la campagne. Je ne voyais plus personne, pas un seul pantalon rouge, quand j'ai entendu des gros pas lourds; et une voix a crié quelque chose, et toutes les crosses des fusils sont tombées en même temps par terre. C'étaient, en bas, dans la rue, *des hommes noirs, petits, l'air sale, avec de grosses têtes vilaines,* coiffées de casques, pareils à ceux de nos pompiers. On m'a dit que c'étaient des Bavarois... Puis, comme je levais les yeux, j'en ai vu, oh! j'en ai vu des milliers et des milliers, qui arrivaient par les routes, par les champs, par les bois, en colonnes serrées, sans fin. Tout de suite, le pays en a été noir. *Une invasion noire, des sauterelles noires,* encore et encore, si bien qu'en un rien de temps, on n'a plus vu la terre'" (*R-M,* 5: 536). Emphasis added.

45. Tiger, *Men in Groups,* p. 213.

46. "Comme Maurice en regardait un, sur la droite, un garçon maigre et chétif, qui emportait un lourd sergent pendu à son cou, les jambes brisées, de l'air d'une fourmi laborieuse qui transporte un grain de blé trop gros, il les vit culbuter et disparaître tous les deux dans l'explosion d'un obus. Quand la fumée se fut dissipée, le sergent reparut sur le dos, sans blessure nouvelle, tandis que le brancardier gisait, le flanc ouvert. Et une autre arriva, une autre fourmi active, qui, après avoir retourné et flairé le camarade mort, reprit le blessé à son cou et l'emporta" (*R-M,* 5: 644).

47. "Un soldat s'avança, un Bavarois trapu, à l'énorme tête embroussaillée de barbe et de cheveux roux, sous lesquels on ne distinguait qu'un large nez carré et que de gros yeux bleus. Il était souillé de sang, effroyable, tel qu'un de ces ours des cavernes, une de ces bêtes poilues toutes rouges de la proie dont elles viennent de faire craquer les os" (*R-M,* 5: 639-40).

48. "Ces hommes ennemis, qui s'étaient rués les uns à la gorge des autres, gisaient maintenant côte à côte, dans la bonne entente de leurs communes souffrances" (*R-M,* 5: 803); "dans le petit cimetière de Remilly, on avait ouvert deux tranchées; et ils dormaient côte à côte, les Allemands à gauche, les Français à droite, réconciliés dans la terre" (p. 804).

49. Gérard Genette, *Figures III* (Paris: Seuil, 1972), p. 129.

50. Gilles Deleuze, *Logique du sens* (Paris: 10/18, 1969), p. 137.

51. "[Maurice] fut très surpris d'apercevoir, au fond d'un vallon écarté, protégé par des pentes rudes, un paysan qui labourait sans hâte, poussant sa charrue attelée d'un grand cheval blanc. Pourquoi perdre un jour? Ce n'était pas parce qu'on se battait, que le blé cesserait de croître et le monde de vivre" (*R-M,* 5: 598).

52. "Et la bataille atroce, souillée de sang, devenait une peinture délicate, vue de si haut, sous l'adieu du soleil: des cavaliers morts, des chevaux éventrés semaient le plateau de Floing de taches gaies; vers la droite, du côté de Givonne, les dernières bousculades de la retraite amusaient l'oeil du tourbillon de ces points noirs, courant, se culbutant; tandis que, dans la presqu'île d'Iges, à gauche, une batterie bavaroise, avec ses canons gros comme des

allumettes, avait l'air d'être une pièce mécanique bien montée, tellement la manoeuvre pouvait se suivre, d'une régularité d'horlogerie. C'était la victoire, inespérée, foudroyante, et le roi n'avait pas de remords, devant ces cadavres si petits, ces milliers d'hommes qui tenaient moins de place que la poussière des routes, cette vallée immense où les incendies de Bazeilles, les massacres d'Illy, les angoisses de Sedan, n'empêchaient pas l'impassible nature d'être belle, à cette fin sereine d'un beau jour" (R-M, 5: 687).

53. Stéphane Mallarmé, "Réponses à des enquêtes: Enquête de Jules Huret," in Oeuvres complètes (Paris: Pléiade, 1970), p. 872.

54. As quoted by Mitterand in the section of his notes ("Etude") dealing with the contemporary critical reception of La Débâcle (R-M, 5: 1443).

55. Ibid., p. 1448.

56. Deleuze, Logique, p. 66.

57. Ibid., pp. 57, 71.

58. Ibid., p. 71.

59. Michel Pierssens, "L'Appareil sériel," Change 16-17 (1973): 283.

60. "Puis, au milieu de cette lutte tragique, il eut tout d'un coup la vision nette de l'empereur, démis de son autorité impériale qu'il avait confiée aux mains de l'impératrice-régente, dépouillé de son commandement de général en chef dont il venait d'investir le maréchal Bazaine, n'étant plus absolument rien, une ombre d'empereur, indéfinie et vague, une inutilité sans nom et encombrante, dont on ne savait quoi faire, que Paris repoussait et qui n'avait plus de place dans l'armée, depuis qu'il s'était engagé à ne pas même donner un ordre" (R-M, 5: 444).

Cf. Karl Marx's assessment of Louis-Napoleon: "Thus it happened...that the most simple-minded man in France acquired the most multifarious significance. Just because he was nothing, he could signify everything save himself" (Class Struggles in France, 1848-1850 [New York: International Publishers, 1964], p. 72). Elsewhere in the same text, Marx refers to Louis-Napoleon as the "neutral man" (p. 109).

61. "C'était bien Napoléon III, qui lui apparaissait plus grand, à cheval, et les moustaches si fortement cirées, les joues si colorées, qu'il le jugea tout de suite rajeuni, fardé comme un acteur. Sûrement, il s'était fait peindre, pour ne pas promener, parmi son armée, l'effroi de son masque blême, décomposé par la souffrance, au nez aminci, aux yeux troubles. Et, averti dès cinq heures qu'on se battait à Bazeilles, il était venu, de son air silencieux et morne de fantôme, aux chairs ravivées de vermillon" (R-M, 5: 579).

62. As quoted by Mitterand in "Etude," R-M, 5: 1433.

63. Michel Serres, Feux et signaux de brume: Zola (Paris: Grasset, 1975), pp. 319, 320, and 321.

64. For a definition of the term idéologème, see Julia Kristeva, Semiotiké (Paris: Seuil, 1969), pp. 62-64 and esp. pp. 113-14. For a survey of the idéologèmes characteristic of these texts, see Lidsky, La Commune, pp. 91-141.

65. Serres, Feux et signaux, pp. 319-20.

66. "D'un geste, Jean le fit taire. 'Tu ne me dois rien, nous sommes quittes... C'est moi que les Prussiens auraient ramassé, là-bas, si tu ne m'avais pas emporté sur ton dos. Et, hier encore, tu m'as arraché de leurs pattes... Tu as payé deux fois, ce serait à mon tour de donner ma vie'" (R-M, 5: 793).

67. "Depuis la mort violente de sa femme, emportée dans un affreux drame, il se croyait sans coeur, il avait juré de ne plus jamais en avoir, de ces créatures dont on souffre tant, même quand elles ne sont pas mauvaises. Et l'amitié leur devenait à tous deux comme un élargissement: on avait beau ne pas s'embrasser, on se touchait à fond, on était l'un dans l'autre, si différent que l'on fût" (R-M, 5: 521-22).

68. "Et ils se serraient d'une étreinte éperdue, dans la fraternité de tout ce qu'ils venaient de souffrir ensemble; et le baiser qu'ils échangèrent alors leur parut le plus doux et

le plus fort de leur vie, un baiser tel qu'ils n'en recevraient jamais d'une femme, l'immortelle amitié, l'absolue certitude que leurs deux coeurs n'en faisaient plus qu'un, pour toujours" (*R-M*, 5: 785).

69. "Ils s'entendirent tout de suite, en causant de Maurice. Si elle se dévouait ainsi, c'était pour l'ami, pour le frère de Maurice, le brave homme secourable envers qui elle payait à son tour une dette de son coeur. Elle était pleine de gratitude, d'une affection qui grandissait, à mesure qu'elle le connaissait mieux, simple et sage, de cerveau solide; et lui, qu'elle soignait comme un enfant, contractait une dette d'infinie reconnaissance" (*R-M*, 5: 796).

70. Genette, *Figures III*, pp. 238-41. Cf. Jacques Neefs, "La Figuration réaliste," *Poétique* 16 (1973): 472.

71. See David Baguley, *"Fécondité" d'Emile Zola: Roman à thèse, évangile, mythe* (Toronto: University of Toronto Press, 1973), pp. 43-44.

72. Canetti, *Crowds*, pp. 42, 46.

73. "Les rosiers, dans les cimetières, épanouissent des fleurs larges, d'une blancheur de lait, d'un rouge sombre. Les racines vont, au fond des bières, prendre la pâleur des poitrines virginales, l'éclat sanglant des coeurs meurtris. Cette rose blanche, c'est la floraison d'une enfant morte à seize ans; cette rose rouge, c'est la dernière goutte de sang d'un homme tombé dans la lutte.

"O fleurs éclatantes, fleurs vivantes, où il y a un peu de nos morts!" (*Nouveaux Contes à Ninon*, in Mitt *OC*, 9: 422).

74. *La Fortune des Rougon*, in *R-M*, 1: 207, 87.

75. Canetti, *Crowds*, p. 47.

76. "Et c'était là le Paris qui voulait mourir, tout le déchet de la vie perdu dans une nuit de Paris, le flot de semence détourné de son juste emploi, tombé au pavé où rien ne poussait, Paris enfin mal ensemencé, ne produisant pas la grande et saine moisson qu'il aurait dû produire" (Mitt *OC*, 8: 73-74).

77. "La divine maternité échouait dans cette boue cachée, l'acte superbe de vie aboutissait à ce cloaque....Tout l'éternel flot de semences qui circule dans les veines du monde, toute l'humanité en germes qui gonfle le ventre des épouses, comme la grande terre au printemps, devenait une moisson déshonorée, corrompue à l'avance, frappée d'ignominie" (Mitt *OC*, 145).

78. "Il ne suffisait pas que la semence humaine fût gâchée, jetée pour le plaisir au pavé brûlant, il ne suffisait pas que la moisson fût mal récoltée, qu'il y eût l'affreux déchet des avortements et des infanticides, il fallait encore que la moisson vivante fût mal mise en grange, que la moitié s'en trouvât détruite, écrasée, tuée. Le déchet continuait, des voleuses et des assassines, flairant le lucre, arrivaient des quatres coins de l'horizon, remportaient au loin tout ce que leurs bras pouvaient tenir de vie naissante, balbutiante, pour en faire de la mort" (Mitt *OC*, 196-97).

79. Claude Lévi-Strauss, "The Structural Study of Myth," in *Myth: A Symposium*, ed. Thomas A. Sebeok (Bloomington: Indiana University Press, Midland Books, 1965), p. 99.

80. Lévi-Strauss, *Structural Anthropology*, trans. Claire Jacobson and Brooke Grundfest Schoepf (Garden City, N.Y.: Doubleday & Co., Anchor Books, 1967), pp. 333, 336.

81. Freud, *Standard Edition*, 17: 130-31.

82. "Et toute une foule riche, moirée d'or, allumée d'un pétillement de bijoux, emplissait l'église: près de l'autel, au fond, le clergé, les évêques crossés et mitrés, faisaient une gloire, un de ces resplendissements qui ouvrent une trouée sur le ciel; autour de l'estrade, des princes, des princesses, de grands dignitaires, étaient rangés avec une pompe souveraine...tandis que les délégations de toutes sortes s'entassaient dans le reste de la nef, et que les dames, en haut, au bord des tribunes, étalaient les vives panachures de leurs étoffes claires. Une grande buée saignante flottait. Les têtes étagées au fond, à droite, à

gauche, gardaient des tons roses de porcelaine peinte. Les costumes, le satin, la soie, le velours, avaient des reflets d'un éclat sombre, comme près de s'enflammer. Des rangs entiers, tout d'un coup, prenaient feu. L'église profonde se chauffait d'un luxe inouï de fournaise" (*R-M*, 2: 101-2).

83. "Mille clartés dansantes s'allumèrent, des éclairs rapides se croisèrent dans les roues, des étincelles jaillirent des harnais secoués par les chevaux. Il y eut sur le sol, sur les arbres, de larges reflets de glace qui couraient. Ce pétillement des harnais et des roues, ce flamboiement des panneaux vernis dans lesquels brûlait la braise rouge du soleil couchant, ces notes vives que jetaient les livrées éclatantes perchées en plein ciel et les toilettes riches débordant des portières, se trouvèrent ainsi emportés dans un grondement sourd, continu, rythmé par le trot des attelages" (*R-M*, 1: 321).

84. "Les soirs d'été, lorsque le soleil oblique allumait l'or des rampes sur la façade blanche, les promeneurs du parc s'arrêtaient, regardaient les rideaux de soie rouge drapés aux fenêtres du rez-de-chaussée; et, au travers des glaces si larges et si claires qu'elles semblaient, comme les glaces des grands magasins modernes, mises là pour étaler au-dehors le faste intérieur, ces familles de petits bourgeois apercevaient des coins de meubles, des bouts d'étoffes, des morceaux de plafonds d'une richesse éclatante, dont la vue les clouait d'admiration et d'envie au beau milieu des allées" (*R-M*, 1: 332).

The comparison of the Saccard mansion to a "big modern shop" ("grands magasins modernes") underscores the newness of this life style. The old rich, represented in *La Curée* by Renée Saccard's father, M. Béraud Du Châtel, or by the Count Muffat's family in *Nana*, do not practice the exhibitionism of the Second Empire *nouveaux riches*. The external display of wealth is culturally marked, as France has a long tradition of taxation on the basis of exterior signs of prosperity.

85. "Les femmes avaient paru, près d'un millier de femmes, aux cheveux épars, dépeignés par la course, aux guenilles montrant la peau nue, des nudités de femelles lasses d'enfanter des meurt-de-faim. Quelques-unes tenaient leur petit entre les bras, le soulevaient, l'agitaient, ainsi qu'un drapeau de deuil et de vengeance. D'autres, plus jeunes, avec des gorges gonflées de guerrières, brandissaient des bâtons; tandis que les vieilles, affreuses, hurlaient si fort, que les cordes de leurs cous décharnés semblaient se rompre. Et les hommes déboulèrent ensuite, deux mille furieux, des galibots, des haveurs, des raccommodeurs, une masse compacte qui roulait d'un seul bloc, serrée, confondue, au point qu'on ne distinguait ni les culottes déteintes, ni les tricots de laine en loques, effacés dans la même uniformité terreuse. Les yeux brûlaient, on voyait seulement les trous des bouches noires, chantant la *Marseillaise*, dont les strophes se perdaient en un mugissement confus, accompagné par le claquement des sabots sur la terre dure. Au-dessus des têtes, parmi le hérissement des barres de fer, une hache passa, portée toute droite; et cette hache unique, qui était comme l'étendard de la bande, avait, dans le ciel clair, le profil aigu d'un couperet de guillotine" (*R-M*, 3: 1435-36).

86. Canetti, *Crowds*, pp. 48-63.

87. "C'était la vision rouge de la révolution qui les emporterait tous, fatalement, par une soirée sanglante de cette fin de siècle....Oui, ce seraient les mêmes guenilles, le même tonnerre de gros sabots, la même cohue effroyable, de peau sale, d'*haleine empestée*, balayant le vieux monde, sous leur poussée débordante de barbares....Oui, c'étaient ces choses qui passaient sur la route, comme une force de la nature, et *ils en recevaient le vent terrible au visage*" (*R-M*, 3: 1436-37). Emphasis added.

"Au coin de la rue Saint-Joseph, près du plateau de la Merlasse, une famille d'excursionnistes, des gens qui arrivaient de Cauterets ou de Bagnères, restaient plantés au bord du trottoir, dans un étonnement profond. Ce devaient être de riches bourgeois, le père et la mère très correctes, les deux grandes filles vêtues de robes claires, avec des visages riants d'heureuses personnes qui s'amusent. Mais, à la surprise première du groupe, succédait une terreur croissante, comme s'ils avaient vu s'ouvrir une maladrerie des temps anciens, un de

ces hôpitaux de la légende qu'on aurait vidé, après quelque grande épidémie. Et les deux filles pâlissaient, le père et la mère demeuraient glacés, devant le défilé ininterrompu de tant d'horreurs, *dont ils recevaient le vent empesté à la face.* Mon Dieu! tant de laideur, tant de saleté, tant de souffrance!" (Mitt *OC*, 7: 119). Emphasis added.

88. "Le *circulus* social est identique au *circulus* vital: dans la société comme dans le corps humain, il existe une solidarité qui lie les différents membres, les différents organes entre eux, de telle sorte que, si un organe se pourrit, beaucoup d'autres sont atteints, et qu'une maladie très complexe se déclare" (*Le Roman expérimental,* in Mitt *OC*, 10: 1189).

89. "La bande s'écoulait, il n'y avait plus que la queue des traînards, lorsque la Mouquette déboucha. Elle s'attardait, elle guettait les bourgeois, sur les portes de leurs jardins, aux fenêtres de leurs maisons; et, quand elle en découvrait, ne pouvant leur cracher au nez, elle leur montrait ce qui était pour elle le comble de son mépris. Sans doute elle en aperçut un, car brusquement elle releva ses jupes, tendit les fesses, montra son derrière énorme, nu dans un dernier flamboiement du soleil. Il n'avait rien d'obscène, ce derrière, et ne faisait pas rire, farouche" (*R-M*, 3: 1437).

"Sous le ciel éclatant. . . le cortège roulait ses damnées des maladies de la peau, à la chair rongée, ses hydropiques enflées comme des outres, ses rhumatisantes, ses paralytiques, tordues de souffrance; et les hydrocéphales défilaient, et les danseuses de Saint-Guy, et les phtisiques, les rachitiques, les épileptiques, les cancéreuses, les goitreuses, les folles, les imbéciles. '*Ave, ave, ave, Maria!*' La complainte obstinée s'enflait davantage, charriait vers la Grotte le flot abominable de la pauvreté et de la douleur humaines, dans l'effroi et l'horreur des passants, qui restaient plantés sur leurs jambes, glacés devant ce galop de cauchemar" (Mitt *OC*, 7: 122).

The equation of poverty and disease is, unfortunately, not a mere figment of Zola's bourgeois imagination. Relying on a combination of statistical and literary evidence, Louis Chevalier has conclusively demonstrated, in *Classes laborieuses et classes dangereuses* (Paris: Plon, 1958), that there is no separating the "biological drama" of infectious diseases from the "economic and political drama" of poverty (p. xvii). His chapter dealing with the great cholera epidemics that ravaged nineteenth-century Paris (pp. 410-39) is of particular interest. Cf. Michel Foucault, *Surveiller et punir: Naissance de la prison* (Paris: Gallimard, 1975), pp. 197-200. Contrasting the different ways in which societies deal with lepers and plague victims, Foucault argues that whereas lepers were rejected, exiled from the polis, plague victims remained in the community but were subjected to a type of surveillance which in time gave rise to the penal system. The fear of *contagion* is the impetus behind the institution of the various "disciplinary systems" which structure contemporary society: prisons, schools, insane asylums, etc.

90. Jean Borie, *Zola et les mythes* (Paris: Seuil, 1971), pp. 17-18.

Chapter 4

1. Michel Butor, *Répertoire II* (Paris: Editions de Minuit, 1964), pp. 82-83.

2. Emile Zola, "Extraits des notes manuscrites," *Paris*, p. 567, Lebl *OC*.

3. J. H. Matthews, *Les Deux Zola: Science et personalité dans l'expression* (Geneva: Droz, 1957).

4. Butor, *Répertoire II*, p. 83.

5. "Does an intermediate vision exist in Zola? Is there anything more individualized than the crowd of sowers, but less isolated than Gervaise in her room?" (Richard B. Grant, "Un Aspect négligé du style de Zola," *Cahiers naturalistes* 42 [1971]: 19).

6. "Pourtant, cette idée du flot de foule que les trains montants et descendants charriaient quotidiennement devant elle, au milieu du grand silence de sa solitude, la laissait pen-

sive....Cela lui semblait drôle, de vivre perdue au fond de ce désert, sans une âme à qui se confier, lorsque, de jour et de nuit, continuellement, il défilait tant d'hommes et de femmes, dans le coup de tempête des trains....Le torrent coulait, en ne laissant rien de lui. Et ce qui la rendait triste, c'était, sous ce roulement continu, sous tant de bien-être et tant d'argent promenés, de sentir que cette foule toujours si haletante ignorait qu'elle fût là, en danger de mort, à ce point que, si son homme l'achevait un soir, les trains continueraient à se croiser près de son cadavre, sans se douter seulement du crime, au fond de la maison solitaire" (*R-M*, 4: 1031-32).

7. "Depuis cinq années qu'ils habitaient là, à chaque heure de jour et de nuit, par les beaux temps, par les orages, que de trains ils avaient vus passer, dans le coup de vent de leur vitesse!...Le monde entier défilait, la foule humaine charriée à toute vapeur, sans qu'ils en connussent autre chose que des visages entrevus dans un éclair....Et voilà que, dans la neige, un train débarquait à leur porte: l'ordre naturel était perverti, ils dévisageaient ce monde inconnu qu'un accident jetait sur la voie, ils le contemplaient avec des yeux ronds de sauvages, accourus sur une côte où des Européens naufrageraient" (*R-M*, 4: 1175-76).

8. See Michael Riffaterre's definition of the process of "expansion" in "Modèles de la phrase littéraire," in *Problèmes de l'analyse textuelle*, ed. R. Léon, Henri Mitterand, and Peter Nesselroth (Montreal: Didier, 1971): "It remains for me to analyze the syntagmatic transformation. It is to this type of transformation that the rule of expansion applies, a rule I would formulate as follows: given a minimal phrase (nuclear, matrix), each of its components engenders a more complex form" (p. 145).

9. "Et [Misard], ainsi que Flore, regardait les cadavres, comme s'ils espéraient les reconnaître, au milieu de la cohue des milliers et des milliers de visages, qui, en dix années, avaient défilé devant eux, à toute vapeur, en ne leur laissant que le souvenir confus d'une foule, apportée, emportée dans un éclair. Non! ce n'était toujours que le flot inconnu du monde en marche; la mort brutale, accidentelle, restait anonyme" (*R-M*, 4: 1264-65).

10. "Je tâcherai de trouver et de suivre, en résolvant la double question des tempéraments et des milieux, le fil qui conduit mathématiquement d'un homme à un autre homme. Et quand je tiendrai tous les fils, quand j'aurai entre les mains tout un groupe social, je ferai voir ce groupe à l'oeuvre comme acteur d'une époque historique" (*R-M*, 1: 3).

11. Zola, "Différences entre Balzac et moi," *R-M*, 5: 1737.

12. Zola, "Notes sur la marche générale de l'oeuvre," *R-M*, 5: 1738.

13. Jean Dubois, *Le Vocabulaire politique en France de 1869 à 1872* (Paris: Larousse, 1962), p. 25.

14. Jean-Paul Sartre, *Critique de la raison dialectique* (Paris: Gallimard, 1960), p. 47.

15. "Les Rougon-Macquart, le groupe, la famille que je me propose d'étudier a pour caractéristique le débordement des appétits, le large soulèvement de notre âge, qui se rue aux jouissances....Historiquement, ils partent du peuple, ils s'irradient dans toute la société contemporaine, ils montent à toutes les situations...et ils racontent ainsi le second Empire à l'aide de leurs drames individuels" (*R-M*, 1: 3).

16. Roland Barthes, *The Pleasure of the Text*, trans. Richard Miller (New York: Farrar, Strauss, and Giroux, Hill and Wang, 1975), pp. 31-32.

17. "D'ailleurs la jeune femme ne regarda pas cette marmaille comme une cause de ruine. Au contraire, elle reconstruisit sur la tête de ses fils l'édifice de sa fortune, qui s'écroulait entre ses mains. Ils n'avaient pas dix ans, qu'elle escomptait déjà en rêve leur avenir. Doutant de jamais réussir par elle-même, elle se mit à espérer en eux pour vaincre l'acharnement du sort. Ils satisferaient ses vanités déçues, ils lui donneraient cette position riche et enviée qu'elle poursuivait en vain. Dès lors, sans abandonner la lutte soutenue par la maison de commerce, elle eut une seconde tactique pour arriver à contenter ses instincts de domination. Il lui semblait impossible que, sur ses trois fils, il n'y eût pas un homme supérieur qui les enrichirait tous. Elle sentait cela, disait-elle. Aussi soigna-t-elle les marmots avec une ferveur où il y avait des sévérités de mère et des tendresses d'usurier. Elle se plut à

les engraisser amoureusement comme un capital qui devait plus tard rapporter de gros intérêts" (*R-M*, 1: 59-60).

18. "Et il sembla un moment que Mathieu, du même rythme dont il confiait aux sillons les germes du blé attendu, les semait aussi, ces chers enfants adorés, les multipliait sans compter, à l'infini, pour que tout un petit peuple de semeurs futurs, nés de son geste, achevât de peupler le monde" (Mitt *OC*, 8: 232).

19. "L'antique Afrique mystérieuse, aujourd'hui découverte, trouée de part et d'autre, l'attirait. Il irait d'abord au Sénégal, puis il pousserait sans doute jusqu'au Soudan, au coeur même des terres vierges, où il rêvait une France nouvelle, cet immense empire colonial qui rajeunirait une race vieillie, en lui donnant sa part de la terre. C'était là qu'il ambitionnait, par de vastes défrichements, de se tailler son royaume, de fonder avec Lisbeth une autre dynastie des Froment, un Chantebled décuplé sous l'ardent soleil, peuplé du peuple de ses enfants" (ibid., pp. 446-47).

20. Cf. this characteristic piece of advice given by Balzac in *Physiologie du mariage* (Paris: Garnier-Flammarion, 1968): "Forswear love. For one thing, no more troubles, no more cares, no more anxieties; no more of those short-lived passions which are a waste of human energy. A man enjoys peace and quiet and, socially speaking, his force is infinitely greater and more intense. *This renunciation of that thing called love is the origin of the power of all men who exercise an influence on the masses"* (p. 307; emphasis added).

21. The band is not, of course, without its literary antecedents; in *Le Décor mythique de "La Chartreuse de Parme"* (Paris: Corti, 1961), Gilbert Durand evokes some of the bands surrounding epic heroes: "One might say in sociological terms that in the epic or the *chanson de geste*, what we have is a heroic 'group effect.' It is the Greeks 'together' who undertake the *Iliad*, and Ulysses' companions, the *Odyssey*. The Argonauts who escort Jason remain the archetype of collective heroism, the symbol of heroic comradeship which will be perpetuated in Western literature by the knights of the round table and Roland's 'compains'" (p. 57).

22. "Ce fut un travail énorme. Chacun prit un rôle. L'entente eut lieu à demi-mots, chez Rougon lui-même, dans les coins, le dimanche et le jeudi. On se partageait les missions difficiles. On se lançait tous les jours au milieu de Paris, avec la volonté entêtée de conquérir une influence. On ne dédaignait rien; les plus petits succès comptaient. On profitait de tout, on tirait ce qu'on pouvait des moindres événements, on utilisait la journée entière, depuis le bonjour du matin jusqu'à la dernière poignée de main du soir. Les amis des amis devinrent complices, et encore les amis de ceux-là. Paris entier fut pris dans cette intrigue. Au fond des quartiers perdus, il y avait des gens qui soupiraient après le triomphe de Rougon, sans savoir au juste pourquoi. La bande, dix à douze personnes, tenait la ville" (*R-M*, 2: 186-87).

23. "Mais ce qu'on apercevait de toute part, des quais, des ponts, des fenêtres, c'était, à l'horizon, sur la muraille nue d'une maison à six étages, dans l'île Saint-Louis, une redingote grise géante, peinte à fresque, de profil, avec sa manche gauche pliée au coude, comme si le vêtement eût gardé l'attitude et le gonflement d'un corps, à cette heure disparu. Cette réclame monumentale prenait, dans le soleil, au-dessus de la fourmilière des promeneurs, une extraordinaire importance" (*R-M*, 2: 86).

24. Jean-Pierre Vernant, "La Catégorie psychologique du double," in *Mythe et pensée chez les Grecs*, 2 vols. (Paris: Maspéro, Petite Collection Maspéro, 1971), 2: 77.

25. "—Tiens! Rougon! Et, debout, de sa main gantée, il saluait. Puis, craignant de ne pas être vu, il prit son chapeau de paille, il l'agita. Rougon, dont le costume de sénateur était très regardé, se renfonça vite dans un coin du coupé. Alors, Gilquin l'appela, en se faisant un porte-voix de son poing à demi fermé. En face, sur le trottoir, la foule s'attroupait, se retournait, pour voir à qui en avait ce grand diable, habillé de coutil jaune. Enfin, le cocher put fouetter son cheval, le coupé s'engagea sur le pont Notre-Dame" (*R-M*, 2: 92).

26. "Et il reprit son rêve caressé d'être un grand propriétaire, avec des troupeaux de bêtes sur lesquels il régnerait. Mais, dans les Landes, son ambition grandissait; il devenait le roi conquérant d'une terre nouvelle; il avait un peuple. Ce furent des détails interminables.

Depuis quinze jours, sans rien dire, il lisait des ouvrages spéciaux. Il desséchait des marais, combattait avec des machines puissantes l'empierrement du sol, arrêtait la marche des dunes par des plantations de pins, dotait la France d'un coin de fertilité miraculeux.... —Hein, c'est une idée! dit-il. Je laisse mon nom à la ville, je fonde un petit empire, moi aussi!" (R-M, 2: 150).

27. Jean Borie, Zola et les mythes (Paris: Seuil, 1971), pp. 78-83.

28. René Girard, Deceit, Desire, and the Novel, trans. Yvonne Freccero (Baltimore: The Johns Hopkins University Press, 1976), p. 17.

29. Ibid., p. 73.

30. "Et jamais il ne s'était senti à ce point mordu par la jalousie inavouée, cette brûlure d'envie orgueilleuse, qu'il avait éprouvée parfois en face de l'empereur tout-puissant. Il aurait préféré Clorinde au bras de ce cocher, dont on parlait à voix basse. Cela irritait ses anciens désirs, de la savoir hors de sa main, tout en haut, esclave d'un homme qui d'un mot courbait les têtes" (R-M, 2: 343).

31. "Mais la plus grande volupté de Rougon était encore de triompher devant sa bande. Il oubliait la France, les fonctionnaires à ses genoux, le peuple de solliciteurs assiégeant sa porte, pour vivre dans l'admiration continue des dix à quinze familiers de son entourage. Il leur ouvrait à toute heure son cabinet, les faisait régner là, sur les fauteuils, à son bureau même, se disait heureux d'en rencontrer sans cesse entre ses jambes, ainsi que des animaux fidèles. Le ministre, ce n'était pas seulement lui, mais eux tous, qui étaient comme des dépendances de sa personne. Dans la victoire, un travail sourd se faisait, les liens se resserraient, il se prenait à les aimer d'une amitié jalouse, mettant sa force à ne pas être seul, se sentant la poitrine élargie par leurs ambitions. Il oubliait ses mépris secrets, en arrivait à les trouver très intelligents, très forts, à son image. Il voulait surtout qu'on le respectât en eux, il les défendait avec emportement, comme il aurait défendu les dix doigts de ses mains. Leurs querelles étaient les siennes. Même il finissait par s'imaginer leur devoir beaucoup, souriant au souvenir de leur longue propagande. Et, sans besoins lui-même, il taillait à la bande de belles proies, il goûtait à la combler la joie personnelle d'agrandir autour de lui l'éclat de sa fortune" (R-M, 2: 219).

32. The simplest and clearest definition of this useful but slippery term comes not from its originator, Greimas, but from one of his disciples: "We term isotope any repetition of a linguistic unit" (François Rastier, "Systématique des isotopies," in Essais de sémiotique poétique, ed. A. J. Greimas [Paris: Larousse, 1972], p. 82). In this instance the linguistic unit is semantic, that is, a seme.

33. "Et, en bas, les chiens achevaient leurs os. Ils se coulaient furieusement les uns sous les autres, pour arriver au milieu du tas. C'était une nappe d'échines mouvantes, les blanches, les noires, se poussant, s'allongeant, s'étalant comme une mare vivante, dans un ronflement vorace. Les mâchoires se hâtaient, mangeaient vite, avec la fièvre de tout manger. De courtes querelles se terminaient par un hurlement. Un gros braque, une bête superbe, fâché d'être trop au bord, recula et s'élança d'un bond au milieu de la bande. Il fit son trou, il but un lambeau des entrailles du cerf" (R-M, 2: 185).

"Il tombait, miné, rongé, dévoré par sa bande....Et, à cette heure, il se rappelait le travail lent de sa bande, ces dents aiguës qui chaque jour mangeaient un peu de sa force. Ils étaient autour de lui; ils lui grimpaient aux genoux, puis à la poitrine, puis à la gorge, jusqu'à l'étrangler; ils lui avaient tout pris, ses pieds pour monter, ses mains pour voler, sa mâchoire pour mordre et engloutir; ils habitaient dans ses membres, en tiraient leur joie et leur santé, s'en donnaient des ripailles, sans songer au lendemain" (pp. 344-45).

34. Elias Canetti, Crowds and Power, trans. Carol Stewart (New York: Viking Press, Compass Books, 1966), pp. 94-95.

35. Girard, Deceit, p. 294.

36. Ibid., p. 312.

37. "—On nous a accusé d'irréligion. On a menti! Nous sommes l'enfant respectueux

de l'Eglise et nous avons le bonheur de croire... Oui, messieurs, la foi est notre guide et notre soutien, dans cette tâche du gouvernement, si lourde parfois à porter. Qu'adviendrait-il de nous, si nous ne nous abandonnions pas aux mains de la Providence? Nous avons la seule prétention d'être l'humble exécuteur de ses desseins, l'instrument docile des volontés de Dieu. C'est là ce qui nous permet de parler haut et de faire un peu de bien... Et, messieurs, je suis heureux de cette occasion pour m'agenouiller ici, avec toute la ferveur de mon coeur de catholique, devant le souverain pontife, devant ce vieillard auguste dont la France restera la fille vigilante et dévouée" (*R-M*, 2: 369).

38. Girard, *Deceit*, p. 314.

39. "A la sortie, Clorinde guetta Rougon. Ils n'avaient plus échangé une parole depuis trois ans. Lorsqu'il parut, rajeuni, comme allégé, ayant démenti en une heure toute sa vie politique, prêt à satisfaire, sous la fiction du parlementarisme, son furieux appétit d'autorité, elle céda à un entraînement, elle alla vers lui, la main tendue, les yeux attendris et humides d'une caresse, en disant: —Vous êtes tout de même d'une jolie force, vous" (*R-M*, 2: 369).

40. "Quand elle eut monté l'escalier, Henriette ne trouva plus Mouret, qui venait de plonger Vallagnosc en pleine foule, pour achever de l'étourdir, et pris lui-même du besoin physique de ce bain du succès. Il perdait délicieusement haleine, c'était là contre ses membres comme un long embrassement de toute sa clientèle" (*R-M*, 3: 492).

41. F. W. J. Hemmings, *Emile Zola* (Oxford: Oxford University Press, Oxford Paperbacks, 1970), p. 147.

42. Zola's "Ebauche," as quoted by Mitterand in *R-M*, 3: 1680, 1685.

43. "—Sans doute, l'idée peut séduire, disait-il. Seulement, elle est d'un poète... Où prendriez-vous la clientèle pour emplir pareille cathédrale?

"Mouret le regarda un moment en silence, comme stupéfait de son refus. Etait-ce possible? un homme d'un tel flair, qui sentait l'argent à toutes les profondeurs! Et, tout d'un coup, il eut un geste de grande éloquence, il montra ces dames dans le salon, en criant:

"—La clientèle, mais la voilà!" (*R-M*, 3: 457).

Cf. the passage from *Le Ventre de Paris*, quoted on p. 31 above, where Claude Lantier calls Florent a "poète" (*R-M*, 1: 849).

44. "Comme elle s'éloignait, elle reconnut près d'elle Mme Marty, accompagnée de sa fille Valentine....

"—Tiens! c'est vous, chère madame?

"—Mais oui, chère madame... Hein? quelle foule!

"—Oh! ne m'en parlez pas, on étouffe. Un succès!... Avez-vous vu le salon oriental?

"—Superbe! inouï!" (*R-M*, 3: 486).

"—Te voilà donc! dit Mme Desforges, en trouvant Mme Bourdelais installée devant un comptoir.

"Tiens! bonjour! répondit celle-ci, qui serra les mains à ces dames. Oui, je suis entrée donner un coup d'oeil.

"—Hein? c'est prodigieux, cet étalage! On en rêve... Et le salon oriental, as-tu vu le salon oriental?

"—Oui, oui, extraordinaire!" (p. 487).

45. "Ces dames, saisies par le courant, ne pouvaient plus reculer. Comme les fleuves tirent à eux les eaux errantes d'une vallée, il semblait que le flot des clientes, coulant à plein vestibule, buvait les passants de la rue, aspirait la population des quatre coins de Paris. Elles n'avançaient que très lentement, serrées à perdre haleine, tenues debout par des épaules et des ventres, dont elles sentaient la molle chaleur; et leur désir satisfait jouissait de cette approche pénible, qui fouettait davantage leur curiosité. C'était un pêle-mêle de dames vêtues de soie, de petites bourgeoises à robes pauvres, de filles en cheveux, toutes soulevées, enfiévrées de la même passion" (*R-M*, 3: 618).

46. "His [Mouret's] creation instituted a new religion; the churches which were gradually being emptied by a loss of faith were replaced by his bazaar" ("Sa création

apportait une religion nouvelle, les églises que désertait peu à peu la foi chancelante étaient remplacées par son bazar" [R-M, 3: 797]).

47. "Mme Desforges arrivait enfin au premier étage, lorsqu'une poussée, plus rude que les autres, l'immobilisa un instant. Elle avait maintenant, au-dessous d'elle, les rayons du rez-de-chaussée, ce peuple de clientes épandu qu'elle venait de traverser. C'était un nouveau spectacle, un océan de têtes vues en raccourci, cachant les corsages, grouillant dans une agitation de fourmilère" (R-M, 3: 631).

48. "Mais ce qui la surprenait surtout, dans la fatigue de ses yeux aveuglés par le pêle-mêle éclatant des couleurs, c'était, lorsqu'elle fermait les paupières, de sentir davantage la foule, à son bruit sourd de marée montante et à la chaleur humaine qu'elle exhalait" (ibid.).

49. "Mme Bourdelais, désireuse de rattraper ses dépenses, avait de nouveau conduit ses trois enfants au buffet; maintenant, la clientèle s'y ruait dans une rage d'appétit, les mères elles-mêmes s'y gorgeaient de malaga; on avait bu, depuis l'ouverture, quatre-vingts litres de sirop et soixante-dix bouteilles de vin....Mme de Boves, suivie de Blanche et de Vallagnosc, avait eu le caprice de demander un ballon rouge, bien qu'elle n'eût rien acheté....Au comptoir de distribution, on entamait le quarantième mille" (R-M, 3: 642-43).

50. "Cinq heures sonnèrent. De toutes ces dames, Mme Marty demeurait seule avec sa fille, dans la crise finale de la vente. Elle ne pouvait s'en détacher, lasse à mourir, retenue par des liens si forts, qu'elle revenait toujours sur ses pas, sans besoin, battant les rayons de sa curiosité inassouvie. C'était l'heure où la cohue, fouettée de réclames, achevait de se détraquer; les soixante mille francs d'annonces payés aux journaux, les dix mille affiches collées sur les murs, les deux cent mille catalogues lancés dans la circulation, après avoir vidé les bourses, laissaient à ces nerfs de femmes l'ébranlement de leur ivresse....Mme Marty s'attardait devant les tables de proposition....La foule flambait sous l'incendie du soleil de cinq heures. Maintenant, Mme Marty avait la face animée et nerveuse d'une enfant qui a bu du vin pur....Il lui fallut se battre pour se dégager de l'écrasement obstiné de la porte" (R-M, 3: 643-44).

51. "L'ecrasement, aux dentelles, croissait de minute en minute. La grande exposition de blanc y triomphait, dans ses blancheurs les plus délicates et les plus chères. C'était la tentation aiguë, le coup de folie du désir, qui détraquait toutes les femmes" (R-M, 3: 790).

"Mme de Boves ne répondait pas. Alors la fille, en tournant sa face molle, vit sa mère, les mains au milieu des dentelles, en train de faire disparaître, dans la manche de son manteau, des volants de point d'Alençon" (p. 791).

"Elle volait avec de l'argent plein sa poche, elle volait pour voler, comme on aime pour aimer, sous le coup de fouet du désir, dans le détraquement de la névrose que ses appétits de luxe inassouvis avaient développée en elle" (p. 793).

52. "Mme Marty et sa fille, emportées au plus haut, vagabondaient parmi les meubles. Retenue par son petit monde, Mme Bourdelais ne pouvait s'arracher des articles de Paris. Puis, venait la bande, Mme de Boves toujours au bras de Vallagnosc, et suivie de Blanche, s'arrêtant à chaque rayon, osant regarder encore les étoffes de son air superbe. Mais, de la clientèle entassée, de cette mer de corsages gonflés de vie,...il finit par ne plus distinguer que le corsage nu de Mme Desforges, qui s'était arrêtée à la ganterie avec Mme Guibal. Malgré sa rancune jalouse, elle aussi achetait, et il se sentit le maître une dernière fois, il les tenait à ses pieds, sous l'éblouissement des feux electriques, ainsi qu'un bétail dont il avait tiré sa fortune" (R-M, 3: 798).

53. "Clorinde, dans ses regards brouillés, s'élargissait toujours, lui bouchait toute la baie, de sa taille de statue géante. Mais il battit des paupières, il la retrouva, bien moins grosse que lui, sur la table. Alors, il eut un sourire; s'il l'avait voulu, il l'aurait fouettée comme une petite fille; et il resta surpris d'en avoir eu peur un moment" (R-M, 2: 67).

54. "Rougon, affolé, effrayant, la face pourpre, se ruait avec un souffle haletant de taureau échappé. Elle-même, heureuse de taper sur cet homme, avait dans les yeux une lueur de cruauté qui s'allumait. Muette à son tour, elle quitta le mur, elle s'avança

superbement au milieu de l'écurie; et elle tournait sur elle-même, multipliant les coups, le tenant à distance, l'atteignant aux jambes, aux bras, au ventre, aux épaules; tandis que, stupide, énorme, il dansait, pareil à une bête sous le fouet d'un dompteur" (*R-M*, 2: 118-19).

55. "Et, dès ce moment, elle devint populaire. On n'ignorait pas les douceurs qu'on lui devait, on l'admirait pour la force de sa volonté. En voilà une, au moins, qui mettait le pied sur la gorge du patron, et qui les vengeait tous, et qui savait tirer de lui autre chose que des promesses! Elle était donc venue, celle qui faisait respecter un peu les pauvres diables!" (*R-M*, 3: 729).

56. "Un nouveau silence régna. On entendit encore, derrière la porte close, le ronflement adouci de l'inventaire. C'était comme un bruit mourant de triomphe, l'accompagnement se faisait discret, dans cette défaite du maître" (*R-M*, 3: 674); "Une dernière rumeur monta du *Bonheur des Dames*, l'acclamation lointaine d'une foule" (pp. 802-3).

57. "L'amour de Philippe était devenu de la rage. Sans cesse obligé de fuir, menacé dans ses rêves de richesse, sous le coup d'un châtiment implacable, le jeune homme se révoltait en pressant Blanche entre ses bras, à la briser. Cette enfant, qui s'abandonnait, était pour lui une vengeance; il la possédait en maître irrité. . . . Son orgueil grandissait dans une jouissance infinie. Lui, le fils du peuple, il tenait enfin, sur sa poitrine, une fille de ces hommes puissants et fiers dont les équipages lui avaient parfois jeté de la boue à la face. Et il se rappelait les légendes du pays, les vexations des nobles, le martyre du peuple, toutes les lâchetés de ses pères devant les caprices cruels de la noblesse. Alors il étouffait Blanche d'une caresse plus rude" (Mitt *OC*, 1: 251-52).

58. "C'était en elle qu'il aimait le peuple souffrant, c'était elle qu'il voulait sauver du monstre. Il l'avait prise la plus misérable, la plus outragée, si près de l'avilissement, qu'elle était sur le point de tomber au ruisseau. Avec sa pauvre main que le travail avait mutilé, elle incarnait toute la race des victimes, des esclaves donnant leur chair pour l'effort et pour le plaisir. Lorsqu'il l'aurait rachetée, il rachèterait avec elle toute la race" (Mitt *OC*, 8: 677).

59. "Elle avait poussé dans un faubourg, sur le pavé parisien; et, grande, belle, de chair superbe ainsi qu'une plante de plein fumier, elle vengeait les gueux et les abandonnés dont elle était le produit. Avec elle, la pourriture qu'on laissait fermenter dans le peuple remontait et pourrissait l'aristocratie. Elle devenait une force de la nature, un ferment de destruction, sans le vouloir elle-même, corrompant et désorganisant Paris" (*R-M*, 2: 1269).

60. "Et tandis que, dans une gloire, son sexe montait et rayonnait sur ses victimes étendues, pareil à un soleil levant qui éclaire un champ de carnage, elle gardait son inconscience de bête superbe, ignorante de sa besogne, bonne fille toujours" (*R-M*, 2: 1470).

61. "Aujourd'hui, elle était l'âme même de ce monde, elle seule importait, elle pouvait d'un mot précipiter ou ralentir le colosse, abattu à ses petits pieds. Cependant, elle n'avait pas voulu ces choses, elle s'était simplement présentée, sans calcul, avec l'unique charme de sa douceur" (*R-M*, 3: 729-30).

62. Borie, *Zola*, p. 128.

63. "Elle continua, elle dit son désir violent de voir le tableau, son escapade au Salon, et comment elle était tombée dans la tempête des rires, sous les huées de tout ce peuple. C'était elle qu'on sifflait ainsi, c'était sur sa nudité que crachaient les gens, cette nudité dont le brutal étalage, devant la blague de Paris, l'avait étranglée dès la porte. Et, prise d'une terreur folle, éperdue de souffrance et de honte, elle s'était sauvée, comme si elle avait senti ces rires s'abattre sur sa peau nue, la cingler au sang de coups de fouet. Mais elle s'oubliait maintenant, elle ne songeait qu'à lui, bouleversée par l'idée du chagrin qu'il devait avoir, grossissant l'amertume de cet échec de toute sa sensibilité de femme, débordant d'un besoin de charité immense" (*R-M*, 4: 139-40).

64. "Maintenant qu'il avait jugé son oeuvre, il écoutait et regardait la foule. L'explosion continuait, s'aggravait dans une gamme ascendante de fous rires. Dès la porte, il voyait se fendre les mâchoires des visiteurs, se rapetisser les yeux, s'élargir le visage; et c'étaient des souffles tempétueux d'hommes gras, des grincements rouillés d'hommes maigres, dominés

par les flûtes aiguës des femmes" (*R-M*, 4: 127).

"Ce fut comme la clameur montant d'une marée. Nana! Nana! Nana! Le cri roulait, grandissait, avec une violence de tempête, emplissant peu à peu l'horizon, des profondeurs du Bois au mont Valérien, des prairies de Longchamp à la plaine de Boulogne....

"Alors, Nana, debout sur le siège de son landau, grandie, crut que c'était elle qu'on acclamait. Elle était restée un instant immobile, dans la stupeur de son triomphe, regardant la piste envahie par le flot si épais, qu'on ne voyait plus l'herbe, couverte d'une mer de chapeaux noirs....

"—Ah! nom de Dieu! c'est moi! pourtant... Ah! nom de Dieu! quelle veine" (*R-M*, 2: 1404-5).

65. "Mais Claude n'entendait que les sourds battements de son coeur, ne voyait que l'*Enfant mort*, en l'air, près du plafond. Il ne le quittait pas des yeux, il subissait la fascination qui le clouait là, en dehors de son vouloir. La foule, dans sa nausée de lassitude, tournoyait autour de lui; des pieds écrasaient les siens, il était heurté, emporté; et, comme une chose inerte, il s'abandonnait, flottait, se retrouvait à la même place, sans baisser la tête, ignorant ce qui se passait en bas, ne vivant plus que là-haut, avec son oeuvre, son petit Jacques, enflé dans la mort. Deux grosses larmes, immobiles entre ses paupières, l'empêchaient de bien voir. Il lui semblait que jamais il n'aurait le temps de voir assez" (*R-M*, 4: 307).

66. Jean Giraudoux, *Pleins pouvoirs* (Paris: Gallimard, 1939), p. 55.

67. Zola, *Le Docteur Pascal*, in *R-M*, 5: 1010.

68. "Oui, il faudrait supprimer la machine à vapeur, la chaudière, qui est l'intermédiaire gênant, entre la houille extraite et l'électricité produite. Il faudrait, en un mot, transformer directement l'énergie calorifique contenue dans le charbon, en énergie électrique, sans passer par l'énergie mécanique" (Mitt *OC*, 8: 855).

69. Henri Hubert and Marcel Mauss, *Essai sur la nature et la fonction du sacrifice*, in *Oeuvres*, by Marcel Mauss, 1 (Paris: Editions de Minuit, 1968): 203.

70. Claude Lévi-Strauss, *The Savage Mind* (Chicago: University of Chicago Press, Phoenix Books, 1966), pp. 224-25.

71. "Le Tartaret, à la lisière du bois, était une lande inculte, d'une stérilité volcanique, sous laquelle, depuis des siècles, brûlait une mine de houille incendiée. Cela se perdait dans la légende, des mineurs du pays racontaient une histoire: le feu du ciel tombant sur cette Sodome des entrailles de la terre, où les hercheuses se souillaient d'abominations; si bien qu'elles n'avaient même pas eu le temps de remonter, et qu'aujourd'hui encore, elles flambaient au fond de cet enfer.... Et, ainsi qu'un miracle d'éternel printemps, au milieu de cette lande maudite du Tartaret, la Côte-Verte se dressait avec ses gazons toujours verts, ses hêtres dont les feuilles se renouvelaient sans cesse, ses champs où mûrissaient jusqu'à trois récoltes. C'était une serre naturelle, chauffée par l'incendie des couches profondes. Jamais la neige n'y séjournait. L'énorme bouquet de verdure, à côté des arbres dépouillés de la forêt s'épanouissait dans cette journée de décembre, sans que la gelée en eût même roussi les bords" (*R-M*, 3: 1395-96).

72. "Les scrupules de sa sensibilité et de son bon sens étaient emportés, rien ne devenait plus facile que la réalisation de ce monde nouveau: il avait tout prévu, il en parlait comme d'une machine qu'il monterait en deux heures, et ni le feu, et ni le sang ne lui coûtaient" (*R-M*, 3: 1380).

73. Another possible revolutionary allusion in the Tartaret text has been noted by Philip Walker in his article, "Prophetic Myths in Zola," *PMLA* 74 (1959): "Tartarus was the profound abysm of the earth where Uranus thrust his fearful children the Hecatonshires and Cyclopes, who were released by Jupiter at the advice of their mother, the earth-mother Gaea, to take part in the war against Cronus. It was here, also, that after ages of struggle the Titans were consigned in their turn, making of Tartarus a symbol of the destructive revolutionary forces that eternally exist deep within the earth itself" (p. 450).

74. "La maison d'habitation, un bâtiment de briques assez étroit, sans style, que le grand-père de Jordan avait construit du temps de Louis XVIII, sur l'emplacement de l'ancien château, brûlé pendant la Révolution, se trouvait adossé contre la rampe des monts Bleuses, une muraille escarpée et géante, qui faisait promontoire, au débouché de la gorge de Brias sur l'immense plaine de la Roumagne. Et le parc, abrité ainsi des vents du nord, exposé en plein midi, semblait être une serre naturelle, où régnait un éternel printemps. Toute une végétation vigoureuse couvrait cette muraille de rochers, grâce aux ruisseaux qui en tombaient de partout, en cascades cristallines; tandis que des sentiers de chèvre montaient, des escaliers taillés dans le roc, parmi des plantes grimpantes et des arbustes toujours verts. Puis, les ruisseaux se réunissaient, arrosaient d'une rivière lente le parc entier, de vastes pelouses, des bouquets de grands arbres, les plus beaux et les plus forts" (Mitt OC, 8: 627).

75. The allusion here is to the title of Leo Marx's book, *The Machine in the Garden* (Oxford: Oxford University Press, 1964).

76. "D'abord il s'était ingénié à supprimer les frais de charrois, en brûlant le charbon au sortir du puit, sous les chaudières, et en amenant par des câbles, à chaque usine, la force électrique obtenue ainsi, *sans trop de déperdition*. Ensuite, il avait imaginé l'appareil si longtemps cherché, il avait pu transformer directement l'énergie calorifique contenue dans le charbon, en énergie électrique, sans passer par l'énergie mécanique. C'était *la suppression de la chaudière*, une amélioration considérable, une économie de plus de cinquante pour cent" (Mitt OC, 8: 944). Emphasis added.

77. "Et, dès lors, pourquoi donc le soleil ne continuerait-il pas, n'achèverait-il pas son oeuvre? Il avait bien, pendant des mille ans, amassé sa chaleur bienfaisante dans les végétaux et dans les arbres, dont la houille était faite. Pendant des mille ans, la houille s'était comme distillé, au sein de la terre, gardant pour nos besoins cet amas immense de chaleur en réserve, nous la rendant enfin en un cadeau inappréciable, à l'heure où notre civilisation devait y trouver une splendeur nouvelle" (Mitt OC, 8: 945).

78. "Ainsi, le problème se posait d'une façon à la fois simple et formidable, il s'agissait de *s'adresser directement au soleil*, de capter la chaleur solaire et de la transformer, à l'aide d'appareils spéciaux, en électricité, dont il faudrait ensuite conserver des provisions énormes dans des réservoirs imperméables" (ibid.). Emphasis added.

79. "Mais un défaut fâcheux persistait pourtant, les immenses réservoirs perdaient beaucoup, et il y avait là un dernier perfectionnement à trouver, la conservation parfaite des réserves hivernales, assez de rayons solidement emmagasinés, afin de rallumer au-dessus de la ville un autre soleil, pendant les longues nuits de décembre" (Mitt OC, 8: 946).

Not in the least unaware that this coda "dialogues" with Borie's, I would suggest that the current decade's critical convergence on Zola's heliophany—I am alluding to Serres's thermodynamic grid—has less to do with academic vampirism than with the critics' shared historical situation, a decadent *Zeitgeist*.

80. Barthes's *S/Z* (Paris: Seuil, 1970) is, of course, the prototype and model for such diverse critical works as Jean Paris, "Modèles balzaciens," in *La Lecture sociocritique du texte romanesque*, ed. Graham Falconer and Henri Mitterand (Toronto: Samuel Stevens Hakkert & Co., 1975), pp. 151-64, and Philippe Bonnefis, "Intérieurs naturalistes," in *Intime, intimité, intimisme*, ed. Raphaël Molho and Pierre Reboul (Lille: Editions Universitaires, Université de Lille III, 1976), pp. 163-98. With reference to the use of translation as a means of auto-nomination, Bonnefis points out that in Italian, *zolla* signifies "lumps of earth"; hence the title page "*La Terre* by E. Zola" is pleonastic; "The signature fades into the title" (p. 173). The initials I allude to are those of Marcel Proust; see Serge Doubrovsky, *La Place de la madeleine* (Paris: Mercure de France, 1974), pp. 119-45.

81. "In Zola's novel of an artist's life, *L'Oeuvre*,...its author, as is well known, introduced himself and his own domestic happiness as an episode. He appears under the name of 'Sandoz'. The transformation was probably arrived at as follows. If 'Zola' is written backwards

...we arrive at 'Aloz'. No doubt this seemed too undisguised. He therefore replaced 'Al', which is the first syllable of 'Alexander' by 'Sand', which is the third syllable of the same name; and in this way 'Sandoz' came into being" (Sigmund Freud, *The Standard Edition of the Complete Psychological Works of Sigmund Freud,* ed. James Strachey and trans. James Strachey, Anna Freud, Alix Strachey, and Alan Tyson, 24 vols. [London: Hogarth Press, 1953-74] 4: 300). As Bonnefis points out, *sand* is derived from Alexandrine (Mme Zola's first name) and not from Alexander ("Intérieurs naturalistes," p. 174).

82. Paris, "Modèles balzaciens," p. 157.
83. Ibid., p. 156.
84. Bonnefis, "Intérieurs naturalistes," p. 174.
85. Ibid., p. 175.

Bibliography

I. Works by Zola

Zola, Emile. *Oeuvres complètes*. Edited by Maurice Leblond. 50 vols. [Unnumbered.] Paris: Bernouard, 1927-29.

———. *Les Rougon-Macquart*. Edited by Henri Mitterand. 5 vols. Paris: Pléiade, 1960-67.

———. *Oeuvres complètes*. Edited by Henri Mitterand. 15 vols. Paris: Cercle du Livre Précieux, 1962-69.

———. *L'Atelier de Zola: Textes de journaux, 1865-1870*. Edited by Martin Kanes. Geneva: Droz, 1963.

———. *The Kill*. Translated by A. Teixeira de Maltos. London: Weidenfeld & Nicolson, 1954.

———. *Germinal*. Translated by L. W. Tancock. Harmondsworth: Penguin Books, 1954.

———. *Thérèse Raquin*. Translated by Leonard Tancock. Harmondsworth: Penguin Books, 1962.

———. *La Débâcle*. Translated by Leonard Tancock. Harmondsworth: Penguin Books, 1972.

———. *Nana*. Translated by George Holden. Harmondsworth: Penguin Books, 1972.

II. Other Works Cited

Baguley, David. *"Fécondité" d'Emile Zola: Roman à thèse, évangile, mythe*. Toronto: University of Toronto Press, 1973.

Balzac, Honoré de. *Physiologie du mariage*. Paris: Garnier-Flammarion, 1968.

Barthes, Roland. *The Pleasure of the Text*. Translated by Richard Miller. New York: Farrar, Strauss, and Giroux, Hill and Wang, 1975.

———. *S/Z*. Translated by Richard Miller. New York: Farrar, Strauss, and Giroux, Hill and Wang, 1974.

Baudelaire, Charles. *The Flowers of Evil.* Selected and edited by Mathiel Mathews and Jackson Mathews. London: Routledge & Kegan Paul, 1955.

————. *Oeuvres complètes.* Paris: Pléiade, 1961.

Bellatorre, André. "Analyse d'un conte de Zola: 'Celle qui m'aime.'" *Cahiers naturalistes* 47 (1974): 88-97.

Beyle, Marie Henri [Stendhal]. *The Red and the Black.* Translated by C. K. Scott-Moncrieff. New York: Modern Library, 1929.

Bonnefis, Philippe. "Intérieurs naturalistes." In *Intime, intimité, intimisme,* edited by Raphaël Molho and Pierre Reboul, pp. 163-98. Lille: Editions Universitaires, Université de Lille III, 1976.

Borie, Jean. *Zola et les mythes ou de la nausée au salut.* Paris: Seuil, 1971.

————. *Le Tyran timide.* Paris: Klincksieck, 1973.

Bremond, Claude. *Logique du récit.* Paris: Seuil, 1968.

Brombert, Victor. *The Intellectual Hero: Studies in the French Novel, 1880-1955.* Chicago: University of Chicago Press, Phoenix Books, 1964.

Butor, Michel, *Répertoire II.* Paris: Editions de Minuit, 1964.

————. "Emile Zola, romancier expérimental, et la flamme bleue." *Critique* 239 (1967): 407-37.

Caillois, Roger. *Man and the Sacred.* Translated by Meyer Barash. Glencoe, Ill.: The Free Press, 1959.

Canetti, Elias. *Crowds and Power.* Translated by Carol Stewart. New York: Viking Press, Compass Books, 1966.

Carter, A. E. *The Idea of Decadence in French Literature: 1830-1900.* Toronto: University of Toronto Press, 1958.

Chevalier, Louis. *Classes laborieuses et classes dangereuses.* Paris: Plon, 1958.

Cuau, Bernard, and Zigante, Denise. *La Politique de la folie.* Paris: Stock, 1974.

Deleuze, Gilles. *Logique du sens.* Paris: 10/18, 1969.

Derrida, Jacques. *La Dissémination.* Paris: Seuil, 1972.

————. *Of Grammatology.* Translated by Gayatri Chakravorty Spivak. Baltimore: The Johns Hopkins University Press, 1976.

————. "The Purveyor of Truth." Translated by Willis Domingo et al. *Yale French Studies* 52 (1975): 31-113.

Dezalay, Auguste. "Ordre et désordre dans les *Rougon-Macquart:* L'Exemple de *La Fortune des Rougon.*" *Travaux de linguistique et de littérature* 11 (1973): 71-81.

Doubrovsky, Serge. *La Place de la madeleine: Ecriture et fantasme chez Proust.* Paris: Mercure de France, 1974.

Dubois, Jean. *Le Vocabulaire politique en France de 1869 à 1872.* Paris: Larousse, 1962.

Durand, Gilbert. *Le Décor mythique de "La Chartreuse de Parme."* Paris: Corti, 1961.

Eliade, Mircea. *Aspects du mythe.* Paris: Gallimard, Idées, 1963.

Ellison, Ralph. *Invisible Man.* Harmondsworth: Penguin Books, 1965.

Flaubert, Gustave. *Oeuvres.* 2 vols. Paris: Pléiade, 1963-66.

————. *Dictionnaire des idées reçues.* Edited by Lea Caminiti. Paris: A. G. Nizet, 1966.

————. *Oeuvres complètes.* Vol. 16, *Correspondance.* Paris: Club de l'Honnête

Homme, 1975.

Foucault, Michel. *Surveiller et punir: Naissance de la prison.* Paris: Gallimard, 1975.

Frazer, James George. *The Golden Bough.* New York: Macmillan Co., Macmillan Paperbacks, 1963.

Freud, Sigmund. *Thé Standard Edition of the Complete Psychological Works of Sigmund Freud.* Edited by James Strachey and translated by James Strachey, Anna Freud, Alix Strachey, and Alan Tyson. 24 vols. London: Hogarth Press, 1953-74.

Frye, Northrop. *Anatomy of Criticism: Four Essays.* Princeton: Princeton University Press, 1957.

Füglister, Robert L. "Baudelaire et le thème des bohémiens." *Etudes baudelairiennes* 2 (1971): 99-143.

Genette, Gérard. *Figures III.* Paris: Seuil, 1972.

Girard, René. *Deceit, Desire, and the Novel: Self and Other in Literary Structure.* Translated by Yvonne Freccero. Baltimore: The Johns Hopkins University Press, A Johns Hopkins Paperback, 1976.

_____. *Violence and the Sacred.* Translated by Patrick Gregory. Baltimore: The Johns Hopkins University Press, 1977.

Giraudoux, Jean. *Pleins pouvoirs.* Paris: Gallimard, 1939.

Grant, Richard B. "Un Aspect négligé du style de Zola." *Cahiers naturalistes* 42 (1971): 13-21.

Greimas, A.-J. *Sémantique structurale: Recherche de méthode.* Paris: Larousse, 1966.

_____. *Du sens.* Paris: Seuil, 1970.

_____. "Les Actants, les acteurs et les figures." In *Sémiotique narrative et textuelle,* edited by Claude Chabrol, pp. 161-76. Paris: Larousse, 1973.

_____. *Maupassant: La Sémiotique du texte.* Paris: Seuil, 1976.

_____., ed. *Essais de sémiotique poétique.* Paris: Larousse, 1972.

Guedj, Aimé. "Les Révolutionnaires de Zola." *Cahiers naturalistes* 36 (1968): 123-37.

Hambly, Peter. "La Pensée socialiste dans les *Rougon-Macquart.*" Thèse de Doctorat d'Université, Paris, 1960.

Hamon, Philippe. "Zola, romancier de la transparence." *Europe* 468-69 (1968): 385-91.

_____. "Pour un statut sémiologique du personnage." *Littérature* 6 (1972): 96-110.

_____. "Du savoir dans le texte." *Revue des sciences humaines* 160 (1975): 489-99.

_____. "Pour un statut sémiologique du personnage." In *Poétique du récit.* Paris: Seuil, Points, 1977.

Hemmings, F. W. J. "Fire in Zola's Fiction: Variations on an Elemental Theme." *Yale French Studies* 42 (1969): 26-37.

_____. *Emile Zola.* Oxford: Oxford University Press, Oxford Paperbacks, 1970.

Hubert, Henri, and Mauss, Marcel. *Essai sur la nature et la fonction du sacrifice.* In *Oeuvres,* by Marcel Mauss, vol. 1. Paris: Editions de Minuit, 1968.

Hugo, Victor. *Les Misérables.* Translated by Isabel F. Hapgood. London: Walter Scott Publishing Co., 1908.

————. *La Légende des siècles.* Paris: Pléiade, 1967.

Kofman, Sarah. *L'Enfance de l'art.* Paris: Payot, 1970.

Kristeva, Julia, *Semiotikè: Recherches pour une sémanalyse.* Paris: Seuil, 1969.

Lacan, Jacques. *Ecrits.* Paris: Seuil, 1966.

————. "Seminar on 'The Purloined Letter.'" Translated by Jeffrey Mehlman. *Yale French Studies* 48 (1972): 38-72.

Lapp, John. *Zola before the "Rougon-Macquart."* Toronto: University of Toronto Press, 1964.

Lévi-Strauss, Claude. "The Structural Study of Myth." In *Myth: A Symposium,* edited by Thomas A. Sebeok. Bloomington: Indiana University Press, Midland Books, 1965.

————. *The Savage Mind.* Chicago: University of Chicago Press, Phoenix Books, 1966.

————. *Structural Anthropology.* Translated by Claire Jacobson and Brooke Grundfest Schoepf. Garden City, N.Y.: Doubleday & Co., Anchor Books, 1967.

————. *The Raw and the Cooked.* Translated by John Weightman and Doreen Weightman. New York: Harper & Row, Harper Torchbooks, 1970.

Lidsky, Paul. *Les Ecrivains contre la Commune.* Paris: Maspéro, 1970.

Malinowski, Bronislaw. *Argonauts of the Western Pacific.* New York: E. P. Dutton & Co., A Dutton Paperback, 1961.

Mallarmé, Stéphane. *Oeuvres complètes.* Paris: Pléiade, 1970.

Marx, Karl. *Class Struggles in France, 1848-1850.* New York: International Publishers, 1964.

Marx, Leo. *The Machine in the Garden.* Oxford: Oxford University Press, 1964.

Massis, Henri. *Comment Emile Zola composait ses romans.* Paris: Fasquelle, 1906.

Miller, Nancy. "Gender and Genre." Ph.D. dissertation, Columbia University, 1974.

Mitterand, Henri. "Corrélations lexicales et organisation du récit: Le Vocabulaire du visage dans *Thérèse Raquin." Nouvelle Critique,* special issue: *Linguistique et littérature* (1968): 21-28.

————. "Système des personnages dans *Germinal." Cahiers de l'association internationale des études françaises* 24 (1972): 155-66.

————. "Fonction narrative et fonction mimétique: Les Personnages de *Germinal." Poétique* 16 (1973): 477-90.

Neefs, Jacques. "La Figuration réaliste: L'Exemple de *Madame Bovary." Poétique* 16 (1973): 466-76.

Paris, Jean. "Modèles balzaciens." In *La Lecture sociocritique du texte romanesque,* edited by Graham Falconer and Henri Mitterand, pp. 151-64. Toronto: Samuel Stevens Hakkert & Co., 1975.

Pascal, Blaise. *Oeuvre.* Paris: Pléiade, 1941.

Perrone-Moisès, Leyla. "Le Récit euphémique." *Poétique* 17 (1974): 27-38.

Pierssens, Michel. "L'Appareil sériel." *Change* 16-17 (1973): 265-85.

Propp, Vladimir. *Morphologie du conte.* Paris: Seuil, Points, 1970.

Proust, Marcel. *Les Plaisirs et les jours.* Paris: Gallimard, 1924.

————. *The Captive.* Translated by C. K. Scott-Moncrieff. New York: Random House, 1970.

Riffaterre, Michael. "Modèles de la phrase littéraire." In *Problèmes de l'analyse textuelle,* edited by Pierre R. Léon, Henri Mitterand, and Peter Nesselroth, pp. 133-48. Montreal: Didier, 1971.

Robert, Guy. *"La Terre" d'Emile Zola: Etude historique et critique.* Paris: Les Belles Lettres, 1952.

Said, Edward W. *Beginnings: Intention and Method.* New York: Basic Books, 1975.

Sartre, Jean-Paul. *Critique de la raison dialectique.* Paris: Gallimard, 1960.

Schor, Naomi. "Zola: From Window to Window." *Yale French Studies* 42 (1969): 38-51.

_____. "Le Sourire du sphinx: Zola et l'énigme de la féminité." *Romantisme* 13-14 (1976): 183-95.

_____."Dali's Freud." *Dada/Surrealism,* no. 6 (1976), pp. 10-17.

_____. "Fiction as Interpretation / Interpretation as Fiction." In *The Reader in Fiction,* edited by Inge Crossman and Susan Suleiman. Princeton: Princeton University Press, forthcoming.

Serres, Michel. *Feux et signaux de brume: Zola.* Paris: Grasset, 1975.

Shapiro, David. *Neurotic Styles.* New York: Basic Books, Harper Torchbooks, 1965.

Sophocles. *Sophocles.* Vol. 1, *Oedipus the King.* Translated by David Greene. Chicago: University of Chicago Press, 1954.

Tiger, Lionel. *Men in Groups.* New York: Random House, Vintage Books, 1970.

Toulouse, Edouard. *Emile Zola: Enquête médico-psychologique sur les rapports de la supériorité intellectuelle avec la névropathie.* Paris: Société d'éditions scientifiques, 1896.

Trilling, Jacques. "James Joyce ou l'écriture matricide." *Etudes Freudiennes,* nos. 7-8 (1973), pp. 7-70.

Turnell, Martin. *The Art of French Fiction.* New York: New Directions Press, 1959.

Vernant, Jean-Pierre. *Mythe et pensée chez les Grecs.* 2 vols. Paris: Maspéro, Petite Collection Maspéro, 1971.

Vernant, Jean-Pierre, and Vidal-Naquet, Pierre. *Mythe et tragédie en Grèce ancienne.* Paris: Maspéro, 1972.

Walker, Philip. "Prophetic Myths in Zola." *PMLA* 74 (1959): 444-52.

Index

Apotheosis: in *Au bonheur des dames*, 165; in *Germinal*, 47-52; and hyperbolization, 36, 47-52; in late novels, 79; leader's, 74, 143; in *Nana*, 77; and silence, 77; and speech, 74; in *Vérité*, 41

Bacchae, The (Euripides), 6, 34, 104, 191 n. 54
Balzac, Honoré de, 3, 10, 59, 179; *Le Colonel Chabert*, 33-34; on convent education, 94; *Le Cousin Pons*, 59; differences between Zola and, xii, 70, 129, 137-39, 168, 179-80; *Eugénie Grandet*, 95; *La Fille aux yeux d'or*, 102; and Hugo, 191 n. 61; name of, 179-80; *Physiologie du mariage*, 140, 203 n. 20; *Sarrasine*, 102
Band: in *Au bonheur des dames*, 153-62; characteristics of, 141-42; and crowd (B/C), 154-58; I/B/C, 155, 162; and individual (I/B), 147-48, 154; literary models of, 203 n. 21; in *Son Excellence Eugène Rougon*, 142-53. *See also* Mediator
Barthes, Roland, 10-11, 60, 102, 139, 182 n. 21
Baudelaire, Charles: and Balzac, 3; *Les Fleurs du mal:* "Abel et Caïn," 27, *Les Fleurs du Mal:* "L'Albatross," 64-65; *Homme-Dieu*, 49; on *Madame Bovary*, 102; *Mon Coeur mis à nu* and *Fusées*, 78; "Le Vieux Saltimbanque," 87-88, 194 n. 10
Bellatorre, André, 194 n. 10
Bellow, Saul, 55
Beyle, Marie Henri [pseud. Stendhal], 59; battle scenes in, 109-10; *Lamiel*, 102; *Le*

Rouge et le noir, 11, 60, 145-46, 183 n. 30; and use of ellipsis, 36; Zola on, 66
Bisexuality, 93-103
Bloom, Harold, xii
Bonnefis, Philippe, 209 n. 80, 210 n. 81
Borie, Jean: on breakdown of architectural barriers, 168; conclusion of, 209 n. 79; on the identification of the natural and the popular, 128-29; on *Lourdes*, 44; on *Madeleine Férat*, 33; on *Nana*, 101; on origin myths, 184 n. 36; on the original crime, 18; on Zola's Oedipus complex, 145
Bremond, Claude, 51
Brombert, Victor, 43
Brunetière, Ferdinand, 128
Butor, Michel, 29, 132-33

Caillois, Roger, 6-7, 182 n. 12
Camus, Albert, 55
Canetti, Elias: on double crowd structure, 87, 105-6; on invisible crowds, 120-21; on the pack, 151; on prevailing crowd emotions, 84-85, 125
Carlyle, Thomas, 79
Céard, Henri, 47
Chevalier, Louis, 201 n. 89
Commune: bourgeois discourse on, 114; in *La Débâcle*, 114, 116, 118; in "Jacques Damour," 33; the "pétroleuses" and, 104
Conversion, 42-46, 47-48, 151-53
Cousin, 94-96
Crane, Stephen, 110
Crowd: all-female, 160; ambiguous, 52; chil-

217

THE JOHNS HOPKINS UNIVERSITY PRESS

This book was composed in Alphatype Baskerville by David Lorton from a design by Charles West. It was printed on 50 lb. Cream White Bookmark and bound by Thomson-Shore, Inc.

Library of Congress Cataloging in Publication Data

Schor, Naomi.
  Zola's crowds.

  Bibliography: pp. 211-15
  Includes index.
  1. Zola, Emile, 1840-1902 — Criticism and interpretation. 2. Crowds in Literature. I. Title.
PQ2538.S34   843'.8   78-1564
ISBN 0-8018-2095-2

D1203671